WITHDRAWN FROM
OHIO UNIVERSITY

PROSPECTS FOR A NEW STRUCTURALISM

AMSTERDAM STUDIES IN THE THEORY AND HISTORY OF LINGUISTIC SCIENCE

General Editor
E.F. KONRAD KOERNER
(University of Ottawa)

Series IV – CURRENT ISSUES IN LINGUISTIC THEORY

Advisory Editorial Board

Henning Andersen (Los Angeles); Raimo Anttila (Los Angeles)
Thomas V. Gamkrelidze (Tbilisi); John E. Joseph (College Park, Md.)
Hans-Heinrich Lieb (Berlin); Ernst Pulgram (Ann Arbor, Mich.)
E. Wyn Roberts (Vancouver, B.C.); Danny Steinberg (Tokyo)

Volume 96

Hans-Heinrich Lieb (ed.)

Prospects for a New Structuralism

PROSPECTS FOR A NEW STRUCTURALISM

Edited by

HANS-HEINRICH LIEB
Freie Universität Berlin

JOHN BENJAMINS PUBLISHING COMPANY
AMSTERDAM/PHILADELPHIA

1992

Library of Congress Cataloging-in-Publication Data

Prospects for a new structuralism / edited by Hans-Heinrich Lieb.
    p.   cm. -- (Amsterdam studies in the theory and history of linguistic science.
Series IV, Current issues in linguistic theory, ISSN 0304-0763; v. 96)
  Includes bibliographical references and index.
  1. Structural linguistics. I. Lieb, Hans-Heinrich. II. Series.
P146.P77   1992
415--dc20   92-33520
ISBN 90 272 3597 X (Eur.)/1-55619-158-8 (US)(alk. paper)   CIP

© Copyright 1992 - John Benjamins B.V.
No part of this book may be reproduced in any form, by print, photoprint, microfilm, or any other means, without written permission from the publisher.

John Benjamins Publishing Co. · P.O. Box 75577 · 1070 AN Amsterdam · The Netherlands
John Benjamins North America · 821 Bethlehem Pike · Philadelphia, PA 19118 · USA

Foreword

The beginnings of this book go back to the Fourteenth International Congress of Linguists, held in Berlin in 1987, in what was then the German Democratic Republic. At the time I organized an official Round Table, already under the title of the present book. A brief report on the Round Table has since appeared in the Congress Proceedings.[1]

Some of the papers in this volume (Sgall, Heger, Bańczerowski et al., Wurzel) go back to contributions submitted to the Round Table but only one (Heger) is virtually unchanged. Three others (Carr, Seiler, Lass) were solicited after the Congress, and the remaining two (by Lieb) are also entirely new (the second Lieb paper replaces a Round Table contribution).

This book has been a long time coming, for reasons that were largely beyond the editor's control:

(i) From the very beginning, this was not to be another collection of round-table papers but an exploration of a new position in linguistics. The philosophical issues raised were to be studied from different angles by different authors, and current linguistic frameworks were to be checked against the position by leading representatives. Securing cooperation on such a project proved to be much more time-consuming than I had suspected. I had eventually to accept that four authors who had been seriously interested were unable to contribute, each for a good reason:
   – Jerrold J. Katz, of the City University of New York, whose paper would have been an asset to Section I: Philosophical Issues

---

[1] Lieb, Hans-Heinrich. 1990. "Rundtisch/Round Table 12. Prospects for a New Structuralism". In: Werner Bahner, Joachim Schildt, and Dieter Viehweger (eds). *Proceedings of the Fourteenth International Congress of Linguists, Berlin/ GDR, August 10 – August 15, 1987.* Vol. I. Berlin: Akademie-Verlag. 325-328.

(however, Katz and Postal[2] may now be read in conjunction with Section I);
- Hans Uszkoreit (Universität Saarbrücken), who at the Berlin Round Table had read a paper on "The status of linguistic objects in GPSG and other Unification Grammars" but who was unable to submit a final version for inclusion in Section II: Frameworks;
- Jacek Fisiak of the University of Poznań and Rolf Haberbeck of Siemens Nixdorf, who could not contribute their papers on, respectively, "Structuralism and applied linguistics" and "Structuralism and technology".

(ii) In 1989 the Berlin Wall came down; in 1990 West Berlin and East Berlin were once again a single city in a united Germany. Since, academic institutions in both parts of Berlin have been subject to dramatic reorganization (in some cases, dissolution); linguistics at my own university, the Freie Universität of West Berlin, was also affected. As a result, I was stopped short in my scientific endeavours.

While it is a loss that some of the papers did not materialize, the delay in publication is hardly a disadvantage: the foundational issues raised in this book have become much more pronounced in the meantime by Carr's[3] and Katz and Postal's independent pleas for realism on the one hand and by the 'connectionist' challenge to recent cognitivism on the other, which may give the book a more interested readership. Still, I am sincerely grateful to the contributors, to the series editor, and to the publisher for their patience.

Berlin, Germany, June 1992   Hans-Heinrich Lieb

---

[2] Katz, Jerrold J., and Paul M. Postal. 1991. "Realism vs. conceptualism in linguistics". *Linguistics and Philosophy* 14.515-554.

[3] Carr, Philip. 1990. *Linguistic Realities*. An Autonomous Metatheory for the Generative Enterprise. Cambridge etc.: Cambridge University Press. (Cambridge Studies in Linguistics 53).

Contents

Foreword	v
Prospects for a New Structuralism: Introduction *Hans-Heinrich Lieb*	1

I. PHILOSOPHICAL ISSUES

An interactionist position *Philip Carr*	17
The case for a New Structuralism *Hans-Heinrich Lieb*	33

II. FRAMEWORKS

Classical structuralism and present-day Praguian linguistics *Petr Sgall*	75
Noematic grammar *Klaus Heger*	91
The functional model of UNITYP dimensions *Hansjakob Seiler*	99
Integrational Linguistics: Outline of a theory of language *Hans-Heinrich Lieb*	127

III. AREAS

A new structuralism in phonology *Jerzy Bańczerowski, Jerzy Pogonowski, and Tadeusz Zgółka*	185
The structuralist heritage in Natural Morphology *Wolfgang U. Wurzel*	225
What are language histories histories of? *Roger Lass*	243
Index of names	273

Prospects for a New Structuralism: Introduction

Hans-Heinrich Lieb
Freie Universität Berlin

1 Nine Principles of New Structuralism

1.1 Introduction

There are two different ways of dealing with linguistics: first and foremost, *doing* linguistics by studying languages; or else, doing metalinguistics (which is a branch of the philosophy of science) by studying linguistics itself. As a matter of fact the two are closely interrelated: no linguistics, no metalinguistics; on the other hand, barely a linguistic study without reflections on 'aims' and 'methods', presupposing a certain stand on foundational issues.

There are periods in the development of any field when foundational issues, buried in day-to-day research under layers of shared beliefs if not prejudice, rise to the surface. This is such a period in linguistics, and the present book is an attempt at reorientation in a changing field.

Currently, the metascientific assumptions of cognitivism stand out prominently in linguistics: the heuristic hypotheses that (i) concepts of perception, cognition, and action apply equally in the study of humans, animals, and machines; (ii) dealing with perception, cognition, and action in the three areas means studying underlying internal mechanisms; and (iii) such mechanisms should be jointly studied from a unified point of view by a number of disciplines that include, in particular, neurophysiology, computer sciences, formal logic, psychology, and linguistics construed as a natural science.

The present book is to document a different orientation in linguistics, an orientation that may be called a New Structuralism, characterized by nine principles.

1.2 The principles

(1) [*Modesty*] The objects of linguistics are the objects actually studied by the practising linguist, of which the theoretician may give a theoretical account. They cannot be prescribed independently of linguistic practice.

(2) [*New mentalism*] Something is an object of linguistics only if it is needed for describing the content of intentional (directed) mental states or events that are connected with
   a. speaking
   b. understanding speech, or
   c. judging speech form a communicative point of view.
   Adequately conceived, the content of such states or events is extramental.

(3) [*Mechanisms*] Neurophysiological or mental mechanisms do not belong to the objects of linguistics.

(4) [*Shared branches*] Relations between objects of linguistics and neurophysiological mechanisms are studied in biolinguistics, a shared branch of linguistics and biology; relations between objects of linguistics and mental mechanisms are studied in psycholinguistics, a shared branch of linguistics and psychology.

(5) [*Ontology 1*] The objects of linguistics, in particular, languages, their systems, and linguistic structures, are abstract and extramental.

(6) [*Ontology 2*] Despite their abstract nature the objects of linguistics may have *derived* spatial and temporal properties, based on spatial or temporal properties of objects or events in spacetime.

(7) [*Diversity*] Linguistic diversity, both within and between languages, is a fundamental linguistic fact. To account for it, objects of linguistics must be allowed to differ in abstractness.

(8) [*Structuralism*] Traditional structuralism was right in — mostly — construing the objects of linguistics as extra-mental and emphasizing their structural (system-based) properties. Traditional structuralism was wrong where it failed to clearly recognize their abstract nature and their basis in human intentionality.

(9) [*Closure*] An optimal conception of linguistics necessarily includes these eight theses.

These principles stand in need of explanation.

1.3 Heuristic nature and modesty (Principles 9 and 1)

PRINCIPLE 9, the *closure principle*, is a factual hypothesis on linguistics not languages; being factual, it may be wrong. The principle determines the status of Principles 1 to 8: these are *heuristic* hypotheses not factual ones, and are to be adopted in the hope that (9) is true (there is also a factual reading of several principles if "linguistics" is understood as "linguistics at [a given time]"). Thus, Principles 1 to 9 jointly define a position to which individual conceptions of linguistics may or may not conform, or may partly conform. The position must of course be consistent, i.e. there must be an interpretation of (1) to (9) on which the nine principles may be jointly held.

PRINCIPLE 1, the *modesty principle*, forces us to respect linguistics as a field that is given through what linguists do (we should of course be generous in deciding who counts as a linguist): it must be a defensible claim that the objects of linguistics as construed by the metalinguist, or by a linguist taking a metalinguistic point of view, are indeed what is studied in linguistics. True enough, we may suggest that linguistics should be reconceived by redefining the objects of linguistic study but even then linguistic practice must be respected. (The modesty principle is not to imply naïve realism; the objects of any field are theory dependant.)

1.4 New mentalism (Principles 2 to 4)

PRINCIPLE 2, the *new mentalism principle*, is obviously heuristic. Once again, there is an implicit relativity to theories: what is necessary for describing mental content in one theory may not be so in another. The mentalism principle may be understood to require necessity with respect to any relevant theory that may be seriously considered in linguistics.

For the mentalism principle to be compatible with the modesty principle, we must make the factual assumption on linguistics that the objects actually studied in linguistics are objects as required by the mentalism principle, or may be reconceived as such without violating linguistic practice. There are good reasons for such an assumption. Linguistics deals with entities such as words, inflexions, sentences, with dialects, languages and their systems. Speaking is an action, hence, has an intention — a mental state — as one of its components. Understanding speech involves perceptions, mental events that are directed towards something (a perception is a perception *of* something). Judging speech relies on mental states connected with knowing entities such as 'languages'; a good case can be made for these states to be 'about' something, too. Since mental states and events of the three types are all 'directed towards' something or 'about' something, each may be assigned a 'content', which should be construed as extra-mental. (The content of a perception of, say, a dead leaf contains the properties of being a leaf and being dead, which are properties of extra-mental objects, and are themselves independent of the perceiver.) Now it is at least plausible that the objects actually studied in linguistics — words, inflexions, languages etc. — are all needed for describing the content of relevant mental states and events (the objects do not have to figure directly in their content).

PRINCIPLE 3, the *principle of mechanisms*, should be implied by the new mentalism principle, i.e. once (2) and its supporting assumptions have been formulated more precisely, (3) should be a logical consequence of (2) and the assumptions. Intuitively, no neurophysiological or mental mechanism underlying a relevant state or event of a person is necessary to describe its content: assuming that an adequate vocabulary is available, the person could in principle give a description without referring at all to any underlying mechanisms. Indeed, such mechanisms are irrelevant to any description that is to mirror basic speaker abilities: barring the most artificial arrangements, speakers — just as anybody else — have no access to any mechanisms underlying their own mental states or events.

The mechanism principle may also be implied by the modesty principle but this is less clear. Of course, (3) can be accepted without subscribing to either (1) or (2).

PRINCIPLE 4, the *principle of shared branches*, relates the study of mechanisms to linguistics. For Principle 4 to be consistent with the principle of mechanisms, any branches shared by linguistics and neighbouring disciplines must be conceived in a way that bars the following consequence: every object of a shared branch is also an object of linguistics; and indeed, such a conception is possible. We may therefore assume that neurophysiological mechanisms underlying speech are objects of biology that are objects of biolinguistics but not of linguistics; similarly, appropriate mental mechanisms are objects of psychology that are also objects of psycholinguistics and yet no objects of linguistics. (Conversely, linguistic objects studied in biolinguistics or psycholinguistics are not, for that reason, objects of biology or psychology.) Such a construal is desirable on independent grounds if reductionism — the attempt (hopeless, it must be feared) to 'reduce' linguistics to either psychology or biology — is to be avoided.

The principle of shared branches guarantees that linguists and non-linguists may jointly pursue the study of relevant mechanisms, without making biological or psychological objects (mechanisms) into linguistic ones or linguistic objects (words etc.) into psychological or biological ones.

1.5 Ontology and linguistic diversity (Principles 5 to 8)

PRINCIPLE 5, the *first ontology principle*, excludes a nominalist position towards linguistics by requiring that the objects of linguistics must be abstract; and excludes a cognitivist or 'conceptualist' position by assigning extra-mental status to all linguistic objects. Furthermore, it would allow drawing a clear distinction between linguistic *data* and linguistic *objects* if the former are construed as concrete objects or events (such as speech objects and events); such a conception is, however, much disputed and is no consequence of either the first ontology principle or any of the other principles.

The first ontology principle should be implied by either the modesty or the mentalism principles once these are restated more formally and supplemented by auxiliary assumptions, but may of course be adopted independently.

PRINCIPLE 6, the *second ontology principle*, ties the abstract objects of linguistics down to space and time without making them spatio-temporal, hence, concrete. A term like "English in 18th century England" must have a good linguistic meaning even if it does not denote an entity of the same type as "Alexander Pope in his 25th year". Indeed, English has the derived temporal *and* spatial property of being *used* in England in the 18th century because Alexander Pope, among others, spoke and wrote in English while *living in* 18th century England. The second ontology principle should be needed for any conception of linguistics that is to avoid separation of 'core branches' of linguistics dealing with linguistic objects *per se* from 'peripheral' ones dealing with their 'temporal and spatial aspects'.

PRINCIPLE 7, the *diversity principle*, precludes certain notorious idealizations in accounting for linguistic data and linguistic objects, idealizations by which linguistic differences within a single language community are treated as irrelevant, or linguistic differences between language communities as something to be abstracted from. Dealing with linguistic diversity may require a sophisticated view of increasingly abstract objects to replace an approach that concentrates on 'ideal' objects obtained in a more or less intuitive way. The diversity principle should be indispensable for any conception that includes applied linguistics among the branches of linguistics.

PRINCIPLE 8, the *structuralism principle*, establishes a relation to traditional or 'classical' structuralism, including its present-day versions. Since classical structuralism is anything but homogeneous, the principle is formulated as a rough generalization; moreover, only two aspects are emphasized. As will be obvious to anybody familiar with the history of linguistics in this century, the first part of the structuralism principle implies a positive evaluation of two basic features shared by most if not all versions of European and American structuralism (extra-mentality is not adopted by Saussure); the second part rejects a feature typical (with some exceptions) of American structuralism: its nominalist slant. The second part of the structuralism principle also takes a stand against the disregard of human action, perception, and cognition in linguistics that is characteristic of many forms of structuralism excepting, in particular, the Prague School and its derivatives.

The structuralism principle, which roughly determines the position of New Structuralism towards classical structuralism, is an obvious consequence of previous principles. Thus, classical structuralism is not used as a point of reference in a definition of New Structuralism, irrespective of the question of historical influences; rather, it is a consequence of underlying principles that New Structuralism is partly structuralist in orientation also in a classical sense.

Finally, Principles 1 to 8 should jointly imply that linguistics is construed as an 'empirical' discipline, in *some* accepted sense. (This very much depends on how "empirical" is understood.)

2 Documenting the principles

2.1 Introduction

The Nine Principles of New Structuralism were formulated by Lieb in 1987 and distributed to the participants in the Round Table on Prospects for a New Structuralism to serve as a basis for the panel discussion. The principles were not named, and no explanations were given, except for a few hints at possible logical relationships. It was hoped that this way differences in position would already appear as differences in the interpretation of individual principles.

While only the new mentalism principle was discussed in any detail at the Round Table, the principles were on the whole favourably received by the panelists; they were more controversial to discussants from the floor. The contributors to this volume were again confronted with the bare principles, not receiving any additional information. Disregarding Lieb, whose commitment to the principles is obvious from his contribution to Section I of the present volume, all contributors except Wurzel reacted to the principles by explicit comments.

Contributions are arranged in three sections: I. *Philosophical Issues*, II. *Frameworks*, and III. *Areas*; a fourth section, *Applications*, which eventually did not materialize, would have shown the relevance of New Structuralism to both applied linguistics and language technology.

2.2 Section I: Philosophical Issues

Section I demonstrates that the metalinguistic issues raised by New Structuralism are of considerable interest, surfacing independently with different authors in similar ways. CARR's 'interactionism' is inspired by Popper's well-known conception of 'three worlds' (since 1972); linguistic objects are placed in the third world of 'objective knowledge'. Ontologically, this is a realist position. LIEB's conception, too, has realism as a defining feature, taking Searle (1983) rather than Popper as a starting-point for relating linguistic objects to the mind. While CARR finds little fault with most of the principles, he hesitates to accept the emphasis placed on variation by the diversity principle, at least if variation is construed as suggested by LIEB; the diversity principle is, however, general enough to allow for other construals.

Not directly represented in the Philosophical Issues section is KATZ's 'Platonism' (since Katz 1981; most recently, Katz and Postal 1991), which shares its realist orientation with New Structuralism but appears to differ in three respects: (i) The new mentalism principle establishes a tie between abstract linguistic objects and mental states or events that may be closer than warranted even by the position adopted in Katz and Postal (1991). (ii) As in the case of CARR, linguistic diversity is not a central but a peripheral phenomenon, contrary to the diversity principle. (iii) The 'core' of linguistics is construed as non-empirical (e.g., Katz and Postal 1991: 538, fn. 11).

I would also suggest that SEARLE's position on linguistics, as it appears from Searle (1990), is germane to New Structuralism, with two qualifications: (i) The extra-mental nature of mental contents (mentalism principle) would have to be more clearly recognized (on this problem, see also Bilgrami 1989). (ii) Searle is too unspecific on questions of detail for us to determine his position towards some of the principles.

All authors mentioned are on record as outspoken critics of the ontological and epistemological stand taken in Chomskyan Generative Grammar. It should be emphasized, therefore, that the Nine Principles are neutral concerning the *format* of linguistic grammars; indeed, CARR attempts nothing less than a 'metatheory for the generative enterprise'.

2.3 Section II: Frameworks

The distinction between 'frameworks' and 'areas' is meant to reflect differences in coverage: ideally, a *framework* is an approach in linguistics that attempts to cover all areas through a comprehensive theory of language; *areas* are, roughly, linguistic disciplines such as phonology, morphology, etc., or historical linguistics and sociolinguistics. (A truly comprehensive theory of language is, of course, a hope for the future.)

Section II characterizes four frameworks in which some or all of the Nine Principles appear to be adopted: present-day Praguian linguistics (SGALL); HEGER's 'noematic' approach; SEILER's UNITYP model for research in universals and typology (which, arguably, might also have been assigned to the Areas section); and LIEB's Integrational Linguistics. Presentation ranges from a brief characterization (HEGER) to a detailed overview (LIEB). Against my own qualms as an editor, I finally decided on a more detailed outline of Integrational Linguistics (or rather, of its theory of language): at least two of the remaining three contributions to this section turned out to be fairly concise so that the entire section might have given an incorrect impression of being partly programmatic, an impression that a more detailed account of one of the frameworks might help to counter.

Whereas LIEB and SEILER simply characterize their approaches, with only a few hints at linguistic tradition in the case of SEILER, both SGALL and HEGER carefully establish the relations between classical structuralism and their respective frameworks. SGALL, HEGER, and SEILER acknowledge their indebtedness, through historical affiliation or thematic closeness, to classical Praguian structuralism.

Not surprisingly, the Nine Principles are simply adopted by LIEB, but HEGER, too, finds all of them acceptable. SEILER welcomes them in a more general way, giving what may be a partial reinterpretation of the mentalism principle. SGALL finds the principles important but suggests that the formulations of the mentalism principle, the second ontology principle, and the structuralism principle should be modified.

Indeed, "the system-oriented character of language" (SGALL) is only implicit in the mentalism principle, especially in (2c): judging speech from a communicative point of view will, as a rule, involve the system aspect of languages. Generally, linguistic objects should presuppose systems insofar as the objects are structured, as made explicit in the first ontology principle. Leaving such assumptions implicit in the mentalism principle has the advantage that the debates on mentalism and on the system aspect of languages can be kept apart.

Again, the second ontology principle may be understood to cover what SGALL calls "the internalizability of language". A more explicit formulation would indeed bring out that there are just two factors to tie abstract linguistic objects down to concrete entities: 'language use', establishing relations to speakers and utterances, and 'language command', establishing relations to speakers and their brain mechanisms.

Finally, recognition of intentionality especially in Praguian linguistics is taken into account in the structuralism principle through the qualifying "where": *not everywhere* in traditional structuralism was there a failure to recognize the role of intentionality.

2.4 Section III: Areas

In their multifacetted paper on 'a new structuralism in phonology', BAŃCZEROWSKI et al. characterize a notion of 'linguistic structuralism' within a carefully laid out philosophical framework. This concept of structuralism is then used to demonstrate that classical structuralist phonology, especially of the Prague School type, has remained influential in more recent and current phonological approaches, in particular, in the generative phonology of *The Sound Pattern of English* (Chomsky and Halle 1968). In the course of the demonstration, essential concepts of Trubetzkoy's phonology are reconstructed in axiomatic form. Use of the axiomatic method is generally seen as a desirable trend in current phonology, especially of a neostructuralist type.

The notion of structuralism proposed by BAŃCZEROWSKI et al. appears to cover traditional structuralism, and it does so independently of a definition of New Structuralism that would result from taking the Nine Principles as a definiens. In their Appendix BAŃCZEROWSKI et al. point out that New Structuralism, so defined, would differ from traditional structuralism: the Nine Principles are partly incorrect if taken as descriptive claims on traditional structuralism. This is important — New Structuralism turns out to be *novel* rather than 'neo'; it is no simple continuation of the past (differently from SPE phonology, if the claims in BAŃCZEROWSKI et al. are correct). The authors do, however, clearly recognize the non-descriptive, heuristic nature of the Nine Principles. Their paper testifies to the fact that the Principles reflect underlying motivation in current developments in phonology.

Analogously, this also holds of WURZEL's paper on Natural Morphology. Although WURZEL does not directly react to the Nine Principles, there is nothing in his nine-point characterization of Natural Morphology to contradict any of the principles, and there is much to support them. WURZEL explicitly acknowledges both Jakobson and Coseriu as sources of inspiration for Natural Morphology, thus placing it within the tradition of European structuralism.

Language change is an issue that looms large in Natural Morphology, and is of course the major topic of LASS's paper on 'what language histories are histories of'. LASS does not, however, approach historical linguistics from the same point of view as WURZEL does. Under the influence of CARR (1990), he adopts Popperian interactionism more decidedly than in his earlier work. However, while CARR (this volume) agrees with LIEB (this volume, Sec. I) in voting for a "non-psychologistic mentalism" (CARR), LASS rejects "even this much 'mentalism'" for historical linguistics, and consequently does not accept the new mentalism principle. (Rejection of the diversity principle appears to be unmotivated; rejection of the shared branches principle, though motivated by rejection of the mentalism principle, is not a necessary consequence.)

LASS's major argument is a weighty one: "linguistic history is a transindividual study, in which the perspective of the participating individual is of little interest." I believe this is essentially correct. However, it may still be compatible with the mentalism principle since this principle does not exclude a transindividual perspective. To bring this out more clearly, the principle should be amended to read: "Something is an object of linguistics only if it is needed for describing — *either from an individual or a transindividual point of view* — the content of ..." Briefly, historical languages are justified as objects of linguistics also from the point of view of the mentalism principle because they are necessary for describing how and why the contents of relevant mental states or events differ with different speakers. The matter requires further discussion.

2.5 Prospects

Obviously, the Nine Principles are broad enough to characterize research conducted in a sizable number of different approaches. Such characterization cuts right through established lines of separation.

For example, New Structuralism cannot be opposed to Generative Grammar in absolute terms. Generative Grammar of the Chomskyan type espouses cognitivism, and this makes it incompatible with New Structuralism; but then Generative Grammar does not have to be wedded to cognitivism. Such a link is tenuous at best in Generalized Phrase Structure Grammar, whose indebtedness to traditional structuralism is an obvious fact, for instance in the role played by the notion of feature.

Nor do the principles follow the traditional divide between mentalism and non-mentalism; rather, they strike a new balance between the mental and the non-mental in the study of language.

The principles do seem to be characteristic of approaches — either to linguistics in general or to specific areas — that are currently pursued most vigorously in Europe. While this may have historical reasons, it is also an accident.

The principles apply to approaches in all areas of linguistics. It is certainly accidental that phonology, morphology, and historical linguistics are singled out in the present volume. As pointed out already by Katz and Postal (1991: 522, fn. 4), Montague Grammar — covering syntax and semantics — is realist in orientation, and it should be rewarding to confront Kac (1992), or the nine current approaches to syntax represented in Droste and Joseph (eds) (1991), with the Nine

Principles; while no approach may be covered completely, most should mark strongly against some of the principles.

Not only are the principles broad enough for actual coverage, they are also specific enough to be controversial. This shows already in the present volume. I conclude that the prospects for a New Structuralism are good: it exists, and it has potential to grow. Reactions are invited.

References

Bilgrami, Akeel. 1989. "Realism without internalism: a critique of Searle on intentionality". *Journal of Philosophy* LXXXVI.57-72.

Carr, Philip. 1990. *Linguistic Realities*. An Autonomist Metatheory for the Generative Enterprise. Cambridge etc.: Cambridge University Press. (Cambridge Studies in Linguistics 53).

Chomsky, Noam, and Morris Halle. 1968. *The Sound Pattern of English*. New York: Harper and Row.

Droste, Flip J., and John E. Joseph (eds). 1991. *Linguistic Theory and Grammatical Description*. Amsterdam/Philadelphia: Benjamins. (CILT 75).

Kac, Michael B. 1992. *Grammars and Grammaticality*. Amsterdam/Philadelphia: Benjamins. (CILT 78).

Katz, Jerrold J. 1981. *Language and Other Abstract Objects*. Oxford: Blackwell.

—, and Paul M. Postal. 1991. "Realism vs. conceptualism in linguistics". *Linguistics and Philosophy* 14.515-554.

Popper, Karl R. 1972. *Objective Knowledge: An Evolutionary Approach*. Oxford: Clarendon Press.

Searle, John R. 1983. *Intentionality*. An Essay in the Philosophy of Mind. Cambridge: Cambridge University Press.

—. 1990. "Consciousness, explanatory inversion, and cognitive science". *Behavioral and Brain Sciences* 13.585-596.

I. PHILOSOPHICAL ISSUES

An Interactionist Position

Philip Carr
University of Newcastle upon Tyne

I give an outline of the interactionist metatheory for generative linguistics described in Carr (1990), followed by a discussion of the way in which some of the issues addressed there relate to structuralist criticisms of generative linguistics. Finally, I consider the Nine Principles of New Structuralism in relation to these issues.

1 Objective knowledge and realism

Let me begin by distinguishing two distinct senses of 'mentalism'. The objects of linguistic theory may be said to be mental (a) in the sense that they constitute a kind of knowledge, or (b) in the more specific sense that they are speaker-internal objects (cognitive states, processes, representations, let's say). This latter notion of mentalism seems a plausible enough ontology for linguistic objects at first glance; it could fairly be labelled 'psychologism' (as discussed in Carr 1987), and rather naturally carries with it the notion that linguistic theory, having speaker-internal cognitive states as its object, is clearly a branch of cognitive psychology. This has been Chomsky's position all along (cf. Chomsky 1986); it has become rather widely accepted in generative linguistics, and probably appears almost self-evident to many of its practitioners.

The first sense of mentalism allows that we may speak of knowledge without its being speaker-internal. Now, since this position probably does not seem at all self-evident, or even comprehensible, to many linguists, it is incumbent upon me to show why it is precisely that kind of mentalism which I propose in the Popperian metatheory for generative linguistics described in Carr (1990). What follows is therefore an attempt briefly to show the rationale for such a position.

Philosophers of science typically attempt, among other things, to note the facts of scientific practice and erect theories about the nature of scientific investigation which explain why they should be the way they are. In the philosophy of linguistics, it can be attested, on inspection of its major journals, that generative linguistics proceeds in the absence of cognitive psychological evidence and testing: there, we find, not the method of cognitive psychological inquiry, with its emphasis on experiment design, control groups, and statistical metrication from corpora of observations gathered under experimental observation, but sets of well-formed and ill-formed expressions, gained via acts of intuitive judgement. Now this fact of the distinction in evidence and testing between cognitive psychology and generative linguistics stands in need of an explanation, and any adequate philosophy of linguistics must be capable of allowing for the existence of this methodological distinction.

It seems to me that one of the great advantages of Popper's (^{2}1979) category of objective knowledge is that it allows us to understand how it can be that a discipline such as theoretical linguistics may successfully investigate a kind of knowledge without adopting the methods of cognitive psychology. Popper points out there that the philosophy of the physical sciences constitutes an investigation into the nature and growth of scientific knowledge. But this is readily achieved without recourse to investigations into the psychology of scientists; rather, it is understood by investigating the logical structure of scientific theories and their relationship to the problem situation in which they are developed. Scientific knowledge grows as a consequence of the interaction between scientists' internal states and processes (such as invention, reflection, deduction), their theories, and the objectively existing problem situations which they are designed to deal with. But it is not just the context which is objective: the theories themselves exist objectively: we may discover properties (consequences, contradictions) of them which always existed but were not noticed, and were thus not scientist-internal properties. Thus, scientific knowledge is crucially objective knowledge: it is not only reasonable, but preferable, to speak of scientific knowledge as a kind of knowledge which is not a cognitive state.

With this conception of objective knowledge, we can begin to see in what sense linguistic knowledge may be taken to be speaker-external: it is, crucially, mutual knowledge. Consider the case of lexical meaning: it is rather difficult to deny that lexical meaning is publicly constituted; as individual speakers, we have only a very limited influence on the publicly established meanings of words. The distinction, so crucial to semantic theory, between the linguistic meaning of lexical items (sense) and associative meaning could not be sustained unless this were so: associative meaning does not constitute part of the sense of an expression precisely because it is non-public, speaker-internal meaning. Now, with a compositionalist account of the nature of sentence meaning, we must allow that, if lexical meaning is speaker-external, then so is sentence-meaning. Given that it is the semantic rules of the language which gets us from lexical meaning to sentence-meaning, we are then committed to allowing that the semantic rules of a language are publicly constituted too. It would be surprising if the semantic and syntactic rules of a language belong to distinct ontological categories, and indeed it seems as if much the same can be said of the syntax of a language as can be said of lexical meaning: we have a choice as to what we say (in terms of choice of lexical meaning, choice of sentence-meaning), but it is the language itself and its rules, syntactic, semantic, morphological and phonological, which determine how this is signalled.

Linguistic objects exist in a public space, rather in the way that scientific knowledge does. They may evolve, and contain the seeds of their own evolution, in a way that parallels scientific knowledge. Now, in neither case does this evolution occur independently of the minds which create such public objects. There is clearly interaction between scientist and theory, and between speaker and linguistic object. But allowing for this interaction does not amount to allowing for an ontological identity between scientists and scientific knowledge, or between speakers and linguistic knowledge. Popper's interactionist account of the relationship between objective knowledge and mental and physical states of affairs can be readily, and profitably, extended to the relationship between cognitive and strictly linguistic states of affairs.

This conception of linguistic objects as belonging to Popper's category of objective knowledge allows us to isolate a third alternative between Chomsky's (1986) E-language and I-language. If I-language is, as Chomsky characterises it, defined by the speaker's internalised grammar, and E-language a speaker-external set of observable, recordable utterances, then we can identify a kind of externality, distinct from the externality of utterance events, which Chomsky has overlooked: taking the term 'grammar$_1$' to denote the linguist's construct and 'grammar$_2$' to denote the linguistic knowledge which grammars$_1$ are intended to characterise, we may say that sentences are speaker-external, as is the grammar$_2$ which defines sentence for a language, but they are not observable spatiotemporal events: they are not utterances. And much of the work carried out in semantic and pragmatic theory presupposes this. Thus, we have objective sentences, and languages, of the Popperian sort, which are not Platonic, but are evolutionary products. This turns out to be important when it comes to considering some of the points on which structuralists have objected to the generative framework, as we will see below.

The credibility of autonomist metatheories for grammatical theory, and doubt about the validity of psychologism, has perhaps been increased by the appearance in the seventies and eighties, of Itkonen's (1978) mutual knowledge metatheory, Lieb's (1983) Integrational Linguistics, Lass' (1980) work on the nature of explanation in historical linguistics, and Katz' (1981) Platonist metatheory, all of which subscribe to the notion that there is a qualitative difference in method between cognitive psychology and theoretical linguistics. This has been accompanied by a certain degree of caution as to psychological realism within linguistic theory itself: there are overt disclaimers as to the psychological reality of much of the work carried out within the generalised phrase structure grammar framework, and associated frameworks.

If we accept the idea that linguistic objects are speaker-external, then interesting questions arise as to the relationship between structuralist and generative linguistics. In order properly to address those questions, I must first say something about the second principal component of Popperian interactionist metatheory: Popper's conjectural realism.

Popper's position can be summed up thus: firstly, falsifiability is the hallmark of scientific hypotheses, and these are tested by means of the hypothetico-deductive method: we deduce the consequences of our conjectures (hypotheses) and test these; the means of arriving at the hypothesis in the first place are of no great significance. Secondly, our hypotheses are tested against descriptive statements which can never be theory-free: even elementary expressions like 'water' are theory-impregnated. Because of this, there can be no such thing as a truly theory-free description language, and thus no description or observation without theory. This latter point is important in discussing structuralist and generative assumptions about the nature of scientific research, as I hope to show. What the nature of reality might be is for our theories to say: we cannot coherently speak of an observational or descriptive reality as if this were *given* prior to our theoretical endeavours, and not theory-impregnated.

This point is an important part which lies at the core of Popperian conjectural realism: it is for the scientist to conjecture upon the nature of reality; when we accept the truth of descriptive statements which are apparently theory-free (such as 'The oil is floating on the water' or 'Specifiers precede their heads in the syntax of English'), we must recognise that there is a large conventional element in such statements: we may assume that they are true, but because they are theory-impregnated (contain theoretical terms), they are subject to revision in the light of theory revision. This means that we may speak of facts, physical, linguistic, and otherwise, but not of theory-free facts. All facts are subject to revision, and may at a later stage in theory development be judged to have been pseudofacts, or simply not facts at all.

In order properly to understand the status of this conjectural realism, we must distinguish between two senses of 'positivism'. In the first, which might be called strong positivism (the positivism of the Vienna Circle), one of the core notions is the idea that a theory-free description language is available to the scientist. This is a crucial point on which Popperian conjectural realism and 'strong' positivism differ, on which realism and positivism are poles in the philosophy of science. But it is on this point precisely that this latter sort of positivism fails: even the most innocent-looking descriptive statements (such as 'the oil is floating on the water') can be shown to be theory-bound. This is of considerable importance when it comes to discussing linguists' uses of the word 'fact', and structuralist objections to generative linguistics, as we will see below.

There is a second, weaker, sense of positivism, and that is the sense in which 'positivist' means upholding some version of the 'unity of method' hypothesis for the natural and human sciences. For those who take it that there is a qualitative gulf between the methods of the natural and human sciences, Popper's position is a positivist one. Popper can only reasonably be construed as a positivist in this latter sense: with regard to the former sense, Popper's work has been consistently anti-positivist. Now, in assessing the question of whether there is unity of method amongst the natural and human sciences, it is important to bear in mind, firstly, that how we decide this depends crucially on how we characterise method in the natural sciences in the first place and secondly, that this need not be an all-or-nothing question: we may reasonably speak of specific points of similarity (and dissimilarity) in method between natural and human sciences.

Some of the major methodological contentions of interactionism in this respect are (a) that falsifiable hypotheses are available to the generative grammarian, (b) that this constitutes an important element of shared method between the natural sciences and linguistic science, (c) that deductive method is also present in linguistic science, and (d) that Popperian conjectural realism is therefore available in the generative enterprise. Where natural science and autonomous linguistics differ is in the type of evidence available to test hypotheses: this is an important difference in method between natural science and linguistics, but it alone does not warrant a wholesale rejection of the idea that there is considerable unity of method between the two. In particular, it cannot reasonably be maintained, in defence of the notion that there is no unity of method between the two, that hypotheses made within a generative framework are heavily theory-dependent, since that is true anyway of scientific hypotheses in the physical sciences.

This observation bears closely on the use in linguistic research of the word 'empirical'. Itkonen's (1975, 1978) work raised something of a storm with its conclusion that grammatical theory is not an empirical discipline. What he meant by this was that empirical testing is testing against evidence which consists of observed spatiotemporal events;

grammatical hypotheses are testable in Itkonen's view, but not against this sort of evidence. Rather, the evidence in grammatical inquiry consists in sets of ill-formed and well-formed expressions, gained via acts of intuitive judgement. Now, since many linguists simply mean 'testable' when they say 'empirical', it was assumed by many that Itkonen (1975) was claiming that grammatical hypotheses were not testable, and thus that linguistics was not a science. But Itkonen made no such claim. Others, notably Sampson (1976), wanted to argue that the evidence in theoretical linguistics was construable as observable spatiotemporal events. I argue in Carr (1990) that his argument is untenable, and that Itkonen is quite correct in his characterisation of the nature of evidence in linguistic theorising. I will not rehearse that argument here, however. The point I want to stress is that testability need not be of the sort which involves spatiotemporal events as evidence, and if 'empirical', used of a discipline and/or its hypotheses, is to mean 'testable', and thus scientific, then linguistic hypotheses may be fully empirical in this sense without being based upon or tested by spatiotemporal observation statements.

Much work on the methodological foundations of grammatical inquiry has sustained some version of autonomism, which of course is incompatible with psychologism. Naturally, the way we go about identifying the methodological status of theoretical linguistics depends on the criteria we pick from the philosophy of science: among those utilised in the literature are: (i) our demarcation criterion for distinguishing empirical science from other discipline types, (ii) our characterisation of the evidential basis of theoretical linguistics and other disciplines, (iii) some clearly defined notion of what counts as scientific explanation, and (iv) ontological arguments supporting the view that the object of grammatical inquiry cannot be speaker-internal.

On the first of these, Itkonen's (1978) demarcation is one between disciplines which may be axiomatised and those that may not. Philosophy, logic, physics, mathematics, grammatical theory and cognitive psychology are thus all describable as sciences. They are further subdivided according to evidence type: grammatical inquiry, having intuitive grammaticality judgements as its evidential basis, is distinct from physics, and from cognitive psychology. Katz (1981), in connection with our second criterion, draws a similar conclusion: empirical sciences are distinct in their evidence type from sciences of the intuition. For Lass (1980), historical linguistics (and, one suspects, linguistics in general) is not a scientific discipline, if scientific explanation is characterised via the deductive-nomological mode of explanation. Katz and Itkonen also supply arguments to the effect that the object of inquiry cannot be speaker-internal; Katz' argument is from the nature of necessary truth, Itkonen's from the Wittgensteinian argument against private rules, and Lieb's (1986, 1987) from the ineradicably intentional nature of utterances. I will not seek to discuss the merits and demerits of these versions of autonomism; rather, I simply suggest that the psychologistic interpretation of grammatical inquiry has an increasingly large number of criticisms to reply to.

While autonomist metatheories have often been accompanied by a rejection of the generative approach to language (in Itkonen's and Lieb's cases), or an abandonment of it (in Lass' case, and apparently, within the New York School of Platonism, in the case of Langendoen and Postal's 1984 work), there is nothing in interactionism which contradicts the generative metaphor of languages as sets of sentences. The generative framework, with its central characterisation of a language as a set of sentences, is perfectly sustainable under an autonomist metatheory, and I intend interactionism to count as a non-psychologistic interpretation of the generative enterprise. Sentences, it seems to me, are linguistic objects of precisely the Popperian objective knowledge category. So too are the linguistic rules which characterise strings as sentences. And if sentences are of this category, then, under a generative framework, so are languages. Linguistic rules, with which the generative grammarian is centrally concerned, are neither events nor cognitive states.

Given the outline of interactionism, let us see what consequences it has for assessing some of the objections raised by structuralist linguists to the generative enterprise.

2 Structuralism and generativity

We have seen that generativity need not be built upon a psychologistic metatheory, and that a non-psychologistic metatheory need not imply a non-realist position. It is clear that structuralist linguistics has traditionally been non-mentalistic, taking the object of inquiry to be external, in the sense of being constituted as (a corpus of) utterance events, that is, external, but not in the interactionist sense. The question then arises: has structuralist linguistics traditionally adopted a realist or a non-realist philosophy of linguistics? To answer this, I want to consider, from a Popperian realist point of view, some of the criticisms of generative linguistics raised by linguists working in the European structuralist tradition.

One dividing point between generative work and other work is its central notion of a language as a set of sentences, and thus of a grammar$_1$ as a definition of 'sentence' for a given string from the vocabulary of that language. This notion is not an empirical hypothesis. Rather, it is akin to what Popper (1959) calls a 'metaphysical research programme', the overall 'picture' or metaphor which underlies an approach to a given domain, and from which falsifiable theories may be derived.

Bearing this in mind, we can see that, with a Popperian deductivist realism, it is for our linguistic theory to tell us, via testing against the relevant (theory-bound) evidence, what the structure of our object of inquiry might be like. Generalisations framed in terms of the theory we adopt are therefore, according to this picture of the way science proceeds, genuinely about the object of inquiry. This bears on one kind of structuralist objection to generative work, which can be found in Coseriu (1974:59-64), Lieb (1975: 1.4) and Lehmann (1982:79) that the study of universals in generative grammar, constituted as universals over the grammars$_1$ which define or generate languages, is a 'shift of interest from the object to its description', as offering 'universals of linguistics instead of universals of language' (Lehmann 1982:79).

Now, this criticism presupposes (though not in the case of Lieb) that there is a distinction to be made between what we know of the object of inquiry and our attempts, via our theories, to describe and explain it. But under a conjectural realist philosophy of science, no such distinction is available, and it seems to me that any philosophy of science that wants to uphold such a distinction faces an uphill struggle in maintaining it in the face of the evidence from the growth of scientific knowledge. What we know of an object of inquiry is *constituted* by our theoretical attempts to describe and explain it; there is no theory-free knowledge. This kind of criticism is therefore seriously weakened if our realist philosophy of science is right.

This notion of a distinction between our descriptive knowledge of a language and our theoretical knowledge of it via our linguistic theories, and thus our grammars$_1$, is especially prominent in the criticisms of generativity in the French structuralist tradition which takes its linguistics-as-semiotics view to follow directly from Saussure. Thus Swiggers (1989:133), in a review of Hagège (1985):

> La vision prophétique de Ferdinand de Saussure — l'insertion de la linguistique dans la science des signes, étudiés dans leur contexte sociale — ne s'est guère concrétisée dans les publications qui ont marqué le développement de la linguistique moderne: tout au contraire, l'évolution a été le plus souvent dans le sens d'une linguistique abstraite, détachée de la réalité sociale et historique, et sacrifiant à la mode des formalismes fort éloignés de la semiosis contextualisée.

Furthermore (136):

> il y a les correspondences (among languages: PC) dans les formes — non dans la forme des grammaires (où l'universalisme n'est que le résultat complaisant d'un raisonnement circulaire) — qui témoignent de *'tendences générales'*

For Swiggers and Hagège, it is circular to construct linguistic theories for natural language, and thus grammars$_1$ as theories of particular languages, and to seek universals in the form of those grammars$_1$, defined by universal linguistic theory. What this accusation of 'circularity' derives from is an awareness that grammars$_1$ are constructed by linguists, they are theoretical devices, and thus our universal linguistic theory is inextricably bound up with theoretical notions from the start. But this is unavoidable in any science: modern linguistic theorising is no more circular than theorising in any other scientific domain, in which the theorist is seeking a generalised theory from which particular descriptions will follow.

The rather strong claim I want to make is that, if we are ever to make any general claims at all about the domains of our theories, then this is the only approach we can take: we have little more than our theoretical, and thus our descriptive, language (in linguistics and all other disciplines) to achieve our goal. And this is made entirely evident when we note that Swiggers does after all want to construct a general theory (136):

> Ces tendances — glissant vers l'universel — se rapportent toutes à l'essence de l'activité linguistique: le problème d'associer des sens ou des contenus à des sons, étant donné certaines contraintes. L'identification des 'universaux' (ou

traits universels/généraux) s'intègre dans un cadre descriptif qui rend compte de cette association complexe à partir de quatre niveaux: la phonologie, la morphologie, le lexique et la syntaxe (p. 55). Ces cadres permettent de situer les énormes divergences entre les langues [...] et de les réduire à certaines *types*.

The most appropriate response to this is to point out that if it is circular to construct universal statements via particular grammars$_1$ based on a linguistic theory, it is equally circular to construct them on the basis of a typology. The point is that typologies are not theory-free, and do not provide an escape from the supposedly problematical 'circularity' constituted by the theory-impregnated nature of description.

We see in this kind of work a rejection, not only of the de facto autonomism of generative linguistics, but also of the explicit autonomism of much continental structuralist work, which investigates linguistic objects independently of their social and historical context. It is an interesting and ironic fact that the French semiotic tradition, with its rejection of generative linguistics on the charge that it makes the positivist error of trying to 'reduce' semiotic phenomena to formal statements, should itself be so thoroughly committed to the core notion of positivism (in the 'strong' sense given above): that a theory-free descriptive language is available to us. It was Chomsky's rejection of this positivist idea that marked the transition to modern generative linguistics; it is in non-generative work in the semiotic tradition that positivism lives on.

In defence of what I have called the 'positivist' idea that there is a clear language/grammar$_1$ distinction available to us, it might be objected that, were there no such distinction, it would be impossible to write grammars$_1$ in the first place. That is, one might object that there is enough of a pre-theoretical notion of 'a language' in phrases such as 'a language called Dutch' to sustain theoretical linguistic inquiry. This position, which runs counter to the Chomskyan notion that 'a language' in such expressions is of purely sociopolitical status, has been expressed in recent years by writers as diverse as Hurford (1988), who takes languages (in this sense) to be countable, Katz (1981), who takes languages to be Platonic objects, Lass (1986), Lieb (1987), and Pateman (1987), who takes languages to be construable in some cases as simultaneously objects of conscious belief and objects of unconscious knowledge. One might put their objection this way: if there is no clear linguistic import to expressions such as 'a language called Dutch', then what is a generative grammar$_1$ of Dutch a grammar$_1$ of? Other formulations are: 'what is a dialect of Dutch a dialect of?' and 'what is a history of Dutch a history of?' (cf. Lass, this volume).

It seems to me that the word 'Dutch' in these expressions does not pick out a set of linguistic objects. Rather, the grammar$_1$ in question identifies a set of linguistic objects, and the term 'Dutch' gives us some rough guide to the spatial and temporal location of the community for whom this mutual knowledge exists. Given that a grammar$_1$ of Dutch picks out some set of intersubjective objects (linguistic rules), we simply have to accept that, with the reality of dialect variation, there will be many communities (themselves non-discrete) sharing, more or less, certain rule systems; but the notion 'community' can only coherently be defined in terms of shared rules and representations (or in a non-generative framework, some other set of linguistic constructs). This 'open-ended' reference for words like 'Dutch' is reflected in the sociopolitical decisions which might alter their use: if communities speaking Flemish dialects of what we refer to as 'Dutch' decide that what they speak is to be called 'the Flemish language', that does nothing to alter the status of our 'grammar$_1$ of Dutch', as a theory of a linguistic object.

What I am denying is that the term 'a language', in expressions like 'a language called Dutch', can be taken simultaneously to refer to an object of conscious belief (such as the belief that one speaks Dutch or Flemish) and an object of unconscious knowledge. Rather, the object of conscious belief in these cases is part of the surface manifestation of unconscious knowledge: conscious beliefs of this sort are not beliefs about grammars$_2$, but about the *effects of grammars$_2$*. Thus the question 'what is a generative grammar$_1$ of Dutch a generative grammar$_1$ of?' amounts to the question 'what is the ontology of linguistic objects?'. The answer supplied by interactionism is that linguistic objects are a kind of objective knowledge, and thus our generative grammar$_1$ of Dutch is a theory of a system of objects of this sort.

It should by now be clear that interactionism shares with traditional structuralist metatheory an opposition to psychologism. But the version of externalism it adopts is not parallel to the structuralist externalism of utterance events, where linguistic generalisations are inductive generalisations over corpora of those events. Rather, interactionism is mentalistic without being psychologistic, in the way I have described. Nor does interactionism share with traditional structuralism the positivistic notion that a theory-free description language is available to the linguist, or the inductivism which naturally combines with this notion. What then of New Structuralism?

3 The Nine Principles

One of the most noticeable points in Lieb's (1990) Nine Principles is his adopting of an explicit externalism which is exactly parallel to the non-psychologistic mentalism I have discussed; this is evidenced in principles 2, 5, and 8 of Lieb's (1990) report. The notion of interaction between autonomous linguistics and neighbouring disciplines is also present in principles 4 and 6, and the autonomist element of interactionism in principle 3. Concerning principle 8, it is clear that New Structuralism and interactionism share the view that traditional structuralism adopted the wrong sort of externalism, and that linguistic objects are properly construed as abstract, aspatial objects, rather than as utterance events. It seems to me, however, that this position can be reasonably characterised as mentalist, albeit in the sense I have discussed, and thus not noticeably structuralist. While there can be no objection to referring to this as a new structuralist notion, there is no reason not to refer to it as a new mentalist, or new generativist, position.

There is one important point on which interactionism is not clearly aligned with the principles of new structuralism, however: the emphasis on variation (principle 7) as central to the nature of linguistic inquiry. It might appear that the radically public ontology in interactionism runs into trouble when faced with the fact of variation (and thus historical change): if individuals figure so little in the ontology of linguistic objects, what is their relation to publicly constituted grammars$_2$? At what point does the individual interact with such public objects, and how are linguistic changes instigated?

The problem here is that while individuals have practically no conscious awareness of the grammar-as-public-object, of which they have internal representations, they are nonetheless aware of the *manifestations* of that grammar$_2$. It is through an interaction with these, rather than through the internal representations per se, that changes may be instigated. I suggest in Carr (1989) that the capacity to abduce rules may well be distributed across individuals as members of a species, in Pateman's (1987) sense, but this capacity is distinct in its ontology from linguistic rules *per se* as intersubjective, i.e. public, objects. A question which arises from this conception of rules vs the rule abduction capacity is, where does this leave the notion 'idiolect'? It seems to me that if we are committed to the idea that sentences and grammars$_2$ are public objects, then idiolects are derivative of, or parasitic upon, intersubjective grammars$_2$. That is, publicly constituted grammars$_2$ are not something abstracted away from sets of idiolects. Rather, idiolects are defined by intersubjective objects: given the system of rules which constitutes a particular idiolect, it may be true that no other individual has that system of rules exactly.

But that is no basis on which to argue that public grammars$_2$ are abstractions over sets of idiolects: the point is that each rule in an idiolect will, by definition, be shared by *some* community, even if no single community can be found which shares exactly the same set of rules. It is the publicly defined nature of a linguistic rule which constitutes it as a rule, and it is from these primary objects that idiolects are derived. Whether principle 7 of New Structuralism entails the primacy of idiolects is open to debate, but it appears to me that one cannot argue for the logical primacy of idiolects with respect to intersubjective grammars$_2$ without seriously damaging the notion 'external linguistic object'. And if New Structuralism's emphasis on variation depends in any way upon a conception of grammars$_2$ as abstractions from sets of idiolects, then it faces a conflict between this emphasis on variation, and its externalism.

Perhaps some kind of rapprochement can be made between structuralist and generative traditions; whether New Structuralism can effect such a convergence remains to be seen. It will perhaps be in computational work on language processing that the difficulties of sustaining an entirely psychologistic metatheory will be borne home; if linguistic objects really are intersubjectively constituted in the way that interactionism and New Structuralism claim, then it should in principle be impossible to achieve many of the aims of AI work on natural language. It will be interesting to see whether the notion of intersubjectivity begins to emerge as a problem in AI in the foreseeable future. I suspect that it will.

References

Carr, P. 1987. "Psychologism in linguistics, and its alternatives". In: Modgil and Modgil (eds). *Noam Chomsky: Consensus and Controversy*. Brighton: Falmer Press. 212-221.
—. 1989. "Autonomism, realism, and linguistic change". *Folia Linguistica* IX,2.13-31.
—. 1990. *Linguistic Realities*. An Autonomist Metatheory for the Generative Enterprise. Cambridge etc.: Cambridge University Press. (Cambridge Studies in Linguistics 53).
Chomsky, N. 1986. *Knowledge of Language*. New York: Praeger.
Coseriu, E. 1974. "Les universaux linguistiques (et les autres)" In: L. Heilmann (ed.). *Proceedings of the XIth International Congress of Linguists*. Bologna: Società editrice il Mulino. Vol. 1. 47-73.
Hurford, J. R. 1988. *Language and Number*. Oxford: Blackwell.
Itkonen, E. 1975. "Transformational grammar and the philosophy of science". In: Koerner (ed.). *The Transformational-Generative Paradigm and Modern Linguistic Theory*. Amsterdam: Benjamins. 381-445. (CILT 1).
—. 1978. *Grammatical Theory and Metascience*. Amsterdam: Benjamins.
Katz, J. J. 1981. *Language and Other Abstract Objects*. Oxford: Blackwell.
Langendoen, D., and P. Postal. 1984. *The Vastness of Natural Languages*. Oxford: Blackwell.
Lass, R. 1980. *On explaining Language Change*. Cambridge: Cambridge University Press.
—. 1986. "Conventionalism, invention, and 'historical reality': some reflections on method". *Diachronica* 3.15-41.
Lehmann, C. 1982. "On some current views of the language universal". In: R. Dirven and G. Radden (eds). *Issues in the Theory of Universal Grammar*. Tübingen: Gunter Narr Verlag. (Tübinger Beiträge zur Linguistik 196). 73-93.

Lieb, H. 1975. "Universals of language: quandaries and prospects". *Foundations of Language* 12.471-511.
—. 1983. *Integrational Linguistics*. Vol. 1: *General Outline*. Amsterdam: Benjamins. (CILT 17).
—. 1986. "Language is external: A reply to Helmut Schnelle". *Theoretical Linguistics* 13.239-255.
—. 1987. "Sprache und Intentionalität: der Zusammenbruch des Kognitivismus". In: R. Wimmer (ed.). *Sprachtheorie*. Jahrbuch des Instituts für deutsche Sprache. Düsseldorf: Schwann. (Sprache der Gegenwart LXXI). 11-76.
—. 1990. "Rundtisch/Round Table 12. Prospects for a New Structuralism". In: W. Bahner, J. Schildt, and D. Viehweger (eds). *Proceedings of the Fourteenth International Congress of Linguists, Berlin/GDR, August 10 – August 15, 1987*. Vol. I. Berlin: Akademie-Verlag. 325-328.
Pateman, T. 1987. *Language in Mind and Language in Society*. Oxford: Clarendon Press.
Popper, K. R. 1959. *The Logic of Scientific Discovery*. London: Hutchinson. [2. revised edition 1968].
—. ²1979. *Objective Knowledge*. Oxford: Clarendon Press.
Sampson, G. 1976. Review of Koerner (ed.), *The Transformational-Generative Paradigm and Modern Linguistic Theory*. Amsterdam 1975. Language 52.961-965.
Swiggers, P. 1989. "Homo loquens: signe, sens, et société". Review of C. Hagège, L'homme des paroles, Paris 1985. *Semiotica* 74.133-144.

The Case for a New Structuralism

Hans-Heinrich Lieb
Freie Universität Berlin

Contents

I. Introduction

1 Problem and aim
  1.1 Realism vs. cognitivism: two opposing claims
  1.2 Aim of this essay
  1.3 Arguing for realism

2 Cognitivist linguistics and linguistic intentionality
  2.1 Representation linguistics
  2.2 The problem of intentionality
  2.3 A connectionist solution?

II. Background

3 Two general claims
  3.1 Linguistic Object Claim and Linguistic Structure Claim
  3.2 Abstract vs. concrete
  3.3 Constructive ontology
  3.4 The notion of extra-mental

4 The intentionality of speech
  4.1 The concept of action
  4.2 Speaking as an action

III. The argument for realism. New Structuralism
5 Arguing the Linguistic Structure Claim
  5.1 Outline of argument
  5.2 The argument
6 Linguistics as an intentional discipline
  6.1 On the Linguistic Object Claim
  6.2 The Intentionality Hypothesis
  6.3 Linguistic interdisciplines
  6.4 Summary
7 New Structuralism

References

I. INTRODUCTION

1 Problem and aim

1.1 Realism vs. cognitivism: two opposing claims

What is linguistics about?

There are at least two ways to understand this question: what is it that linguists study — which may not be what they claim or believe to be studying? And, what is an optimal way of construing the objects of linguistics — optimal for further developing linguistics as a field that, while closely cooperating with other fields, makes its own contribution to human knowledge? While the two questions are linked, the second may still be studied independently of the first, as will indeed be done in the present essay. I will be dealing with the following problem:

(1.1) What is linguistics about? that is, what is an optimal way of construing the objects of linguistics?

I will argue for

(1.2) *The Realist Claim.* The objects of linguistics are abstract, extra-mental entities.

This claim is opposed to

(1.3) *The Cognitivist Claim*. The objects of linguistics are mental mechanisms, which may or may not be construed as neurophysiological in nature.

The two claims do not exhaust possible answers to question (1.1). They are, however, the only ones to be considered in the present essay.

The Cognitivist Claim has been part and parcel of Chomskyan Generative Grammar since the early sixties (prominently, since Chomsky 1965); as such it has been discussed extensively. Explicit formulations of the Realist Claim have been rare and have had little impact so far. Best known is Katz (1981), on "Platonism" (the term is replaced by "realism" in Katz and Postal 1991); but this is not the only interpretation of the claim and may not yet be an optimal one.

Logically, the two claims are incompatible, assuming the same sense of "mental" in both (1.2) and (1.3). Hence, a conclusive argument *for* one claim is a conclusive argument *against* the other. On the other hand, neither claim is implied by the negation of the other. Therefore, a conclusive argument *against* one claim is no conclusive argument *for* the other.

1.2 Aim of this essay

It is my aim in the present essay to provide a cogent argument for the Realist Claim. This cannot be achieved by 'disproving' the Cognitivist Claim. If I am successful in my attempt, the Cognitivist Claim is automatically shown to be untenable but this is just a by-product of my essay (desirable, I believe), it is not a major objective. Differently from Lieb (1987a), there will be no independent argument against the Cognitivist Claim.

There is a two-pronged attack against the Realist Claim on its Katzian (1981) interpretation in Chomsky (1986): first, there are arguments *for* the Cognitivist Claim, which, if accepted, rule out the Realist Claim on any interpretation; second, there are arguments directed specifically at the Katzian version. Arguments of the second if not the first type are, to my mind, successfully countered in Katz and Postal (1991); moreover, it could be shown that they do not apply to the Realist Claim as interpreted in the present essay. But this is immaterial:

Chomsky's more general objections are countered automatically if I successfully demonstrate that the Realist Claim should be accepted.

A version of the Realist Claim has been embodied in my own work since Lieb (1968), (1970) (see, in particular, Lieb 1983; the opposition of Realist vs. Cognitivist Claim is the major topic of Lieb 1987a, b). Katz and coauthors developed their own versions independently (esp. Katz 1981, Langendoen and Postal 1984, Katz and Postal 1991, see also Soames 1984); and so did Carr (esp. 1990), partly reacting to Katz. Both my interpretation of and my argument for the Realist Claim differ from the versions offered by these authors (I am closest to Carr).

Katz and Postal (1991) and also Carr (1990) take a large step beyond Chomsky (1986) in explicitness of argumentation. I will go even further and present an argument whose logical structure is made completely transparent. In particular, all non-logical assumptions on which the argument rests, even minor ones, will be stated. Thus, anybody who objects to the conclusions has a chance to find some premise he would reject. If, however, there is none; and if the argument is valid; *and if one is willing to act rationally*, then objections must be dropped, and the conclusions accepted.

Both the Realist Claim and the Cognitivist Claim are ontological in nature; they define two types of conceptions of linguistics that are ontologically opposed. Conceptions are neither true nor false; they may be more or less adequate. My argument for the Realist Claim may also be understood as an attempt to demonstrate that any conception of linguistics that is to meet basic standards of adequacy must be realist in ontological matters and should indeed subscribe to the Realist Claim.

More specifically, the Realist Claim is naturally integrated into a conception that may rightly be called a *New Structuralism*. Thus, my argument for realism is also an argument for a fundamental aspect of New Structuralism (other aspects, like the epistemological, will only be touched upon). While the argument is involved and may be demanding, the conception of New Structuralism is informally characterized at the end of this essay and should be intelligible independently of the argument.

1.3 Arguing for Realism

My argument in support of the Realist Claim centers around a key problem in the theory of linguistics: how to account for *linguistic intentionality*, the 'directedness' or 'aboutness' of mental states and events in the areas of speaking, understanding speech, and knowing a language.

Part II of this essay develops the background to the argument, itself presented in Part III. As a first step, two important claims are formulated and explained (Sec. 3): for a proper treatment of linguistic intentionality it must be assumed that certain objects of linguistics are abstract and extra-mental (*Linguistic Object Claim*), which must be true in particular of 'linguistic structures' (*Linguistic Structure Claim*). As a second step, a framework is outlined that allows to deal with the intentionality of speech (Sec. 4).

Part III presents the argument for the Realist Claim, again in two steps:

(i) A detailed argument based on the nature of linguistic intentionality is formulated in Sec. 5 that supports the Linguistic Structure Claim. This argument, if accepted, is sufficient for rejecting the Cognitivist Claim (1.3); it is not yet sufficient support for the Realist Claim.

(ii) Sec. 6 first considers all objects covered by the Linguistic Object Claim and goes on to argue that any object not covered by this claim must also be abstract and extra-mental, which completes the argument for the Realist Claim. To the extent that Sec. 6 goes beyond the Linguistic Object Claim, the argument is based on an additional 'intentionality hypothesis' (6.1) and on a demonstration that non-linguistic objects such as relevant mental mechanisms may be fruitfully studied in 'interdisciplines', shared branches of linguistics and other disciplines.

In both steps (i) and (ii) the problem of how to deal with linguistic intentionality is of prime importance. This problem has figured prominently in discussions of cognitivism, and I conclude Part I by considering its role in a cognitivist framework (Sec. 2), where I believe it is unsolvable. It should be remembered, though, that my argument for the Realist Claim in no way depends on first demonstrating that the Cognitivist Claim is untenable. Sec. 2 is therefore not essential to the argument in Part III.

2 Cognitivist linguistics and linguistic intentionality

2.1 Representation linguistics

Cognitivist linguistics is linguistics conceived so as to conform to the *cognitive science program*: the heuristic assumptions that (i) notions of perception, cognition, and action apply equally to man, animal, and machine, and (ii) perception, cognition, and action in all three areas can and should be studied from a unified point of view by a group of disciplines working in close cooperation, a group that includes, in particular, psychology, neuroanatomy and neurophysiology, logic, linguistics, and computer sciences. I here presuppose familiarity with the more essential features of the program.

After a shaky start in the sixties and seventies, the cognitive science movement gathered momentum in the eighties as *symbolic cognitivism*, concentrating on the manipulation of 'symbol configurations' ('representations') by 'programs' (see Pylyshyn 1984 for a classic formulation).

In linguistics, cognitivism has had a tradition under the heading of *mentalism*, advocated by Chomsky since the early sixties and rejected as *conceptualism* in Katz (1981), Katz and Postal (1991); Chomsky continues to be a major proponent. By and large mentalist linguistics as inspired by Chomsky represents symbolic cognitivism, despite a certain vagueness and ambiguity on this point in Chomsky's more recent (since Chomsky 1981) 'Principles and Parameters' model; mentalism in linguistics has thus been *cognitivist mentalism*. Let us call *representation linguistics* the type of cognitivist linguistics that adopts symbolic cognitivism (with its emphasis on mental 'representations'). In representation linguistics, the Cognitivist Claim (1.3) is understood as follows.

The objects to be studied in linguistics are 'mental mechanisms'. These are more abstract — farther removed from objects or events in space-time — than neurophysiological mechanisms. In a different but equivalent formulation, the linguist studies neurophysiological mechanisms 'at a certain level of abstraction'; it can be shown that such study consists in characterizing abstract mechanisms that are based on the neurophysiological. (On this conception of abstract mechanisms, see Lieb 1987a,b.)

Mental mechanism that have been considered in representation linguistics are of one of three types:

(2.1) a. Production devices, i.e. abstract mechanisms whose states — or terminating states — are connected with representations that underlie utterance events.
b. Recognition devices, i.e. abstract mechanisms whose states — or terminating states — are connected with representations that underlie events of understanding.
c. Acquisition devices, i.e. abstract mechanisms whose states — or terminating states — are connected with representations that satisfy the following condition: they are again mechanisms — or components of such, e.g., algorithms — that are related to production devices and recognition devices in a fixed way.

Chomsky, in particular, has been advocating the following theses, in one form or other, for nearly thirty years:

(2.2) a. The objects studied in linguistics are acquisition devices, to be studied, in particular, for their states and associated representations called *internalized grammars* or, more recently (since Chomsky 1986), *internalized languages* (I-languages).
b. A correct *linguistic* grammar describes — or, more weakly, corresponds to — an internalized grammar.

2.2 The problem of intentionality

Symbolic cognitivism was severely attacked by Searle, most prominently in his famous 1980 'Chinese room' article and in his 1984 book. The essential points of his arguments can be summarized as follows:

(2.3) a. On any reasonable account cognitive states and events are *intentional*, i.e. directed at something in a sense that is adequate for describing human mental states and events.
b. (Searle's thesis) Instantiating a computer program is not sufficient for intentionality.

From (2.3b) it eventually follows that

(2.4) Symbolic cognitivism cannot deal with the intentionality of cognitive states or events.

Let us loosely define

(2.5) *Linguistic intentionality* = intentionality in the areas of speaking, understanding speech, and knowing a language.

It then follows from (2.4) and the definition of "respresentation linguistics" (Sec. 2.1) that

(2.6) Representation linguistics cannot deal with linguistic intentionality.

In order to defuse (2.6), we may question either (2.3a) or (2.3b). Indeed, either claim has been rejected in the extensive discussion following Searle's attack. In particular, if (2.3a) is given up and some cognitive states are not intentional, linguistics may have to deal only with non-intentional cognitive states, which makes (2.6) irrelevant even if true, a position that may be attributed to Chomsky. On the whole, however, Searle's arguments in support of (2.3) appear to have stood up remarkably well (for a recent evaluation, see Penrose 1989: Ch. 1).

Searle's arguments may have to be reevaluated, though, in the light of current developments. The cognitive science movement has been shaken from within by the advent of *connectionism*: symbolic cognitivism is being challenged by the *connectionist* conception that emphasizes — for mechanisms of a specific type — the role of a mechanism's structure for its functioning (construed in a specific way), rather than the role of any 'programs' operating on 'representations' (cf. e.g. Feldman and Ballard 1982; the shock-wave really started from Rumelhart et al. (eds) 1986, McClelland et al. (eds) 1986). Subsequent discussion (e.g. Fodor and Pylyshyn 1988) has hardly been conclusive regarding the adjustments that may be required in the cognitive science program but details need not concern us here.

Let us call *connectionist linguistics* the type of cognitivist linguistics that adopts connectionism. It may be suggested that connectionist linguistics provides a solution, or partial solution, to the problem of dealing with linguistic intentionality.

2.3 A connectionist solution?

Searle's attack against cognitivism may no longer apply to its connectionist version. Suppose we modify (2.3) by exempting connectionist mechanisms; (2.3) then takes the form

(2.7) a. On any reasonable account cognitive states and events are *intentional*, i.e. directed at something in a sense that is adequate for describing human mental states and events. (= (2.3a))
b. (Searle's thesis, *modified*) Instantiating a computer program is not sufficient for intentionality *but operation of a connectionist mechanism of the right type is.*

It follows that

(2.8) Connectionist cognitivism (connectionism) can deal with the intentionality of cognitive states and events to the extent that such intentionality is due to connectionist mechanisms.

And with special reference to linguistics:

(2.9) Connectionist linguistics can deal with linguistic intentionality to the extent that such intentionality is due to connectionist mechanisms.

Indeed, (2.8) appears to be adopted by some authors, and (2.9) corresponds to the position taken in Schnelle (1991). However, the clause added in (2.7b) may well be false, for the following reason.

Connectionist mechanisms are 'cellular automata', or systems of such (see Farmer et al. (eds) 1984, on such automata). The differences between cellular and non-cellular automata, it may be argued, are irrelevant at the level of generality that must be assumed for computational mechanisms presupposed in (2.3b); i.e. operation of a cellular automaton is a special case of instantiating a computer program; in this case, Searle's thesis also applies to connectionism. Indeed, this is the position taken by Searle as early as in (1980:420) and as late as in (1990a); his position appears to have changed in (1990b:594). I believe that this argument has considerable force. It would follow, then, that connectionist linguistics cannot deal with linguistic intentionality either.

But suppose that (2.7b) is adopted, and it is allowed that connectionist linguistics can, to some extent, deal with linguistic intentionality. *This would still not force us to accept the Cognitivist Claim* that the objects of linguistics are mental mechanisms, now understood as connectionist ones. Taking a thoroughly intentionalist stand we may require:

(2.10) Something is an object of linguistics only if it is needed for describing linguistic intentionality.

Even allowing that connectionist linguistics *can* deal with linguistic intentionality, it is conceivable that connectionist mechanisms *need not be considered in describing linguistic intentionality*. Indeed, I eventually adopt (2.10) in arguing for the Realist Claim. I begin by providing some necessary background for the argument.

II. BACKGROUND

3 Two general claims

3.1 Linguistic Object Claim and Linguistic Structure Claim

Linguistic intentionality, it will be remembered, is intentionality in the three areas of speaking, understanding speech, and knowing a language. "Speaking", "speech", and "language" are to be understood in a general sense where they do not imply restriction to the oral mode; there are, however, non-trivial problems involved in covering all 'realization modes' simultaneously. For simplicity's sake I may at times restrict myself to the oral mode.

As announced in Sec. 1.3, I will argue for the following position:

(3.1) *Linguistic Object Claim*. For a proper treatment of linguistic intentionality it is necessary to postulate at least the following entities as abstract, extra-mental objects studied in linguistics:
   a. *linguistic structures*, i.e.
      (i) potential phonetic-syntactic forms that may be forms of speech events,
      (ii) certain proper 'parts' of such forms,
      (iii) structures of proper 'parts' of such forms (this is to cover morphology);
   b. *linguistic meanings*, i.e. meanings of linguistic structures that may be, or may underlie, meanings of speech events;
   c. idiolects (in a defensible sense of the term) that are more abstract than sets of speech events; and idiolect systems that are more abstract than idiolects and determine idiolects, linguistic structures, and linguistic meanings;
   d. languages that are abstractions from idiolects; and systems of languages that are abstractions from idiolect systems.

In speaking of a *phonetic-syntactic* form I wish to include all phonetic-phonological and syntactic aspects. These forms are entities that may be 'forms of' speech events. Note that two concepts of form are involved: 'x is a phonetic-syntactic form', and the relational 'x is a form of [speech event] y' — a phonetic-syntactic *form* may be a *form of* some speech event. This *may* but need not be the case: for many of the forms, no corresponding speech event may exist. For this reason I speak of *potential* phonetic-syntactic forms. All this carries over to 'forms of' speech objects in writing, where "phonetic" may be replaced by "graphic". (3.1a) and (3.1b) are meant to cover both 'spoken' and 'written language'. The details would have to be clarified in a theory of language; different explications may be envisaged for any of the concepts in (3.1a) and (3.1b), depending on one's theory.

In the same way, no particular solution is presupposed in (3.1c) and (3.1d) for the problems surrounding the notions of idiolect and language (for *one* possible approach, see Lieb 1983; for general discussion, Lieb forthc.: Sec. 6); however, certain types of solutions, such as Chomsky's, are ruled out.

My argument for realism in Part III will center around the following subclaim of the Linguistic Object Claim:

(3.2) *Linguistic Structure Claim.* For a proper treatment of linguistic intentionality it is necessary to postulate, as objects studied in linguistics, potential phonetic-syntactic forms that are abstract, extra-mental entities.

The term "Linguistic Structure Claim" is motivated by the informal definition of "linguistic structure" in (3.1a): *if* (3.2) is true and all potential phonetic-syntactic forms are ontologically of the same type, then (3.1) must obviously hold for *any* linguistic structure, given a reasonable theory of language.

Let me emphasize that in arguing for (3.2) I am moving at the metascientific level, speaking of linguistics not languages. I am trying to prove that any conception of linguistics that is to account for linguistic intentionality must necessarily commit itself to a certain view of linguistic structures.

There are two general (non-linguistic) concepts in the two claims that stand in need of explanation: "abstract" and "extra-mental".

3.2 Abstract vs. concrete

The opposition of *abstract* vs. *concrete* is an ontological one, and abstractness allows for degrees. The comparative or degree nature of abstractness is recognized in the Linguistic Object Claim: while all postulated entities are abstract, some are more so than others, with language systems occupying the position of maximal abstractness. The distinction between concrete and abstract in this sense can be made more precise by referring to a *hierarchy of ontological levels.* Allowing for minor variations, such a hierarchy may have to conform to the following conditions to be useful for linguistics.

At the lowest or *zero level*, the level of *ontological individuals*, there are objects and events in space-time such as persons (speakers) and sound events. Actually, objects and events should be treated as individuals of different *sorts*.

Intentionality is attributed to mental states or events, in particular, cognitive ones. On a materialist account mental states and events can be ontologically reduced to objects or events in space-time; hence, no additional individuals would be needed. Proposals for such reductions have so far remained speculative and highly controversial. It is therefore advisable to simply place mental states and events at the lowest ontological level taking them as individuals of a *third* sort. This is provisional and does not imply a decision for dualism rather than materialist monism.

Technically, three *domains of ontological individuals* are postulated, the domains of spatiotemporal objects, spatiotemporal events, and mental states and events. (Certain other domains may have to be added.)

The lowest or zero level now contains individuals of three sorts; in addition, n-tuples of individuals (of any sort) are assigned to this level. (This means that n-tuples of individuals are taken as basic entities rather than sets of a specific type, which would place them at a higher level. Generally, n-tuples are here construed as belonging to the same level as their highest-level components.)

At the *first level* we have sets and properties of individuals of a single sort, relations-in-extension and relations-in-intension among individuals (not necessarily of a single sort), and n-tuples whose components are entities of the first and, possibly, the zero level.

The *second level* again builds on the first and may also involve entities form the zero level for its relations and n-tuples. In the same way, the *third* and following levels are based on the lower levels. The hierarchy may be restricted to only a few levels.

The *entities allowed by* the hierarchy are the individuals, n-tuples, sets, relations-in-extension, properties, and relations-in-intension that belong to one of the levels of the hierarchy.

The letter "H" will be used for any hierarchy of ontological levels as just specified, and "w", "x", and "y" for any entity allowed by any hierarchy H. The notions of abstract and concrete may now be defined as follows:

(3.3)   *Definitions*. Let x be any entity allowed by H.
       a. x is *concrete* in H iff x belongs to the zero level of H.
       b. x is *abstract* in H iff x is not concrete in H.

By these definitions, individuals of all sorts — objects in space-time, events in space-time, and mental states and events — and n-tuples of individuals are concrete; any other entity is abstract. Moreover, all abstract entities are related to the level of concrete entities in a systematic way.

Consider, once again, the Linguistic Object Claim. Speech events (sound events) are concrete, and so are speakers and the mental states and events associated with them. On the other hand, linguistic structures and meanings are to be abstract, and this is also true of idiolects and their systems, of languages, and of language systems.

To cover differences in abstractness between various entities, a concept *is-more-abstract-than* could be defined by criteria such as, entities higher up in the ontological hierarchy are more abstract than lower-level entities, and at a single level, intensional entities such as properties are more abstract than the corresponding extensional ones like sets of the same type (e.g. properties of individuals vs. sets of individuals). We may even allow differences of abstractness between concrete entities; thus, events might be considered as more abstract than objects; and if entities such as numbers are admitted at the zero level (a frequent move in the empirical sciences), these would certainly be more abstract than spatiotemporal events. The comparative concept is-more-abstract-than may then be used in a definition of a degree concept, *degree of abstractness*.

3.3 Constructive ontology

A hierarchy of ontological levels is *constructive* in the following weak sense: entities of higher levels are *ontological constructs* based on lower-level entities. For example, a specific theory of English (or rather, of a given English idiolect system) might construe 'the phonetic word form *not*' as

(i) the sequence of phonetic sounds [n] [ɒ] [t].

Understanding "sequence" in one of its mathematical senses as a function whose arguments are the positive integers 1,...,n, for some n > 0; construing a function as a binary relation; and conceiving a binary relation set-theoretically as a set of ordered pairs, we obtain:

(ii) *not* = {(1, [n]), (2, [ɒ]), (3, [t])}.

Moreover, the theory of English might take a standard approach and construe phonetic sounds as sets of properties of sound events, e.g.,

(iii) [n] = {Nasal, Voiced, Alveolar,...}.

where

(iv) Nasal = the property of being a sound event that has been produced by a person with release of air exclusively through his or her nose,

etc. In this case,

(v) *not* is a set of ordered pairs whose first components are positive integers and whose second components are sets of properties of sound events.

Assuming a hierarchy in which not only sound events but positive integers belong to the zero level, it follows that

(vi) *not* is an entity of the third ontological level.

(Properties of sound events are level 1; sets of such properties are level 2; so are pairs involving such sets as highest-level components; and sets of such pairs are level 3.)

The following point is worth emphasizing. A theory that semantically presupposes an ontological hierarchy of more than two levels is not committed for its formulation to a higher-order logic. Suppose that all entities referred to in the theory can be understood as sets. Now set theory can be axiomatized in a first-order language, i.e. a language without predicate variables, put differently, a language that does not require quantification over properties of basic entities (see, for example, Carnap 1958: § 43c, for such an axiomatization). All sets are individuals in the logical sense (basic entities with respect to the language) but different sets may still be placed at different levels in a hierarchy of ontological levels depending on their status as, for example, spatiotemporal events, sets of such events, sets of such sets, etc. Ontological hierarchies may thus be assumed even for theories formulated in a first-order language. (For a related if much more elaborate view of constructive ontology, see Fine 1991.)

Next, consider the concept of extramentality.

3.4 The notion of extra-mental

Roughly, entity x is *mental in a general sense* if it ontologically involves mental states or events. x *ontologically involves* y means that a proper or improper part of y is a proper or improper part of x. An object x is *mental in a cognitive science sense* if x ontologically involves some mental mechanism; x may, in particular, be a mental representation. x is *mental* if x is mental in a general sense or in a cognitive science sense, and *extra-mental* if it is not mental.

More precisely, we have the following five definitions:

(3.4) *Definition*. x *ontologically involves* y iff some proper or improper part of y is a proper or improper part of x.

"Part" is used as a cover term for any part-like relation. The element relation is counted among the part-like relations; therefore, x ontologically involves y if y is an element of x. In the case of a mental state or event, the 'content' of the state or event — see § 4, below — is not considered one of its parts; and if a mental state or event has a content of a certain kind, then the property of having this content is no part of the state or event either. The relational product or concatenation of two part-like relations is again a part-like relation.

(3.5) *Definition*. x is *mental in a general sense* iff for some y,
   a. y is a mental state or event;
   b. x ontologically involves y.

(3.6) *Definition*. x is *mental in a cognitive science sense* iff for some y,
   a. y is an abstract representational mechanism or an 'equivalent' connectionist mechanism in some robot or organism w;
   b. x ontologically involves y.

x and y are any entities allowed by any hierarchies of ontological levels. An abstract representational mechanism y may be expected to be an n-tuple whose components are, among others, an algorithm, a system of 'symbols', and a functional architecture. A *mental representation* connected with a given state of mechanism y is a construct of symbols of y; the representation therefore ontologically involves the mechanism. Representations are thus covered by (3.6). "Equivalent" in

(3.6a) abbreviates a requirement that the connectionist mechanism should produce results comparable to the results of an abstract representational mechanism. Mechanisms may be simple or complex; in particular, representational mechanisms may be based on connectionist ones that may or may not qualify independently in the context of (3.6a) — I avoid taking sides in the connectionist debate.

(3.7) *Definition.* x is *mental* iff (a) or (b):
   a. x is mental in a general sense;
   b. x is mental in a cognitive science sense.

I allow two cases of being mental; their precise relationship may be left undetermined as long as both are covered.

(3.8) *Definition.* x is *extra-mental* iff x is not mental.

The essential concepts in the Linguistic Structure Claim have now been explained, and the claim itself can be considered: the claim that potential phonetic-syntactic forms must be postulated as abstract, extra-mental entities if linguistic intentionality is to be accounted for. Linguistic intentionality is intentionality in the areas of speaking, understanding speech, and knowing a language. I will use the intentionality of (oral) speaking for my demonstration although either of the other types would have served, too. What, then, are the key intentional features of speaking?

4 The intentionality of speech

4.1 The concept of action

Speaking is a physical action, and the intentionality of speaking is a special case of the intentionality of actions. There is a vast literature on action. In the early eighties, Searle outlined a theory of action as part of a theory of intentionality (Searle 1983). I believe that Searle's action theory, somewhat modified, is a suitable framework for dealing with the intentionality of speaking. Let's have a look at the basic concepts of the modified theory (see already Lieb 1987a).

Very roughly, a physical action by somebody is a pair consisting of a mental state and a bodily movement of that person; the mental state is an intention and the movement is caused by the state.

More precisely, let "V", "V_1", etc. stand for any objects in space-time; "e", "e_1", etc. for any events in space-time; and "z", "z_1", etc. for any mental states or events. We define:

(4.1) *Definition.* (z,e) is an *action* by V iff
   a. z is an intention-in-action of V;
   b. e is a movement of V caused by z.

The notion of intention-in-action is to be understood as in Searle (1983); in particular, intention-in-action z is not prior to movement e but is a mental state that sustains the movement.

An intention-in-action is intentional, it is directed at something, namely, at a movement with specific properties; the movement is to be *caused* by the intention. More specifically, I make the following assumption, which contains certain improvements on analogous assumptions made by Searle:

(4.2) *Assumption 1: intentions-in-action.* For every intention-in-action z of V, there is exactly one greatest set of properties of spatiotemporal events such that:
   a. the set contains the property of being a movement of V caused by z;
   b. V wants that there is an e_1 that has every property in the set.

Given Assumption 1 we may introduce the notions of *content* and *object set* for intentions-in-action: the content is the set of properties postulated in Assumption 1, the object set is the set of movements that have all the properties in the content (this modifies Searle's 1983 account; in Searle 1990b, Searle postulates 'aspectual shapes' for 'intrinsic intentional states', apparently recognizing the need for *some* notion of content in our sense):

(4.3) *Definitions.* For any intention-in-action z of V:
   a. *the V-content of* z = the set of properties that is guaranteed by Assumption 1;
   b. *the V-object set of* z = the set of all e_1 such that e_1 has every property in the V-content of z.

From these definitions and Assumption 1 it follows that

THE CASE FOR A NEW STRUCTURALISM

(4.4) For any intention-in-action z of V,
   a. every element of the V-content of z is a property of spatiotemporal events;.
   b. any element of the V-object set of z is a movement of V.

While any intention-in-action has a non-empty content by (4.2a), the object set — normally, a unit set — may be empty: there need not be an appropriate movement of V.

An action as defined in (4.1) is a pair (z,e) such that e has at least the property that analogously occurs in the content of *any* intention-in-action: e has the property of being a movement of V caused by z. (z,e) is a *successful* action by V if (z,e) is an action such that e has *every* property in the V-content of z, that is, e belongs to the object set of z.

Consequences (4.4) may be informally summarized as, the content of any intention-in-action of a person consists of properties of movements of that person (no appropriate movement may exist). It is important to realize that these movement properties need not be properties of movement *form* but may be properties of any type. In particular, the content of an intention-in-action may contain *effect* properties: the property of being a movement that has a certain effect, either directly or indirectly.

On a reasonable conception of actions, an actor must have control over his movement. This should mean, among other things, that every property that the movement is meant to have is 'accessible' to the actor. I tentatively explicate this notion as follows: the actor is able in principle to recognize if his movement does or does not have the property. Generally,

(4.5) a. *Definition*. For any property α of spatiotemporal events (analogously, objects), α is *accessible* to V iff it is not excluded by α that, for any e,
   (i) if e has α, V recognizes that e has α;
   (ii) if e does not have α, V recognizes that e does not have α.

   b. *Assumption 2: intentions-in-action*. For any intention-in-action z of V and any property α in the V-content of z, α is accessible to V.

The import of Assumption 2 ultimately depends on how "recognize" in the definition of accessibility (4.5a) is understood. I suggest that recognition may be construed as a type of perception, in a very broad sense of this term.

A notion similar to accessibility in the sense of (4.5a) has recently been introduced also by Searle: there are unconscious intentional states "that are in principle accessible to consciousness", where "accessible in principle" means that "given the right circumstances — [they] are capable of generating conscious states" (1990b:588; insofar Chomsky's criticism, who sees no interpretation of "in principle", is beside the point — Chomsky 1990). Similarly to (4.5b), Searle assumes that there are no intentional states that are "inaccessible even in principle" (l.c.). My own concept, developed independently of Searle's, is non-committal on questions of consciousness.

Speech actions are actions of a special type.

4.2 Speaking as an action

I assume that

(4.6) *Assumption 3: speech actions.* Any speech action of V is a pair (z,e) such that
a. (z,e) is an action by V;
b. e is an articulatory movement of V.

Movement e is as a rule quite complex. z is a *speech intention* of V in the following sense: z is an intention-in-action whose content consists of properties of articulatory movements of V.

On formal grounds alone Assumption 3 cannot be construed as a definition of "speech action". A definition would have to contain further conditions on the content of the speech intention. What should be assumed for the content under normal circumstances?

We might suggest that the content should contain a property of movement *form*; after all, the form of the articulatory movement has to be determined. Sure enough, if there is a property of movement form in the content of the speech intention, then the form is directly determined. Such determination is, however, an exception.

Unless I am involved in an articulation exercise, I do not, in speaking, intend to make articulatory movements of a specific form: I do not intend to close my lips, keep my vocal chords from vibrating, etc. All this is a by-product of what I am really trying to do. Under normal circumstances, there is no property of movement form in the content of a speech intention.

Part of what I really intend to do in normal speaking is this: I want to make a movement that *results in* a sound event that has a certain form. If, for example, I wish to say "Get out!" rather than "Get in!", then I want to make a complex articulatory movement that results in a sound event of a Get-out!-form rather than a Get-in!-form.

It is the sound event that has this form not the articulatory movement. There is, however, a general relationship that must be postulated:

> (4.7) *Assumption 4: normal speech actions.* A sound event caused by the movement part of a *normal* speech action (i.e. one whose intention-in-action does not contain a form property of articulation events in its content) has its intended form only if the movement has a certain form; more briefly: movement form is implied by intended form of movement result.

(A more formal restatement, which would be rather technical, is here unnecessary.) Although no particular form of the movement is intended, movement form is automatically determined by the intended form of the movement result; articulation is automated and is controlled by checking the form of the resulting sound event.

What normally figures in the content of a speech intention is an *effect property* defined by a form property of sound events.

Let "F", "F_1", etc. be variables that range over entities such as forms of sound events, in an appropriate sense of "is a form of" (see also the comments on (3.1), above). We may then define:

> (4.8) *Definitions*
> a. *The* F-*property* = the property of being a sound event e_1 such that F = the form of e_1.
> b. *The effect property relative to* F *and* V = the property of being an articulatory movement e of V that causes some sound event e_1 that has the F-property, i.e. whose form is F.

In defining the notion of F-property I made the simplifying assumption that any sound event has exactly one 'form'. This gets us around some non-trivial problems, in particular, around the following quandary. "The form of" is most naturally understood as "the overall form of", where all relevant form aspects are covered. But then we run into the problem of partial automatization in speech — I may wish to realize a syntactic sentence without precisely planning the phonetic shape of the sound event. Using concepts (4.8) in subsequent assumptions thus means a non-trivial idealization that in a fuller account should be avoided. ("The form of" must also be relativized to 'linguistic systems', a point to which I return in Sec. 6.1.)

Any speech intention that does not contain a property of articulation form in its content contains an effect property defined by a property of sound event form:

(4.9) *Assumption 5: normal speech intentions.* For any normal speech intention z of V (i.e. any speech intention z that does not contain a form property of articulation events in its content), there is an F such that the effect property relative to F and V is an element of the V-content of z.

This assumption is fundamental to my argument for the Linguistic Structure Claim: it is forms F on which the argument hinges. (It may be objected that even *syntactic* form may only be 'implied by an intended meaning'; hence, (4.9) should require existence of an effect property relative to a 'meaning' not a form. This is doubtful but even if correct, an argument concerning sound-event form could still be formulated, be it in a more complicated way. Moreover, it would be possible to argue for meanings themselves as abstract, extra-mental entities, see Sec. 6.1, below.)

III. THE ARGUMENT FOR REALISM. NEW STRUCTURALISM

5 Arguing the Linguistic Structure Claim

5.1 Outline of argument

The Linguistic Structure Claim says that

(5.1) = (3.2)
For a proper treatment of linguistic intentionality it is necessary to postulate, as objects studied in linguistics, potential phonetic-syntactic forms that are abstract, extra-mental entities.

I now demonstrate that there are entities F of the required type.
Assume that

(5.2) (z,e) is a successful normal speech action of V, i.e.
a. (z,e) is a speech action of V;
b. e has all properties in the V-content of z;
c. z is a normal speech intention of V (the V-content of z does not contain a form property of articulation events).

Then, by (c) and Assumption 5 (4.9),

(5.3) there is an F — say F^* — such that the V-content of z contains the effect property relative to F and V, i.e. the property of being an articulatory movement of V that causes a sound event whose form is F.

I demonstrate that

(5.4) A. F^* partly determines the intentionality of z.
B. F^* is a potential phonetic-syntactic form.
C. F^* is abstract (in any hierarchy H of ontological levels).
D. F^* is extra-mental.

Let me first characterize my arguments for A to D in a general way.

Assertion A is directly supported by (5.3). My argument for B hinges on the fact that in a normal speech action the intended form of the resulting sound event must indirectly determine the form of the articulatory movement; for this, both phonetic-phonological and syntactic aspects must be considered.

My argument for C — the abstract nature of F^* — is based on the fact that it must be possible for different sound events to have the same phonetic-syntactic form, which requires such forms to be abstract.

My argument for D — the extra-mental nature of F^* — is the most complex of the four. Its essential point is this: the effect property relative to F^* and V must be *accessible* to V, by Assumption 2 (4.5b); this requires that the F^*-property — the property of being a sound event whose form is F^* — is accessible, too; and this appears to be impossible if F^* is mental in the sense of (3.7).

In this way, the Linguistic Structure Claim is, in principle, proved: the intentionality of normal speech actions is a case of linguistic intentionality; for a proper treatment of the intentionality of such actions it is necessary to postulate potential phonetic-syntactic forms that are abstract and extra-mental; these are, of course, studied in linguistics.

5.2 The argument

A. F^* *partly determines the intentionality of* z. — The object set of z — see above, following (4.2) — is determined by the content of z, and there is one element of the content, viz. the effect property relative to F^* and V, that is partly determined by F^*.

B. F^* *is a potential phonetic-syntactic form.* — I am presupposing a concept of potential phonetic-syntactic form such that (*Auxiliary Assumption I*), for all F_1, F_1 is a potential phonetic-syntactic form iff,

(i) it is not excluded by F_1 that there is some sound event e_1 such that F_1 = the form of e_1;
(ii) F_1 is both phonetic-phonological and syntactic.

(This need not be construed as a definition of the term. The concept should be further relativized to 'idiolect systems', see § 6.1, below.) By (5.2b) and (5.3), there is a sound event e_1, say e_1^*, such that F^* = the form of e_1^*; hence, existence of such a sound event is not excluded by F^*; this satisfies (i). By Assumption 4 (4.7), e_1^* has F^* only if articulatory movement e has a certain form. Now it is well-known (*Auxil-*

iary Assumption II) that articulation is simultaneously determined by phonetic-phonological and syntactic factors. Hence, F^* is both phonetic-phonological and syntactic, as required by (ii). It follows that F^* is a potential phonetic-syntactic form.

C. F^* *is abstract.* — Suppose that F^* is concrete (in some hierarchy H of ontological levels that allows only the three domains of ontological individuals mentioned in 3.2 — a non-essential restriction that simplifies the argument; reference to H will be omitted). Then F^* is either a spatiotemporal object or event, or a mental state or event, or a tuple of such entities, by (3.3a). In the first case, we are forced into the position of extreme nominalism combined with physicalism, in the second case into the position of extreme nominalism combined with mentalism (I am using "nominalism" in a broader sense to cover all restriction to zero-level entities). But the position of extreme nominalism necessarily fails in linguistics: it must be possible for different sound events to have the same phonetic-syntactic form (*Auxiliary Assumption III*). If such forms are concrete, this is out of the question for the forms of sufficiently complex sound events (*Auxiliary Assumption IV*). Since all phonetic-syntactic forms should have the same ontological status (*Auxiliary Assumption V*), F^* cannot be concrete. Hence, F^* is abstract, by (3.3b).

D. F^* *is extra-mental.* — For reasons that will soon be obvious, I begin by introducing an additional hypothesis that may be somewhat surprising:

(i) V dies before the beginning of 1992.

Assume that F^* is mental. Then F^* is mental in a general sense or in a cognitive science sense, by (3.7).
Suppose that

(ii) F^* is mental in a general sense.

Then there is a mental state or event y such that F^* ontologically involves y, i.e. some proper or improper part of y is a proper or improper part of F^*, by (3.5) and (3.4).

By (5.3) the V-content of speech intention z contains the effect property relative to F^* and V, the property of being an articulatory movement that causes a sound event whose form is F^*. By Assumption 2 (4.5b),

(iii) the effect property relative to F^* and V is accessible to V,

i.e., by (4.5a), it is not excluded by the effect property that, for any movement e_2, if e_2 has the effect property, then this is recognized by V, and if e_2 does not have the effect property, then this, too, is recognized by V. On the other hand, (iii) cannot be true, as appears from the following argument.

F^* has a part that is part of the mental state or event y (see above). It is certainly safe to make the following *Auxiliary Assumption VIa*: for any person V_1 that dies before the beginning of 1992 and any mental state or event y_1, V_1 does not know y_1. (I here presuppose a materialist conception of mental states and events; such states and events must not be confused with their contents.) Because of (i), F^* or some part of F^* is therefore unknown to V. This again implies — assuming a reasonable relation between knowing and recognizability (*Auxiliary Assumption VII*) — that V cannot recognize whether the form of any given sound event is or is not F^*. Recognition is excluded by the F^*-property itself, viz. by the fact that F^* has a part not known to V. It follows that the F^*-property (the property of being a sound event whose form is F^*) is not accessible to V, by (4.5a).

The effect property is the property of being a movement that causes a sound event that has the F^*-property. We may certainly assume (*Auxiliary Assumption VIII*): for any F_1 and V_1, if the F_1-property is not accessible to V_1, then V_1 cannot recognize whether a movement has the property of causing a sound event that has the F_1-property. Therefore, V cannot recognize whether any movement has the effect property relative to F^* and V. Moreover, this is excluded by a fact about the effect property: being determined by an inaccessible sound-event property. If follows from (4.5a) that

(iv) the effect property relative to F^* and V is not accessible to V,

in contradiction to (iii). Therefore, (ii) does not hold: F^* is not mental in a general sense.

F^* could still be mental in a cognitive science sense. This is excluded by a strictly analogous argument: reference to a mental state or event y is replaced by reference to a mental (representational or connectionist) mechanism y (which leads to a new *Auxiliary Assumption VIb* analogous to VIa). This is the only change. (See also Lieb 1987a: § 5.3, for an argument against the cognitive science case.)

Therefore, F^* *is extra-mental*, by (3.8).

This result still depends on (i) V dies before the beginning of 1992: we did *not* assume, in Auxiliary Assumptions VIa and VIb, that mental states and events and mental mechanisms will never be known but only that nobody before 1992 knew them. However, it would be linguistically absurd to allow that potential phonetic-syntactic forms might differ in 'mentality status' depending on a speaker's death before or after the beginning of 1992; this, then, should be excluded by an appropriate requirement (*Auxiliary Assumption IX*). It then follows that F^* is extra-mental also if V does not die before the beginning of 1992, i.e. F^* *is extra-mental unconditionally*. (Q.E.D.)

This concludes my argumentation in support of (5.4) and thus, of the Linguistic Structure Claim in general. Let us briefly consider the assumptions to which I had to commit myself.

The general basis of the argument is Assumption 5 on normal speech intentions (4.9) by which the content of any normal speech intention contains the effect property relative to some F; it is this Assumption that justifies the initial transition from (5.2) to (5.3).

In addition, the phonetic-syntactic nature of F^* (5.4B) also depends on Assumption 4 (4.7) (in normal speech actions, movement form is implied by intended form of movement result). To prove the extra-mentality of F^*, Assumption 2 (4.5b) has to be brought in (it is true of any intention-in-action that all content elements are accessible).

Proofs of B, of C, and of D also depend on Auxiliary Assumptions I and II; III to V; and VIa,b, VII to IX, respectively. I consider as incontrovertible both Assumptions 2, 4, and 5 and the ten Auxiliary Assumptions.

I now return to the Linguistic Object Claim, of which the Linguistic Structure Claim is an essential part.

6 Linguistics as an intentional discipline

6.1 On the Linguistic Object Claim

So far I have argued only for some potential phonetic-syntactic forms as abstract, extra-mental entities. By Auxiliary Assumption V (Sec. 5.2, end of C), all such forms must have this status. Linguistic structures in the sense of (3.1a) may then be included generally.

The Linguistic Object Claim also commits us to linguistic meanings that may be, or may underlie, meanings of speech events and are abstract and extra-mental. Naturally, an argument for such meanings cannot be based on a form-related effect property. There is, however, a corresponding meaning-related 'semantic' property that belongs to the content of normal speech intentions; this semantic property may be used in an argument for abstract, extra-mental meanings (where "extra-mental" is understood in the technical sense of (3.8), which, surprisingly, is compatible with a partly 'psychological' conception of lexical meanings; see Lieb 1992). Moreover, a corresponding 'pragmatic' property gives rise to abstract, extra-mental 'pragmatic senses'. (Both properties are addressee-dependant; we are not arguing purely from the speaker's point of view. See Lieb, 1987a: § 4.3, for details of these properties.)

In addition, the Linguistic Object Claim has us committed to 'idiolects' and 'idiolect systems' (3.1c). As a matter of fact, if we postulate potential phonetic-syntactic forms, or speak of 'the form' of a sound event, we cannot avoid postulating some sort of 'linguistic system' to justify formulations such as in § 4.2, Auxiliary Assumption I (ii): "F_1 is both phonetic-phonological and syntactic". Concepts like "phonetic-phonological" and "syntactic" make sense *only if relativized* to linguistic systems S. This means that the notion of potential phonetic-syntactic form — analogously, linguistic structure and linguistic meaning — must be relativized in the same way. I have argued elsewhere (Lieb 1987a: § 5.5) that (i) the abstract, extra-mental nature of forms and meanings carries over to systems that involve such forms and meanings, and (ii) the systems must be construed as speaker-relative, as systems of 'idiolects', in a *defensible* sense of "idiolect" (see also Lieb forthc.: Sec. 6). Again, if languages are abstractions from idiolects and language systems abstractions from idiolect systems, then both must also be abstract and extra-mental.

It should be emphasized that the Linguistic Object Claim is neutral as to a 'static' or a 'dynamic' conception of systems.

I have only hinted at the reasons for adopting not just the Linguistic Structure Claim but the Linguistic Object Claim in its entirety. To be really convincing we may have to construct a framework that conforms to this claim and in which forms, meanings, idiolects, idiolect systems, languages, and language systems are formally related (for an outline of one possible framework, see Lieb 1983: Part A). Moreover, the Linguistic Object Claim, which is strictly ontological, should be shown to be compatible with reasonable answers to epistemological questions such as, what does it mean to 'know' a language? (For my own answers, see Lieb 1987a: § 6.)

The Linguistic Object Claim covers all objects that have been at the core of traditional linguistic interest, in particular, languages and their systems. In this respect, then, the Linguistic Object Claim is inclusive: *all* linguistic objects at the core of traditional linguistic interest must be abstract and extra-mental. This is the very opposite of the cognitivist position that all linguistic objects, or those of primary importance, are neurophysiological or mental mechanisms.

Still, the Linguistic Object Claim was not formulated so as to *exclude* neurophysiological and mental mechanisms as objects of linguistics: the claim as it stands allows for objects studied in linguistics that are not abstract and extra-mental — accepting the claim means rejecting the Cognitivist Claim (1.3), but the Linguistic Object Claim is not yet equivalent to the Realist Claim. Exclusion of mechanisms is a consequence of an additional hypothesis.

6.2 The Intentionality Hypothesis

I propose that the following should be adopted as a fundamental heuristic hypothesis for linguistics:

> (6.1) *Hypothesis of linguistics as an intentional discipline (Intentionality Hypothesis)*. Something is an object of linguistics only if it is needed for describing the content of intentional

mental states or events that are connected — in a non-contingent way — with
(i) speaking,
(ii) understanding speech, or
(iii) judging speech from a communicative point of view.

"Speaking" and "speech" are used in a general sense where no restriction to oral communication is implied. In the case of a speech action, it is first of all the intention-in-action that is connected with the action in a non-contingent way. Mental states of 'knowing a language' are not mentioned in (6.1) because they are connected with each of (i) to (iii).

We may indeed assume that all theoretical constructs mentioned in the Linguistic Object Claim are permitted by the Intentionality Hypothesis, but this may *not* be assumed of neurophysiological and mental mechanisms connected with speaking, understanding speech, or judging speech from a communicative point of view. Such mechanisms may or may not underlie most or all relevant mental states and events; even if they do, *they are not needed for describing their content*. This simply follows from the fact that knowing the content of these mental states and events is compatible with total ignorance of the underlying mechanisms; such ignorance must indeed be assumed for normal communication.

Adoption of the Intentionality Hypothesis may appear as overly restrictive: aren't we excluding from linguistics what many linguists claim to be interested in most of all? The hypothesis does rule out neurophysiological and mental mechanisms as objects of linguistics but not as objects to be studied in an interdisciplinary way by non-linguists cooperating with linguists. This is seen more clearly once the notion of 'interdiscipline' has been introduced and explained.

6.3 Linguistic interdisciplines

I begin by introducing two concepts of interdiscipline, where the second is based on the first:

(6.2) *Definitions*. Let "d", "d_1",... stand for any scientific disciplines.
   a. d is an *interdiscipline* of d_1 and d_2 iff
      (i) d is a branch of both d_1 and d_2;

(ii) there is no d_3 such that both d_1 and d_2 are branches of d_3;
(iii) neither is d_1 a branch of d_2 nor conversely.
b. d is a d_1-*interdiscipline* iff for some d_2, d is an interdiscipline of d_1 and d_2.

For example, it may be proposed that *psycholinguistics* is an *interdiscipline of linguistics and psychology*: a shared branch of both, which are neither branches of a single other discipline nor branches of each other. In this case, psycholinguistics is a *linguistic* (and also a psychological) *interdiscipline* (d_1 = linguistics, or d_1 = psychology), by (b).

Any scientific discipline is partly characterized by its *domain* and its *subject matter*: the domain is composed of, in some way or other, some or all objects studied in the discipline, and the subject matter, of the properties *for which* objects in the domain are studied. "Composed of, in some way or other" allows for different set-theoretical relationships. "Some or all objects" allows for a construal where only the most basic or representative objects are considered for the domain; for branches of linguistics other than linguistic interdisciplines, these may be complete languages rather than linguistic structures etc. For simplicity's sake I will here take the position that *all* objects studied in a discipline are included in its domain.

In the case of an interdiscipline of d_1 and d_2, both the domain and the subject matter are *inhomogeneous*: the domain of the interdiscipline includes objects from the domain of d_1 and objects from the domain of d_2; its subject matter includes properties from the subject matter of d_1 and the subject matter of d_2. At the same time, certain *relations* hold between objects from d_1 and objects from d_2, and conversely; and the subject matter of the interdiscipline consists of properties based on these relations: each property is the property of being related in a certain way to some object from d_2, or is the property of being related in a certain way to some object from d_1. We may say that the interdiscipline studies the d_2-objects in its domain *from the point of view of* d_1, and the d_1-objects *from the point of view of* d_2. Psycholinguistics would study the linguistic objects in its domain from a psychological point of view and the psychological objects in its domain from a linguistic point of view: for example, a syntactic construction might be studied for its learnability, and a mental mechanism for its involvement in learning the construction.

More precisely, suppose that d is an interdiscipline of d_1 and d_2, and only of d_1 and d_2. Assume that the domains of d_1 and d_2 are *sets* composed of, in some way or other, the objects studied in d_1 and d_2, respectively.

The domain of d may then be construed as a set of two sets. One set is a subset of the domain of d_1, and is therefore composed of, in some way or other, objects studied in d_1; the other set is related in the same way to objects studied in d_2.

The subject matter of d is also construed as a set of two sets. *One set* is composed of, in some way or other, properties of the following kind:

(i) it is d_1-objects figuring in d's domain that are studied in d for these properties;
(ii) each property consists in a d_1-object being related in a certain way to some d_2-object figuring in d's domain.

To characterize the *second set* in the subject matter of d, "d_1" and "d_2" are interchanged in (i) and (ii). It is in this way that the subject matter of d accounts for relations that hold between objects of d_1 and objects of d_2 or conversely. (For various aspects of the notions of interdiscipline as applied to linguistics, see also Lieb 1976: § 7, 1983: § 29.2.)

The study of neurophysiological and mental mechanisms that are connected with speaking, understanding speech, with judging speech, or with language learning now finds a natural place in two linguistic interdisciplines:

(6.3) *Place of neurophysiological and mental mechanisms.* Consider any mechanism connected with speaking, understanding speech, judging speech from a communicative point of view, or with language learning. Either (a) or (b):
   a. The mechanism is neurophysiological and belongs to the biological part (element) of the domain of *biolinguistics*, an interdiscipline of linguistics and biology.
   b. The mechanism is mental and belongs to the psychological part of the domain of *psycholinguistics*, an interdiscipline of linguistics and psychology.

The point of (6.3) is this.

Both biolinguistics and psycholinguistics are construed as interdisciplines in the sense of (6.2a), which implies specific conditions on their subject matters. In particular, the *biological* objects in the domain of biolinguistics, such as neurophysiological mechanisms, are studied from a *linguistic* point of view: they are studied for properties they may have because of their relations to linguistic objects; and conversely, the *linguistic* objects in the domain of biolinguistics such as linguistic structures are studied from a *biological* point of view: they are studied for properties they may have through their relations to biological objects, such as neurophysiological mechanisms. *These statements depend on a prior distinction between linguistic and non-linguistic objects in the domain of biolinguistics*; they simply cannot be made if the biological objects — specifically, neurophysiological mechanisms — are identified with the linguistic.

The situation is of course analogous for *psycholinguistics*, where mental mechanisms take the place of the neurophysiological, and is essentially the same for arbitrary linguistic interdisciplines (e.g., for sociolinguistics).

Mechanisms, then, need not be construed as objects of linguistics to account for their linguistic relevance; they belong to the non-linguistic parts of the domains of linguistic interdisciplines in which they are studied from a linguistic point of view.

6.4 Summary

We have considered all types of abstract entities, both mental and extra-mental, that have been proposed as linguistic objects. It is only extra-mental entities that have stood up to scrutiny. This, then, supports the Realist Claim:

(6.4) = (1.2) The objects of linguistics are abstract, extra-mental entities.

I argued in considerable detail for the claim that *most* types of linguistic objects are abstract and extra-mental. My argument for *all* types being of this kind was sketchier and depended on the hypothesis of linguistics as an intentional discipline. This hypothesis cannot be proved; it is a heuristic hypothesis that must prove itself by its fruitfulness. To the extent that the argument for the Realist Claim uses the Intentionality Hypothesis, this claim, too, is construed as heuristic. One point in favour of the Realist Claim, understood as partly heuristic, is a metascientific consequence: it avoids reductionism, leading to an *integrative* conception of linguistics.

All aspects of linguistic objects, be they 'purely linguistic' in a traditional sense or of a 'mixed' type, are accounted for and still linguistics retains its identity within a system of interrelated disciplines. Cognitivist linguistics, on the other hand, is one of several *reductionist* conceptions: essential parts of the traditional domain of linguistics are declared irrelevant ("epiphenomenal" — Chomsky), and linguistics as a whole is reduced to a branch of a discipline (psychology or biology) with which, on our view, it may only have *shared branches*. Since there are several disciplines to choose from (sociology, psychology, and biology), reduction is arbitrary unless also applied to these disciplines, an endeavour with a long history of failure (for a relevant discussion of reduction problems, see Carrier and Mittelstraß 1989, esp. Ch. 2; on the most recent reduction attempts, Bickle 1992). I would allow linguistics as a branch of semiotics; this is the only conception that leaves the traditional domain of linguistics unaffected.

More specifically, the Realist Claim is an essential component of the following position.

7 New Structuralism

The most prominent metascientific positions in current linguistics should be cognitivism, in particular, cognitivist mentalism; functionalism; and realism. Cognitivism and realism are diametrically opposed, and functionalism coexists in an uneasy neighbourhood with cognitivism and realism. Accepting the Realist Claim, the underlying Intentionality Hypothesis, and the notion of linguistic interdiscipline, we may at once transcend this fragmentation and arrive at a unified view of linguistics.

Our position is realist in a broad sense — the objects of linguistic study are abstract and extra-mental — but differs from realism in its Katzian form. On our view the abstract objects of linguistics are indeed non-spatial and non-temporal but not 'aspatial' and 'atemporal';

it is not true, on our conception, that they have "no temporal or spatial properties" (Katz 1981:186): abstract objects exist only as entities of a hierarchy of ontological levels; as such they are systematically related to concrete ones, in particular, to spatiotemporal objects and events, and there are independent relations (such as, 'is spoken by') between the abstract objects of linguistics and concrete entities (which is of course recognized by Katz). For this reason the abstract objects of linguistics may be assigned *derived* temporal and spatial properties, a fundamental fact for historical and areal linguistics. (Identification of relevant properties is a major topic in Lieb 1970; see also Lieb 1983: Part A, Lieb forthc.)

The objects of linguistics are extra-mental but they are still dependant on the contents of mental states and events. Thus, I cannot accept without qualification the Katzian view of abstract objects by which their existence is "independent of mind and matter" (Katz 1981:12); nor do I subscribe to its epistemological consequence, postulation of a separate faculty of 'intuition' by which abstract objects are known.

I am proposing a position of what may be called *constructive realism*; the position implies a constructive ontology. It appears to be closer to Popper (1972), Popper and Eccles (1977), and Carr (1990), than to Katz. (I would hesitate, though, to subscribe to the details of Popper's arguments, competently criticized by Carrier and Mittelstraß in 1989: Ch. 4, who at the same time argue for their own version of 'interactionism'.) While proposing a realist position, I am also taking a mentalist stand, and this is no contradiction.

Realism and cognitivism are indeed incompatible. Cognitivist mentalism is, however, only one possible form of mentalism, and this seems to have been overlooked not only in linguistics. A mentalist position may consist in concentrating not on mental mechanisms (which may or may not be construed as neurophysiological ones) but on the contents of intentional mental states and events. Surprisingly only to the cognitivist, the contents turn out to be extra-mental. (True, this is not clearly recognized by Searle, either.) Thirty years ago Chomsky took the wrong turn, leading linguistics into the dead-end of cognitivist mentalism rather than down the open road of intentionalist studies. I am advocating a position, then, that combines constructive realism with *non-cognitivist mentalism* or *intentionalism*.

Finally, consider functionalism. This is a many-faceted position which may, however, reduce to four basic points:

(i) The 'function' of linguistic properties of speech events is to be defined in terms of speaker intentionality.
(ii) The 'function' of an element of a linguistic system is to be defined in terms of relations that connect the element with other elements of the system (more restrictively, only 'forms' are allowed to have functions, which are to be defined in terms of relations that connect 'forms' with 'meanings').
(iii) Every non-peripheral element of a linguistic system has a 'function'.
(iv) 'Function' in (ii) is ultimately determined by 'function' in (i).

(i) is easily accepted. (iv) has remained programmatic; no determination relation has ever been specified. I propose to take a neutral stand towards (ii) and (iii), due to the unresolved problems connected with (iv). The position I am advocating may therefore be construed as *weaker functionalism*, a weak form of functionalism that adopts a functional view of speech and does not exclude a functional view of elements of linguistic systems but does not commit itself to such a view.

I am advocating, then, *combining constructive realism, non-cognitivist mentalism (intentionalism), and weaker functionalism into a unified position that may rightly be called a New Structuralism.*

First, realism is essentially a structuralist position. Linguistic structures and systems are key objects of linguistic study. True, these are abstract, and American structuralism used to have great problems with abstract entities, due to its nominalist slant. This, however, should be considered a degeneration rather than a characteristic of a structuralist position.

Second, functionalism itself is part of the structuralist tradition in Europe, and is normally combined with non-cognitivist mentalism.

The essentially new feature is the fundamental role assigned to non-cognitivist mentalism: linguistic intentionality is moved to the center of linguistics. This provides a framework for solving two basic problems of linguistics with which traditional structuralism struggled unsuccessfully.

First, there is the language vs. speech quagmire from which formalist structuralism tried to extract itself on the language side and functionalism on the side of speech, both ending up, all too frequently, in fruitless confrontation. Linguistic intentionality now turns out to justify both the ontological position of formalist structuralism (as far as it did not subscribe to extreme nominalism) and the communicative orientation of functionalism, which should end the confrontation.

Second, there is the problem of justifying theoretical constructs in linguistics from an empirical point of view. In American structuralism the unsolvable controversy of God's truth linguistics vs. hocus-pocus linguistics (cf. Joos in Joos (ed.) 1966 [1957]:80) highlighted, for a brief historical moment, a fundamental problem: linguistic analyses remain arbitrary unless both the objects of and the data for linguistic studies are clearly defined. It is Chomsky's historical merit that he kept drawing attention to the problem by untiringly offering an inadequate solution: the objects of linguistic study are mental mechanisms. This may now be confronted with the following consequence of the Intentionality Hypothesis:

(7.1) Theoretical constructs are objects of linguistics only if they are needed for describing the content of intentional mental states or events that are connected — in a non-contingent way — with (i) speaking, (ii) understanding speech, or (iii) judging speech from a communicative point of view.

New Structuralism as here characterized is not anybody's theory, or any theory at all. It is an integrative, non-reductionist position in linguistics that may be made specific in many different ways. In particular, it allows for an indefinite number of theories of language, each giving its own answers to questions such as, what is a linguistic structure? what is a language? what is it that determines or explains structures and languages? What I am claiming is this: on an optimal conception of linguistics, different answers to the same questions will still agree with the principles of New Structuralism.

References

Bickle, John. 1992. "Mental anomaly and the new mind-brain reductionism". *Philosophy of Science* 59.217-230.
Carnap, Rudolf. 1958. *Introduction to Symbolic Logic and Its Applications*. New York: Dover.
Carr, Philip. 1990. *Linguistic Realities. An Autonomist Metatheory for the Generative Enterprise*. Cambridge etc.: Cambridge University Press. (Cambridge Studies in Linguistics 53).
Carrier, Martin, and Jürgen Mittelstraß. 1989. *Geist, Gehirn, Verhalten. Das Leib-Seele-Problem und die Philosophie der Psychologie*. Berlin/New York: de Gruyter.
Chomsky, Noam. 1965. *Aspects of the Theory of Syntax*. Cambridge, Mass.: The M. I. T. Press.
—. 1981. *Lectures on Government and Binding*. Dordrecht: Foris.
—. 1986. *Knowledge of Language: Its Nature, Origin, and Use*. New York etc.: Praeger. (Convergence).
—. 1990. "Accessibility 'in principle'." *Behavioral and Brain Sciences* 13.600-601.
Farmer, Doyne; Tommaso Toffoli; and Stephen Wolfram. 1984 (eds). *Cellular Automata. Proceedings of an Interdisciplinary Workshop, Los Alamos, New Mexico, USA, March 7-11, 1983*. Amsterdam etc.: North Holland Physics Publishing.
Feldman, J. H., and Dana H. Ballard. 1982. "Connectionist models and their properties". *Cognitive Science* 6.205-254.
Fine, Kit. 1991. "The study of ontology". *Νοῦς* XXV.263-274.
Fodor, Jerrold A., and Zenon W. Pylyshyn. 1988. "Connectionism and cognitive architecture: a critical analysis". *Cognition* 28.3-71.
Joos, Martin. 1966 (ed.). *Readings in Linguistics I. The Development of Descriptive Linguistics in America 1925-56*. London/Chicago: The University of Chicago Press. [1st ed. 1957].
Katz, Jerrold J. 1981. *Language and Other Abstract Objects*. Oxford: Blackwell.
Katz, Jerrold J., and Paul M. Postal. 1991. "Realism vs. conceptualism in linguistics". *Linguistics and Philosophy* 14.515-554.
Langendoen, D. Terence, and Paul M. Postal. 1984. *The Vastness of Natural Languages*. Oxford: Blackwell.

Lieb, Hans-Heinrich. 1968. "Zur Kritik von N. Chomskys Theorie der Ebenen". *Lingua* 19.341-385.
—. 1970. *Sprachstadium und Sprachsystem.* Umrisse einer Sprachtheorie. Stuttgart: Kohlhammer.
—. 1976. "On relating pragmatics, linguistics, and non-semiotic disciplines". In: Asa Kasher (ed.). *Language in Focus: Foundations, Methods and Systems.* Essays in Memory of Yehoshua Bar-Hillel. Dordrecht: Reidel. (Boston Studies in the Philosophy of Science XLIII). 217-249.
—. 1983. *Integrational Linguistics.* Vol. I.: *General Outline.* Amsterdam: Benjamins. (CILT 17).
—. 1987a. "Sprache und Intentionalität: der Zusammenbruch des Kognitivismus". In: Rainer F. Wimmer (ed.). *Sprachtheorie: Jahrbuch 1986 des Instituts für deutsche Sprache.* Düsseldorf: Schwann. (Sprache der Gegenwart 71). 11-76.
—. 1987b. "Language is external — a reply to Helmut Schnelle". *Theoretical Linguistics* 13 (1986). 239-255. [Published 1987].
—. 1992. "Integrational semantics: an integrative view of linguistic meaning". In: Maxim Stamenov (ed.). *Current Advances in Semantic Theory.* Amsterdam/Philadelphia: Benjamins. (CILT 73). 239-268.
—. forthc. *Linguistic Variables.* Towards a Unified Theory of Linguistic Variation, with Special Reference to Syntax.
McClelland, James L.; Rumelhart, David E., and the PDP Research Group (eds). 1986. *Parallel Distributed Processing: Explorations in the Microstructure of Cognition.* Vol. 2: *Psychological and Biological Models.* Cambridge, Mass./London, Engl.: The M. I. T. Press. (A Bradford Book).
Popper, Karl R. 1972. *Objective Knowledge: An Evolutionary Approach.* Oxford: Clarendon Press.
—, and John C. Eccles. 1977. *The Self and Its Brain.* Berlin etc.: Springer Verlag. (Springer International).
Penrose, Roger. 1989. *The Emperor's New Mind.* Concerning Computers, Minds, and the Laws of Physics. Oxford: Oxford University Press.

Pylyshyn, Zenon W. 1984. *Computation and Cognition: Toward a Foundation for Cognitive Science*. Cambridge, Mass.: The M. I. T. Press. (A Bradford Book).

Rumelhart, David E.; McClelland, James L., and the PDP Research Group (eds). 1986. *Parallel Distributed Processing: Explorations in the Microstructure of Cognition*. Vol. 1: *Foundations*. Cambridge, Mass./London, Engl.: The M. I. T. Press. (A Bradford Book).

Schnelle, Helmut. 1991. *Die Natur der Sprache*. Die Dynamik der Prozesse des Sprechens und Verstehens. Berlin/New York: de Gruyter. (Grundlagen der Kommunikation und Kognition).

Searle, John R. 1980. "Minds, brains, and programs". *Behavioral and Brain Sciences* 3.417-424.

—. 1983. *Intentionality*. An Essay in the Philosophy of Mind. Cambridge: Cambridge University Press.

—. 1984. *Minds, Brains, and Science*. Cambridge, Mass.: Harvard UP.

—. 1990a. "Is the brain's mind a computer program?" *Scientific American* 262,1.20-25.

—. 1990b. "Consciousness, explanatory inversion, and cognitive science". *Behavioral and Brain Sciences* 13.585-596.

Soames, Scott. 1984. "Linguistics and psychology". *Linguistics and Philosophy* 7.155-179.

II. FRAMEWORKS

Classical Structuralism and Present-day Praguian Linguistics

Petr Sgall
Charles University, Prague

The classical Prague School, founded at the end of the 1920's by a group of Czech and Russian linguists and aestheticians, has been called a school of functional structuralism. In the present contribution I would like to characterize the importance of its methods and insights for present-day linguistics, rather than the influence of the School on linguistic thinking of the middle third of this century and the links connecting it with Hjelmslevian, Bloomfieldian and other trends. Some of the principles which were formulated by the School have not yet lost their validity, although they were set up in a period where no precise methods of linguistic description were available. They may be criticized today for various shortcomings and inconsistencies. It is possible to say that at that time questions were asked, rather than answered. The results of research were not formulated clearly enough for such differences as the one between assertions (stating what was found or assumed) and definitions (characterizing the notions used) to be explicit. The issues analysed were often tackled just presystematically rather than accounted for within carefully formulated frameworks. Nevertheless, many insights of the School remain important and are responded to in present-day Czech linguistics and elsewhere. Their importance for contemporary linguistics should not be overlooked and attention should be paid to the open questions involved in each of them. I would like to recall just a few insights that are rarely discussed and appear to be directly relevant to the topic of the Round Table.

The first of these questions concerns the character of the language system: its openness and its stratification into varieties (Sec. 1). The next issue is that of autonomy of language (Sec. 2); finally, the use or functioning of language (Sec. 3) and the teleological approach (Sec. 4) are discussed.

1 Character of the language system

1.1 Openness and complexity of the system

The central concept of the School has always been the language system; the term "language" was used only in the sense of language system, never just to denote a set (or collection) of sentences or a set of pairs of expressions and their meanings. This notion, based on de Saussure's 'langue', differs from Chomsky's 'linguistic competence' in that it cannot be reduced to something attributed to an 'ideal speaker'. A language is understood, in this tradition, as an open and complex system.

A language is open: this means it always contains variation (Mathesius 1911), and only its centre can be assumed to have a fully fixed structure; the centre or core of a language constitutes a relatively stable system, economical enough to be learned and flexibly used. However, it is a system flexible enough for improvisation, enrichment and other changes. The system has its periphery, it contains obsolete and innovative phenomena and gives room to stylistic, poetic, and other differences.[1] This notion of flexible stability or of dynamics within synchrony comes close to recent views; see, e.g., Margolis (1986), who speaks of language as accommodating improvisation.

The other side of the coin is the complexity of a language. A natural language (national language, in the classical terminology) is complex, it is a system of different codes, registers, or norms. It should be recalled that 'norms' were understood (esp. by Havránek 1932) as inherent to a language; norms differ from codification (which may be more or less adequate). The norm of a standard code is followed more or less closely by (official) codification; non-standard codes typically exist without their norms being codified.

The *codes* (*jazykové útvary*, i.e. "language formations") differ from *styles* or *registers*: each code is relatively complete, it might exist as a language by itself. In our societies we usually have a standard code; possibly, a central substandard code; interdialects (used by speakers of dialects whenever they want to use a code with a higher prestige than the dialect has; see Havránek 1932, 1942); and local dialects. Social varieties and individual idiolects may belong to one code or other. It should also be noted that a speaker regularly has more than one idiolect (where an idiolect is not conceived as a collection of norms defined by the usage of an individual; in this case, it would be rather remote from a code).

More importantly, the functionally determined differences between a standard and a central substandard, or between a dialect and an interdialect do not always directly correspond to differences between codes; the functional boundaries are often supported just by differences between registers or styles (see Sec. 1.2).

In any case, a language is understood here as intersubjective, extramental;[2] an individual speaker typically does not know the language as a whole; the internalization of a language enables the speaker to make improvisations and to use deviations of different kinds; speakers want to be understood as easily and as precisely as possible but often they also want something else — they want to impress, amuse, surprise, and so on. Chomsky's theory of grammar, even if understood as one of the corner-stones of linguistic theory, would still have to be combined with theories reflecting the social and functional aspects of language.

1.2 On the stratification of a language

One of the most urgent questions is how to distinguish a *code* (see above) from a *register* or a linguistic *style*. In the case of a style the prototypically significant relationships concern statistics, numbers of occurrences of individual expressions and numbers of their classes; in the case of a code, the presence of units is crucial. A set of well-defined concepts is needed for the study of different types of language stratification (from the basic situation with a standard and several local dialects through more complex stages to Ferguson's diglossia). A situation typical of modern national languages can be seen in French, with the standard, with *français parlé* as a central substandard code, with areal dialects of northern France, furthermore with the cognate, though not fully homogeneous codes of southern France, and also with backgrounded languages like Breton and Basque, which are no codes of French. The presence of a central substandard is even more pronounced in Czech. A different situation is that of German (with several centres, having different relations to the standard), and still other conditions characterize English (with the American and other varieties) or again, languages with rather recent standard codes. Luelsdorff's (1986) 'metagrammars' presuppose such a set of basic notions.

2   On the autonomy of a language

In the classical Prague School the most relevant question concerning language description used to be whether a given opposition is present within the language system, whether it is patterned by morphemic or other means of the language system, reflected in its syntax, etc. Distributional and other criteria were first used for this purpose in Trubetzkoy's phonology, then in other areas. Jakobson's (1936) approach to meaning, by which every morphemic unit corresponds to a single invariant meaning, was further elaborated by Pauliny (1943) and more recently by Schooneveld (1974, 1986) and others, including Běličová (1985). This view was challenged especially by Kuryłowicz (1949), who allows several (syntactic or semantic) functions of morphemic cases and other units but still assumes that one of these functions is primary while each of the secondary ones is present only in a domain defined by positive contextual criteria. There are more or less similar approaches followed by de Groot (1939), Skalička (1949), Dokulil (1958), and even the notion of a disambiguated level in Montaguean semantics (as well as in the writings by Partee, Gazdar, and others) seems to get relatively close to these views.

It is important to realize that the question of linguistic structuring concerns not only phonemics and grammar in the narrow sense but also the area of meaning, i.e. of semantic and pragmatic patterns. Here it is crucial to ask whether a given difference in the cognitive domain is rendered, in a given language, simply by lexical means or is patterned by the language system itself.[3] In this way the classical Prague School contributed to the endeavour to overcome psychologism by an inter-subjective approach to *meaning* (see Posner 1984). How many, and which, tenses, aspects, or modalities are represented in a given language, such questions are typically asked in this context. For example, the category of reported speech is represented in German but not in English (where its content can be rendered only optionally by lexical means such as *It is said..., We are told*, etc.). Whenever a cognitive difference is not patterned by the language system itself, it does not have to be expressed by lexical means; and retrieving the difference may then be left to natural language inferencing or to the hearer's own interpretation (who may use factual knowledge in addition to the transmitted text).

Another aspect of this issue consists in a more precise delimitation of the notion of a (well formed) sentence of a language. Such English sentences as (1) through (6) show that linguistic patterning must be kept apart from factual knowledge.[4]

(1) You cannot buy a house with a sum you just expect to inherit.

(2) Jones annoyed me by the abrupt manner in which the dinner ended.

(3) She cannot become my mother.

(4) Ashtrays don't shoot.

(5) I know that I know nothing.

(6) Round squares don't exist.

Using testable criteria it should be decided where the boundary line is to be drawn between de Saussure's form and substance of content, cf. also Hjelmslev's 'sense' or Coseriu's (1973) *Bedeutung* vs. *Bezeichnung*, or, in more recent terms, between linguistic meaning and cognitive (ontological) content (between linguistic and non-linguistic knowledge). It is now widely recognized (cf. Montague's 'disambiguated language', or more recently, Bierwisch 1987) that language dependent meaning differs from factual knowledge (and from the output of semantic interpretation) especially with respect to complex units (sentences, derived words).[5]

In the Praguian tradition, several levels of the language system are recognized as consecutive steps on the way from meaning to expression (see esp. Trnka 1964). Two levels of sentence structure have been assumed, first in individual presystematic formulations (Mathesius 1924) and subsequently in a more systematic way (Dokulil and Daneš 1958; Sgall 1964; Sgall, Hajičová and Panevová 1986).

Although the difference between linguistic structure and cognitive content is often neglected in the logical analysis of natural languages and in several linguistic schools, there are also trends in which this difference is indeed analysed. It is especially the research conducted by Seiler and his colleagues that is close to Praguian approaches by studying cognitive 'continua' (such as possession, aspect, modality) in view of various kinds of grammatical patterning that renders them in individual languages; see esp. Seiler and Brettschneider (eds) (1985).

Linguistic meaning comprises not only semantic but also pragmatic oppositions (especially oppositions connected with the morphological categories of tense, aspect and modality, with indexicals, and with the area of topic and focus). It appears therefore inappropriate to divide a linguistic description into a syntactic, a semantic, and a pragmatic component. The boundary between linguistic meaning and nonlinguistic domains of cognition differs from the borderline between semantic and purely pragmatic relations. This boundary is also relevant for separating ambiguity (simultaneous occurrence of several linguistic meanings) from indistinctness (where a single meaning is not fully specified within the system of a language).[6] Such an approach to natural language semantics also allowed to show that valency slots (theta roles, deep cases) are distinct from cognitive roles; in particular, Actor/Bearer — or Tesnière's (1959) premier actant — is a unit of linguistic meaning (i.e. of underlying structure) whereas the differences between Agentive, Experiencer, Theme, etc. are derived by inferencing from the context (which also includes the lexical meaning of the given verb); see Hajičová and Panevová (1984).

Using dependency syntax rather than constituent structure, we may then account for the structure of sentences in a relatively economical way (see Sgall, Hajičová, and Panevová 1986), including the topic-focus articulation (expressed by the position of the intonation centre, by word order and other means; and relevant not only to contextual or stylistic appropriateness but also to such semantic phenomena as the scope of negation and other operators).[7] Cases of paradoxical or self-contradictory meanings can also be described by a framework of this kind if the assignment of reference is taken as specific to individual occurrences of sentences in a discourse (and understood as partly restricted by context). For example, a sentence formulating the Liar's paradox can be accounted for by assuming a meaning for which no reference assignment is possible such that the resulting sense of the sentence maps into a proposition (where the mapping from senses into propositions — in Carnap's terminology — is a partial function). In sentence (6), above, lexical meanings should be assumed for *round* and *square* such that the semantic interpretation of the sentence assigns to it (for every reference assignment) a proposition that maps every possible world into the value 'true'; for sentence (5), we should get 'false' for every possible world.

3 Language use

The Prague School has always recognized the impact of the *communicative function* on the language system. This function may not be primitive[8] but has been of great importance in the development of language and should be taken into account in any inquiry into natural language (see esp. Koj 1984).

If, in addition to the language system, communicative competence and the patterning of discourses are also to be described in a systematic way, then linguistics should contribute to this interdisciplinary endeavour by including in its conception and description of languages (a) the pragmatically based aspects of their structure (major linguistic theories still fail to provide a systematic account of topic and focus), and (b) language variation (see Sec. 1, above), which is, to some extent, functionally conditioned and exploited. Otherwise, the gap between 'formal' and 'functional' linguistics will not be closed, and no 'new paradigm' of linguistics can be achieved. However, neither would it be appropriate to try and collect all pragmatic aspects of language structure into a 'pragmatic component' of a language system or its description, nor does it seem advisable simply to abandon the study of language structure altogether, cf. Lieb (1983:49).

Following this direction, the main goal of contemporary linguistics is seen as formulating descriptions of language and languages in such a way that they may form part of an interdisciplinary account of communication and cognition. Both classical linguistics as well as Chomsky and Montague may be criticized for not paying proper attention to communication, thus failing to examine language from all essential points of view. On the other hand, analyzing communication with no notion of language system may be compared to constructing a roof without a basement — even if a basement alone is a bad place to live in.

The *formal* and the *functional* viewpoints do not, on this conception, exclude each other. They may and should be combined, with the formal approach included in the functional: whenever possible, results of empirical research should be formulated as correct formal systems; points of motivation, comparison of different approaches, inquiry into questions not yet amenable to formal analysis — all this has its place in functional studies alongside of formal frameworks.

From a certain point of view the *internalized* form of existence of a language can be understood as secondary (cf. Lieb 1986, 1987; it should also be noted that an extinct language may be fully reinstated, even if it must first be deciphered). Still, the possibility to be internalized is an essential property of languages. Combining the principles of Lieb's integrational view with Schnelle's (1981, 1986) neural-net linguistics might offer a promising approach to the question of how to describe a language as an extramental, although internalizable object.[9]

Characteristically, a link between Schnelle's approach and dependency syntax has been found possible (Petkevič 1987). Understanding a "theta-grid" of a verb as now proposed by adherents of GB theory as similar to Tesnière's valency and Fillmore's case frames, we may also use dependency syntax in combination with many findings of generative grammar. It may prove useful, for this purpose, to deal with sentence structure by means of a pushdown-like patterning of elementary and complex symbols (perhaps using insights of the theory of attributed grammars), since this way sentence-structure trees are not unnecessarily complicated even if coordination, topic-focus, and the values of morphological categories are included in the representations of sentence meanings (construed as representations of the sentences' underlying, tectogrammatical structure). These representations, which are disambiguated, can serve as a suitable starting-point for a semantic interpretation in the sense of intensional logic, cf. Materna et al. (1980, 1984, 1986).

4 On the teleological approach

The links between language and intentionality, recently discussed by Searle (1983) and Lieb (1987), were at the basis of Praguian functionalism, which, besides paying attention to the communicative function of language, also concerned itself with the structure of language and its development. A detailed analysis of the Praguian approach to 'teleology' was published by Leška (1986), who distinguishes (i) synchronic functionalism (closely connected with Mathesius' ideas on variation) from the means-end model of language development, elaborated most prominently by Jakobson, and (ii) changes oriented towards a common goal (e.g. 'therapeutic' ones) from those having a functional (e.g. stylistic) motivation.

With respect to synchrony, functionalism must take a stand on whether the function of a linguistic unit should be seen primarily as its role within more complex units (e. g, the function of the morpheme as its role within the word-form and of the latter as its role within the sentence), or as its relationships to units of a higher (deeper, for Chomsky) level (cf. a series such as phoneme — morpheme — syntactic relation — theta-role). While Daneš (1987) stresses function in the first sense, Sgall (1987) offers arguments in support of also analysing and describing function in the second sense.

For a proper treatment of speaker intention in language development two points must be clarified:

(a) Due attention should be paid to the fact that typological change corresponds to Gabelentz's "Spirallauf" rather than to Jespersen's "progress". The main difference between Sumer, Latin, and the modern languages, or between Warlpiri and Russian, or classical Chinese and Modern English, appear to reside in the richness of the lexicon; neither in the structure of the language, nor in discourse patterning, conversational maxims, and so on, substantial progress has been achieved since Homer. Differences between cultures or uneven progress of civilization should not be confused with differences between languages and stages of their development, especially if the differences are related to the typological cycle.

(b) It remains to be established how individual intentions contribute to the development (and thus the shape) of languages. The teleological approach has so far failed to explain by features of the communication process the major components of the postulated goal-directed features of language development, especially the source or 'central unit' and the mechanisms regulating the enrichment of linguistic structures.

5 Conclusion

I would like to emphasize that the 'Nine Principles of New Structuralism' as presented by Lieb are of great importance to the perspectives of theoretical linguistics. My remarks, rather marginal, concern just the formulation of three of them:

In Principle 2 the system-oriented character of language which implies the requirement of naturalness (including psychological realism), might also be mentioned.

Principle 6 should perhaps also cover the internalizability of language, see Sec. 3, above.

It might be brought out more clearly in Principle 8 that Praguian structuralists differed from descriptivists in that they were aware of human intentionality as the basis of the objects of linguistics; however, they were not able to answer the question of how individual intentions of speakers and abstract properties of their language were interconnected (cf. Sec. 4, above). In this area, as in several others, questions were asked rather than answered in the classical period of European structuralism. Some of the most interesting questions still appear to ask for discussion.

Notes

[1] It is demonstrated by the volume edited by Vachek (1966) that in the second generation of the School the systematic character of the core of language and the variation concerning its periphery were integrated into a single and unified approach to the nature of language. This integration has rich sources in the classical period

of the School; differences of degree between individual views should therefore not be exaggerated.

2   We cannot but subscribe to Lieb's (1983, 1987) view that a language is abstract and cannot be reduced to the individual speaker's linguistic competence in a mentalist sense and that such idealizations as a homogeneous speech community offer no real alternative.

3   The point is that, due to the universality of natural language, every cognitive difference can be rendered in any natural language by lexical means, if it is not expressed grammatically: either a single word is sufficient (such as *two* or *pair* in languages lacking the Dual number), or lexical collocations can be used (e.g. *I and you* as an equivalent of an inclusive plural).

4   Our examples should show that it is inappropriate to "asterisk away" (e.g. McCawley 1978, Postal 1976) sentences which can be used either with or without negation, even if it may not always make sense to call them either true or false.

5   We should seriously consider the possibility that the level of linguistic meaning is much closer to the surface structure of individual languages, i.e. is language specific and equipped with an intrinsically linguistic structure (lacking overt variables, prenex quantifiers or other operators). If such a level is included in the description, the levels of D-structure and of logical form may no longer be necessary.

6   Thus, the meaning of *we* is indistinct (the speaker and someone else are included, and determining 'who else' is left to inferencing). So-called systematic ambiguity (e.g. a book as a text and as a physical object) also belongs to indistinctness in this sense.

7   Firbas' (1971) scale of communicative dynamism allows for a more complete description of the 'functional perspective' or 'information structure' of the sentence than the mere dichotomy of topic (theme) and focus (rheme, comment) would provide. Apparently, not only the underlying order of sentence parts, including the positions of focalizers (see Koktova 1986), but also, among others, the semantic differences determined by the internal structure of NPs (as in *big European butterfly* vs. *European big butterfly*) can be accounted for by this scale, appropriately interpreted.

8   See esp. Kuroda (1979), who analyses this function from a logical point of view.

[9] As Dressler (1986) states in another context, it is now possible to bridge the abyss between the neurological or biological microlevel and the linguistic macrolevel, although neither of these levels can be reduced to the other.

References

Běličová, H. 1985. "Ještě k podílu předložek na konstituování sémantické struktury věty" [More on the role of prepositions in the semantic structure of the sentence]. *Slavia* 54.8-21.
Bierwisch, M. 1987. "Some aspects of semantic form in natural language". In: M. Nagao (ed.). *Language and Artificial Intelligence*. Proceedings of an International Symposium on Language and Artificial Intelligence held in Kyoto, Japan, 16-21 March, 1986. Amsterdam: North Holland. 35-50.
Coseriu, E. 1973. *Probleme der strukturellen Semantik*. Vorlesung gehalten im Wintersemester 1965/66 an der Universität Tübingen. Autorisierte und bearbeitete Nachschrift von Dieter Kastovsky. Tübingen: Fotodruck Präzis. (Tübinger Beiträge zur Linguistik 40).
Daneš, F. 1987. "On Prague school functionalism in linguistics". In: Dirven and Fried (eds) 1987. 3-38.
Dirven, R., and V. Fried (eds). 1987. *Functionalism in Linguistics*. Amsterdam/Philadelphia: Benjamins. (LLSEE 20).
Dokulil, M. 1958. "K otázce morfologických protikladů" [On the question of morphological oppositions]. *Slovo a slovesnost* 19.81-103. [Translated into English in Luelsdorff (ed.). (in press)].
—, and F. Daneš. 1958. "K tzv. významové a mluvnické stavbě věty a výstavbě výpovědi" [On the so-called semantic and grammatical structure of the sentence]. In: *O vědeckém poznání soudobých jazyků*. Prague. 231-246.
Dressler, W. 1986. "Complementarity in linguistic observation, description and explanation". In: J. de Boch, E. Dal and Ghocck (eds). *The Lesson of Quantum Theory*. Amsterdam: North-Holland. 315-324.
Firbas, J. 1971. "On the concept of communicative dynamism in the theory of functional sentence perspective". *Brno Studies in English* 7.12-47.

Groot, A. W. de. 1939. "Les oppositions dans les systèmes de la syntaxe et des cas". In: *Mélanges de Linguistique offerts à Charles Bally*. Geneva.
Hajičová, E., and J. Panevová. 1984. "Valency (case) frames of verbs". In: Sgall (ed.). 1984. 147-188.
Havránek, B. 1932. "Úkoly spisovného jazyka a jeho kultura" [The tasks of the Standard language and its culture]. In: *Spisovná čeština a jazyková kultura*. Prague. 32-84. [Translated into German in: J. Scharnhorst and E. Ising (eds). *Grundlagen der Sprachkultur*. Beiträge der Prager Linguistik zur Sprachtheorie und Sprachpflege. Part 1. Berlin: Akademie-Verlag 1976. 103-141].
—. 1942. "K funkčnímu rozvrstvení spisovného jazyka" [On the functional stratification of the Standard language]. *Časopis pro moderní filologii* 28.409-416. [Translated into German in: J. Scharnhorst and E. Ising (eds). *Grundlagen der Sprachkultur*. Beiträge der Prager Linguistik zur Sprachtheorie und Sprachpflege. Part 1. Berlin: Akademie-Verlag 1976. 150-161].
Jakobson, R. 1936. "Beitrag zur allgemeinen Kasuslehre". *Travaux du Cercle linguistique de Prague* 6.240-288.
Koj, L. 1984. "Non-compositional semantics". In: J. Pelc, T. A. Seboek, E. Stankiewicz and T. G. Winner (eds). *Sign, System and Function*. Papers of the 1st and 2nd Polish-American Semiotics Colloquia. Berlin/New York/Amsterdam: Mouton. (Approaches to Semiotics 67). 117-122.
Koktova, E. 1986. *Sentence Adverbials in a Functional Description*. Amsterdam/Philadelphia: Benjamins. (Pragmatics and Beyond 7,2).
Kuroda, S. 1979. "Some thoughts on the foundations of the theory of language use". *Linguistics and Philosophy* 3.1-17.
Kuryłowicz, J. 1949. "Le problème du classement des cas". *Bulletin de la Société polonaise de linguistique* IX.20-43.
Leška, O. 1986. "Poznámky k teleologickému pojetí jazyka" [Remarks on the teleological approach to language]. In: *Teoretické otázky jazykovědy*. K. vyd. připr. J. Nekvapil a O. Šoltys. Prague: Ústav pro jázyk česky ČSAV. (Linguistica XVI). 63-100.
Lieb, H. 1983. *Integrational Linguistics*. Vol. 1: *General Outline*. Amsterdam: Benjamins. (CILT 17).

—. 1986. "Language is external — a reply to Helmut Schnelle". *Theoretical Linguistics* 13.239-256.
—. 1987. "Sprache und Intentionalität: Der Zusammenbruch des Kognitivismus". In: R. Wimmer (ed.). *Sprachtheorie*. Jahrbuch des Instituts für deutsche Sprache. Düsseldorf: Schwann. (Sprache der Gegenwart LXXI). 11-76.
Luelsdorff, P. 1986. *Constraints on Error Variables in Grammar*. Amsterdam/Philadelphia: Benjamins.
—. (ed.). In press. *Praguiana* 2. Amsterdam.
Margolis, J. 1986. "Intentionality, institutions, and human nature". *The Monist* 69.546-567.
Materna, P., and P. Sgall. 1980. "Functional sentence perspective, the question test and intensional semantics". *SMIL — Journal of Linguistic Calculus* 1-2.141-160.
—, and P. Sgall. 1984. "Optional participants in a semantic interpretation". In: Sgall (ed.). 1984. 51-62.
—, Hajičová, E., and P. Sgall. 1986. "Redundant answers and topic-focus articulation". *Linguistics and Philosophy* 10.101-113.
Mathesius, V. 1911. "O potenciálnosti jevů jazykových" [On the potentiality of language phenomena]. *Věstník české královské společnosti nauk 1911-12, třída filosoficko-historico-jazykozpytná*. No. 2.1-24.
—. 1924. "Několik poznámek o funkci podmětu v moderní angličtině" [Some remarks on the function of the Subject in Modern English]. *Časopis pro moderní filologii* 10.244-248.
McCawley, J. 1978. "'World-creating' predicates". *Versus* 19/20.77-93.
Pauliny, E. 1943. *Štruktúra slovenského slovesa* [The Structure of the Slovak Verb]. Bratislava: Slovenská akadémia vied a umení.
Petkevič, V. 1987. "A new dependency based specification of underlying representations of sentences". *Theoretical Linguistics* 14.143-172.
Posner, R. 1984. "Vom russischen Formalismus zur Glossematik". *Zeitschrift für Semiotik* 6.383-395.
Postal, P. 1976. "Linguistic anarchy notes". In: J. McCawley (ed.). *Syntax and Semantics*. Vol. 7: *Notes from the linguistic undergound*. New York/San Francisco/London: Academic Press. 201-216.

Schnelle, H. 1981. "Elements of theoretical net-linguistics". *Theoretical Linguistics* 8.67-100.
—. 1986. "Different approaches to integrational linguistics". *Theoretical Linguistics* 13.225-238.
Schooneveld, C. H. van. 1978. *Semantic Transmutations: Prolegomena to a Calculus of Meaning.* Vol. 1: *The Cardinal Semantic Structure of Prepositions, Cases, and Paratactic Conjunctions in Contemporary Standard Russian.* Bloomington, Indiana: Bloomington Distribution Group. (Physsard Series in Prague Linguistics 1/1).
—. 1986. "A sign-theoretical model of semantic structure in language". In: W. Lenders (ed.). COLING 86. Bonn.
Searle, J. 1983. *Intentionality.* An Essay in the Philosophy of Mind. Cambridge etc.: Cambridge University Press.
Seiler, H., and G. Brettschneider (eds). 1985. *Language Invariants and Mental Operations.* International Interdisciplinary Conference held at Gummersbach/Cologne, Germany, September 18-23, 1983. Tübingen: Gunter Narr Verlag.
Sgall, P. 1964. "Generative Beschreibung und die Ebenen des Sprachsystems". In: *Zeichen und System der Sprache.* Vol. 3: *Veröffentlichung des II. Internationalen Symposions "Zeichen und System der Sprache" vom 8.9. bis 15.9.1964 in Magdeburg.* Berlin: Akademie-Verlag 1966. 225-239.
—. (ed.). 1984. *Contributions to Functional Syntax, Semantics and Language Comprehension.* Prague: Academia / Amsterdam: Benjamins.
—. 1987. "Prague functionalism and topic vs. focus". In: Dirven and Fried (eds) 1987. 169-189.
—, Hajičová, E., and J. Panevová. 1986. *The Meaning of the Sentence in Its Semantic and Pragmatic Aspects.* Ed. by J. Mey. Prague: Akademia / Dordrecht etc.: Reidel.
Skalička, V. 1950. "Poznámky k theorii pádů". *Slovo a slovesnost* 12.134-152.
Tesnière, L. 1959. *Eléments de syntaxe structurale.* Paris: Klincksieck.
Trnka, B. 1964. "On the linguistic sign and the multilevel organization of language". In: J. Vachek (ed.). *Travaux linguistiques de Prague.* Vol. 1: *L'École de Prague d'aujourd'hui.* Prague: Academia / Paris: Klincksieck. 33-40.

Vachek, J. (ed.). 1966. *Travaux linguistiques de Prague*. Vol. 2: *Les problèmes du centre et de la périphérie du système de la langue.* Prague: Academia / Paris: Klincksieck.

Noematic grammar

Klaus Heger
Universität Heidelberg

0. The term "Noematic Grammar" (proposed by Lieb as the title of my contribution to the Round Table on New Structuralism) has three advantages: it might serve as a concise slogan for publicity, it calls for explanations by combining two apparently incompatible attributes, and it implicitly alludes to one of the points where I feel most indebted to traditions of European structuralism. In order to make this allusion explicit by giving the explanations required by this term, I have to begin by stating that the overall aim of my efforts, first as a student of Romance languages and then for nearly twenty years within general linguistics, has been to make explicit the phenomenon of the diversity and comparability of natural languages. This aim implies the necessity of working with explicit *comparanda* on the one hand, and with explicit *tertia comparationis* on the other, and of avoiding any confusions between the two.

1. For this purpose I adopted a distinction made by Erwin Koschmieder which I found extremely useful: the distinction between *grammatical* categories of a given individual language and what he called the universal *noemic* categories of what the speaker intends to say (cf. Koschmieder 1951). Reinterpreting *grammatical* categories as the *comparanda*, and *noemic* categories as the *tertia comparationis* in language comparison immediately brings out the way in which the expression "noematic grammar" combines two incompatible attributes: it must certainly not be misread as confusing *comparanda* with *tertia comparationis*. However, the relation between the two is a relation not

only of strict opposition but also of closest complementarity, and it is with reference to the aspect of complementarity that "noematic grammar" does make good sense: as an abbreviated formula that covers the two complementary tasks of

- analysing, in an inductive or semasiological way, the signs of a given individual language independently of other languages, and
- projecting, in a deductive or onomasiological way, such analyses for different languages on the common *tertium comparationis* constituted by the various *noemic* categories.

There are two preconditions for solving these tasks (cf. Heger 1983): first, analysing the signs of a given individual language presupposes that an ordered collection of these signs, representative if not exhaustive, is available (a requirement not easily met as any specialist on so-called 'exotic' languages knows only too well); second, projecting analyses on a common *tertium comparationis* presupposes availability of the necessary systems of *noemic* categories that are to serve as *tertia comparationis*.

In order to make the combination of these four tasks as effective as possible, I have generalized Koschmieder's *grammatical* categories "to the point where they comprise everything that can be referred to the *signifié*-side of language signs. *Noemic* categories, on the contrary, have to be — as far as possible — sufficiently independent of particular languages in order to be real *tertia*, and at the same time sufficiently related to 'language in general' — something like Saussure's *langage* — in order to be capable of serving as *tertia comparationis* in the comparison of different languages. In other words, they can neither be found in some so-called extra-linguistic domain, nor be derived inductively from the analysis of particular languages. The safest way to get to them, therefore, seems to me to construct them deductively, and to consider them mere theoretical constructs which only exist within the frame of a given theory, and the only justification of which lies in their usefulness as *tertia comparationis*" (Heger 1986:262).

2. As for the degree to which solving the four interdependent tasks enumerated above is more than wishful thinking, and as for the degree to which I might have contributed something useful to their solution, the situation varies considerably with these four tasks.

(1) While establishing ordered collections of the signs of a given individual language, for which I use the technical term *semantic paradigmatization*, remains to be done for many languages, it has been achieved for many others for quite a long time. In particular, the student of Romance languages might easily get the impression that little remains to be done.

(2) Again, there is a tradition of several centuries, or more, in the *semasiological analysis* of paradigmatically ordered signs of individual languages, and no doubt, during its long history it has arrived at results that may lack in exhaustiveness but are more than satisfactory in many respects.

(3) As to *onomasiological projection* on a common *tertium comparationis*, the very term *onomasiological* shows that it dates back at least to pre-structuralist onomasiological dialectology. Implicitly, however, the century-old habit of projecting any language on the categories of Latin grammar was just as much onomasiological *avant la lettre*; its shortcomings were due not to any inherent fault of onomasiological projection as such but to inadequate *tertia comparationis*.

(4) On the other hand, establishing partial systems of *noemic* categories seems to me a task still largely to be tackled. There is only one implicit exception that I have come across in both traditional and modern descriptions of languages, viz. the sections dedicated in our grammars to numerals, which are usually given in arithmetical order, rather than arranged by language-specific criteria.

In this situation it was only a natural consequence for me to concentrate my own research efforts mainly on this fourth task so as to reach a point where I might profit, at least partially, from existing work in the three other fields. Most of my publications are concerned, either exclusively or in parts, with this task: constructing partial systems of noemic categories that exemplify both the independence of such systems with respect to individual languages and their usefulness as *tertia comparationis*. As for the first requirement, I readily confess that I have exploited the possibility of choosing domains where independence was easy to prove by relating the premises of noemic systems to characteristics of 'language in general' (in the sense of Saussure's *langage*), to anthropological universals, or the like. As for the second requirement, usefulness of noemic categories, there are a few onomasiological projections where I have tried to show how noemic categories can be used in language comparison. Most detailed are my projection of Latin, French, and Spanish tense systems on the noemic categories of temporal deixis (cf. Heger 1963); the projection of the systems of personal pronouns of ten widely different languages on a system that combines noemic categories of personal deixis and of quantity (cf. Heger 1980, based on Heger 1965); and the distinction of at least seven different existing types of ergativity/accusativity, a distinction made possible by the projection on a system of noemic categories that is based on the definition of three different actant functions (cf. Heger 1983/85, based on Heger 1966 and 1976 as well as on Heger and Mudersbach 1984).

As for the two complementary tasks (1) and (2), I have not worked at all on semantic paradigmatization, and only recently have I proposed a sample semasiological analysis — of just one simple German sentence — that exemplifies the way in which such an analysis can be directly projected on the relevant noemic *tertia comparationis* (cf. Heger 1985). In other words, I am fully aware of the fact that I am only doing part of the job implied by a correct reading of "noematic grammar". I hope, however, that it is a useful part, and I do believe that it is the part that most urgently needed elaborating in order to match the standards reached by others in the other parts.

3. After this presentation of what I think "noematic grammar" is (or rather: should be), the question has to be asked as to what the relations are between this "noematic grammar" and "structuralism". Indeed, such relations do exist — in both senses of "structuralism" assumed at the Round Table, traditional and new structuralism.

3.1. As mentioned before, I am indebted to various traditions of European structuralism; reference was made to Ferdinand de Saussure more than once. My thinking, both in general and for the important place it assigns to noemic categories of deixis, was also decisively influenced by Karl Bühler's *Sprachtheorie* (Bühler 1934). Indirect access to the classical Prague School of structuralism was provided by both Bühler and Koschmieder (mentioned above). Likewise, my work on actant functions would not have been possible without Lucien Tesnière's inspirational *Eléments de syntaxe structurale* (Tesnière 1959). Through him, but not only through him, I also feel highly indebted to the French school or schools of structuralism.

As for the missing centre of European structuralism, namely the Copenhagen School, Knud Togeby's work proved most suggestive when I tried to project French and Spanish tense systems on my noemic *tertia comparationis* of temporal deixis (cf. Togeby's publications quoted in Heger 1963). On the other hand, the Copenhagen School also embodies what I consider as the most serious shortcoming of certain types of traditional structuralism: after all that I have said so far about the four tasks of "noematic grammar", it will not come as a surprise that I have never felt much attracted by linguistic schools that define themselves as "asemantic". For this reason, I cannot feel indebted to the Copenhagen School in the same manner as to other European schools of structuralism and have never been attracted by American structuralism of the Bloomfieldian vein. This does not mean that I automatically agree with the reaction to Bloomfieldian structuralism: when, after its asemantic beginnings and under the influence of Quine and others, generative grammar rediscovered (or reinvented) semantics, this turned out to be a purely extensionalist type of semantics — a type that I am sorry to say is even worse in linguistics and more inadequate than the asemanticism of the Copenhagen School.

3.2. The other sense in which the question as to what relations exist between "noematic grammar" and structuralism has to be asked, concerns what I consider to be "structuralist" components in my own approach. If the term "structuralist" refers to structural, i.e. system-based, properties of the objects of linguistics — see Principle 8 of the Nine Principles of New Structuralism — then it may rightly be claimed that

- semantic paradigmatization and semasiological analysis are structuralist since their objects are systems and their components, in the sense of "system" introduced by Ferdinand de Saussure and further developed by Lieb (cf. Lieb 1970 and Heger 1971); and

- onomasiological projection and establishing partial systems of noemic categories are structuralist in a derived sense since noemic categories must be "sufficiently related to 'language in general' in order to be capable of serving as *tertia comparationis*" (above, § 1); this implies that the theoretical frameworks of (language) systems and of noemic categories have to be compatible (cf. Heger 1981:72) and must be located at the same level of abstraction.

There is just one consideration that might make me hesitate to subsume "noematic grammar" fully under "New Structuralism": it might be objected that "noematic grammar" is too heavily indebted to classical structuralism to deserve this label.

4. Summarizing what I have said so far, I can fully subscribe to principles 5, 7, and 8 of the Nine Principles of New Structuralism; even before they were formulated, these were guiding principles of "noematic grammar". This does not mean that I would be unwilling to subscribe to the remaining six which at first may appear to have less direct bearing on problems to be solved in order to justify "noematic grammar". On closer inspection, they, too, turn out to be relevant, generally because all nine principles are interdependent but also for the more specific reasons of

- justifying the level of abstraction at which I try to construct noemic categories, and

- allowing for a satisfactory answer to the question of where to locate, within linguistics in general, my overall aim: making explicit the phenomenon of the diversity and comparability of natural languages.

I do agree, then, with all the nine principles of New Structuralism.

References

Bühler, Karl. 1934. *Sprachtheorie*. Jena: Fischer. [Second edition Stuttgart: G. Fischer 1965].
Heger, Klaus. 1963. *Die Bezeichnung temporal-deiktischer Begriffskategorien im französischen und spanischen Konjugationssystem*. Tü-

bingen: Niemeyer.
—. 1965. "Personale Deixis und grammatische Person". *Zeitschrift für romanische Philologie* 81.76-97,
—. 1966. "Valenz, Diathese und Kasus". *Zeitschrift für romanische Philologie* 82.138-170.
—. 1971. Rezension zu: Lieb 1970. *Zeitschrift für romanische Philologie* 87.550-560.
—. 1976. *Monem, Wort, Satz und Text.* Tübingen: Niemeyer.
—. 1980. *Sprachvergleich und Semantik — Das Beispiel der grammatischen Kategorien 'Person' und 'Numerus'.* Heidelberg: Winter. (Sitzungsberichte der Heidelberger Akademie der Wissenschaften, philosophisch-historische Klasse, Jahrgang 1980, 10. Abhandlung).
—. 1981. "Außersprachlichkeit — Außereinzelsprachlichkeit — Übereinzelsprachlichkeit". In: Geckeler, H., B. Schlieben-Lange, J. Trabant and H. Weydt (eds). *Logos Semantikos.* Studia linguistica in honorem Eugenio Coseriu 1921-1981. Berlin: de Gruyter / New York/Madrid: Gredos. Vol. 2. 67-76.
—. 1983. "Zum Verhältnis von Semantik und Noematik". In: Stimm, H., and W. Raible (eds). *Zur Semantik des Französischen. Beiträge zum Regensburger Romanistentag.* Wiesbaden: Steiner. (*Zeitschrift für französische Sprache und Literatur.* Beiheft 9). 40-44.
—. 1983/85. "Akkusativische, ergativische und aktivische Bezeichnung von Aktantenfunktionen". In: Planck, F. (ed.). *Relational Typology.* Berlin/New York/Amsterdam: Mouton 1985. [First in: *Arbeiten des Kölner Universalien-Projekts (akup)* 54. Cologne: Universität, Institut für Sprachwissenschaft 1983].
—. 1985. *Flexionsformen, Vokabeln und Wortarten.* Heidelberg: Winter. (Abhandlungen der Heidelberger Akademie der Wissenschaften, philosophisch-historische Klasse, Jahrgang 1985, 1. Abhandlung).
—. 1986. "Fifty Years of Linguistics — Four examples". *Folia Linguistica* 20.251-264.
—, and Klaus Mudersbach. 1984. *Aktantenmodelle — Aufgabenstellung und Aufbauregeln.* Birkenau: Bitsch. (Abhandlungen der Heidelberger Akademie der Wissenschaften, philosophisch-historische Klasse, Jahrgang 1984, 4. Abhandlung).
Koschmieder, Erwin. 1951. *Die noetischen Grundlagen der Syntax.*

München: Beck. (Sitzungsberichte der Bayerischen Akademie der Wissenschaften, Jahrgang 1951, Heft 4).

Lieb, Hans-Heinrich. 1970. *Sprachstadium und Sprachsystem*. Stuttgart etc.: Kohlhammer.

Tesnière, Lucien. 1959. *Eléments de syntaxe structurale*. Paris: Kliencksieck.

The Functional Model of UNITYP Dimensions

Hansjakob Seiler
Universität Köln, Germany / Lenzburg, Switzerland

1 Introduction

In this paper I should like to present the UNITYP model in such a way as to assure maximal comparability with other coexisting models, especially those of European structuralism. It is hoped that this will meet with the intentions of the editor of the present volume.

After highlighting some basic thoughts (section 2) I shall outline an exemplary case of dimension, the dimension of participation (section 3). Basic notions and the problems connected with their definition will be discussed in section 4. A glimpse on the gradual unfolding of the model will be presented in section 5. In section 6 some basic features of the model will be examined in the light of H. Lieb's "principles of a new structuralism".

2 Basic thoughts

The UNITYP model has been developed by this writer and the "Cologne research group on language universals and typology with particular reference to functional aspects".[1] It seems to be of primary importance that one states one's goals: why should we engage in language universals research and typology? What do we want to explain?

It is a fact that, although languages differ significantly and considerably indeed, no one would deny that they have something in common: how else could they be labelled "language"? How would translations from one language into any other be possible if there were not a common basis? There is obviously unity among them, no matter how vaguely felt and for what reasons. Neither diversity nor unity is what we want to explain. We consider both as given. What we want to explain are such facts as the comparability of languages, the translatability from one language into another, the learnability of any language, language change — all of which presuppose that speakers intuitively find their ways from diversity to unity, and back again to diversity — and this is a highly salient process that deserves to be brought into our consciousness. Generally then, our basic goal is to explain the ways in which language-specific facts are connected with a unitarian concept of language — "die Sprache", "le langage".

The foremost notion here is that of a process, as against the conception of language as an "object" — "formal" or "abstract" — in short, a thing. This can be exemplified with translation, where the processual nature is, perhaps, most immediately evident. We know the input and the output. But what goes on in between? It was said above that speakers intuitively find their ways from diversity to unity and back again to diversity, and that it will be the linguists' task to bring these pathways into our scientific consciousness. This entails an approach from two sides and in two opposite directions: one inductive, the other deductive.

The deductive aspect has to do with positing a certain cognitive conceptual apparatus, to which, e.g., the concept of a situation with its relation between the entities involved and the entity that involves them (our Participation, see below section 3), belong. Indeed, this is what grammarians have been doing all along, no matter how subconsciously. The cognitive conceptual apparatus can either be intuitively posited or made explicit by a formal theory. Klaus Heger's noematic framework offers such an explication (see this volume and 1983:40ff), although he would not be inclined to attribute his "noemes" a conceptual-cognitive status (Heger 1985:97ff). However, Heger and myself agree in postulating abstract entities as *tertia comparationis* as a necessary prerequisite for both language universals research and language typology — in short — for any comparison between languages. To the extent that these *tertia comparationis* are applicable to all the languages of the world, they truly deserve the status of universality. The cognitive-conceptual content should not be confused with the meanings of particular linguistic structures. The latter, as we know, differ from one language to another, no matter how much they may have in common in particular instances. But difference and sameness must be judged on the basis of one common ground — the *tertia comparationis*.

The inductive aspect of our research concerns the ordering of data assembled under a common concept. Here, we make generalizations regarding their form and their meaning, and we try to bring them into an order according to sameness and difference. The construct of DIMENSIONS and SUBDIMENSIONS based on the notion of a continuum, and respectively structured by the gradience of two negatively correlated functional principles — viz. indicativity vs. predicativity: see section 3 — is our most important tool in this task. Once a dimension or subdimension is established, we can then extract a common functional denominator representing the INVARIANT, while the positions on the dimension are the corresponding VARIANTS. Universals and invariants are not the same; they differ in their epistemological status. The former pertain to deduction and apriorism, the latter to inductive generalization. But they can and must be matched with one another, and where they match is the domain of function.

FUNCTION, then, is the key notion of the entire model. Its key role derives from its Janus-like character: Under the aprioristic, deductive view it represents the purpose to be fulfilled, i.e. the problem to be solved — while the diversified structures in the diversified languages represent the corresponding solutions. Under the inductive aspect it represents the invariance/variation complex as related to a common cognitive content.

Here follows a simplified iconic representation of the UNITYP model. As can be expected with models, it is open to further differentiation and refinement:

(S 1)

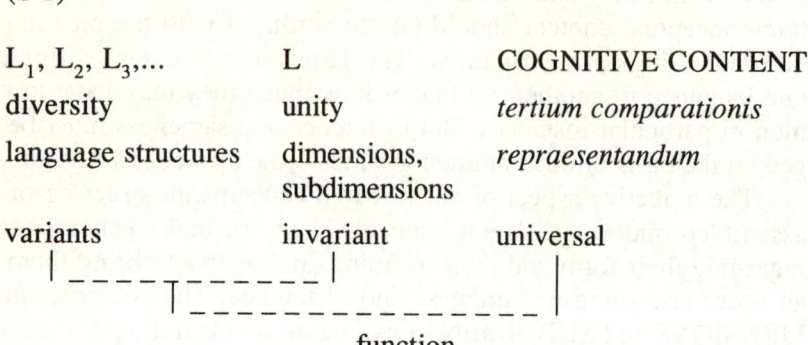

function

The chart is to be interpreted in a dynamic, goal-directed sense corresponding to the above described bidirectionality. The cognitive-conceptual content is not only the *tertium comparationis* but also the *repraesentandum*, i.e. that which is to be represented or expressed by means of language. This representation is not a matter of course but a constant problem to be solved by the speaker and listener. There is no gap nor break between universal *repraesentanda* and language-specific structures. They are linked by virtue of the dimensions and subdimensions and their corresponding invariants.

3 An example of a dimension: Participation (overview)

3.1 Introduction

The reader is referred to a special volume on this topic (Seiler and Premper (eds) 1991) as well as to numerous relevant *akup* publications by members of the UNITYP research group: Numbers 54 (1983), 56 (1984), 57 (1984), 58 (1984), 59 (1984), 60 (1984), 61 (1985), 62 (1986), 63 (1986), 64 (1986), 66 (1987), 67 (1987), 68 (1987), 70 (1988), 71 (1988), 72 (1988), 73 (1988), 74 (1988), 75 (1988).

To facilitate access to the argumentation, it may be convenient to guide the reader by the "rear entrance" of grammatical categories involved in this particular dimension. They are, roughly speaking: 1. one-word clauses, nominal clauses; 2. noun/verb distinction; 3. verb classes; 4. valency; 5. voice (verbal gender); 6. transitivity; 7. case marking; 8. verb series; 9. causativity; 10. complex sentences. That these categories are more or less closely interrelated is an opinion shared by many linguists. The problem consists in determining the nature and the degree of their interrelatedness. Here the dimensional model comes in as an important and powerful device for bringing the problem closer to a solution.

From the array of grammatical categories enumerated above it is not altogether too difficult to extract a common denominator: they all — except 1., which seems problematic, but see on this problem further below — seem to have to do with representing a relation: a relation between participants of some sort, and "that which is participated in", which, for convenience, we shall call the participatum.

Let us now switch our point of view from the grammatical to the conceptual, i.e. to the cognitive content. Here we are confronted with any kind of situation that may be conceived by humans and that would have to be represented by the means of language. How can we describe our conceiving of a situation independently of language? We cannot. Yet we know that beside language there are other ways of access to cognitive content: gestures and other kinds of non-verbal interaction. Thus, language and cognition overlap to a large extent, but they are not coterminous. We can agree in this respect with Lieb's principles nos. 2 and 5 that the objects of linguistics are extra-mental (Lieb 1990).

Since language is not the sole access to cognitive content, we can at least intuitively grasp and describe it. In our particular case, viz. the conception of a situation, there is a basic correlation between the entities involved in the situation and "that which involves them in the situation". Our next question, then, is: how is this correlation represented by the means of language? This is the functional question. We note that the cognitive content as outlined above and the common denominator of the linguistic categories involved in the representation of a situation are compatible. There is an interface between the invariants of linguistic representation and cognitive content, and it is functional. We shall use the following terms to refer to this interface: PARTICIPATION for the correlation as a whole; PARTICIPANTS for the entities involved in the situation; PARTICIPATUM for "that which involves them in the situation".

We shall keep apart these and further functional terms from current semantic, syntactic and morphological terminology, as in the following chart:

(S 2)

functional	semantic	syntactic	morphological
Participation	Case Grammar	Grammatical or Functional Relations Valency Voice Case	
Participatum	Action, Event, State	Predicate	Verb
Participants	(Case)-Roles	Actants, Circumstants	
Initiant	Agent	Subject	
Undergoer	Patient	Object	

Note that the functional terms are not meant to replace either the semantic or the syntactic or morphological ones. The latter three continue to be needed just as the former. But the former comprise the latter. In much of the current literature no importance is attributed to making clearcut terminological distinctions. Thus, e.g., "object" is used where "patient" is meant; or "patient" is used instead of "undergoer". That "patient" and "undergoer" are not coterminous, we know at least since Foley and Van Valin (1984:53ff); instead of their "actor" we use "initiant".

Initiant is that entity which initiates a situation. This can semantically be an agent, as in

(1) *George killed the dragon*

an instrument, as in

(2) *The key opens the door*

an experiencer, as in

(3) *He felt a pain in the back*

Undergoer is that entity which undergoes a situation. This can semantically be a patient, as *the dragon* in (1), a beneficiary, as in

(4)   *He voted for Bush*

a location, as in

(5)   *The arrow missed the mark*

3.2 The techniques as bundles of subdimensions

We have established that participation is about the correlation between the participants in a situation and the corresponding participatum, and that it is about the linguistic representation of such a correlation. We still have not shown what the modes of representation are.

For convenience of exposition let us once more go by the "rear entrance" of the grammatical categories as enumerated in 3.1. They are important as a basis for further orientation.

No doubt, these categories differ both in their form and in their meaning. Case marking, e.g., conveys a semantic aspect that differs from the semantics of verbal voice. Yet, both as well as all the remaining categories pertain to participation. We would say that participation is the invariant, and that voice, case marking etc. are corresponding variants of representation. Can we bring some order into this variational multiplicity? This is a possible re-phrasing of the above question about the different modes of representation — and of the question formulated in 3.1 about the interrelation between these categories.

In order to find the answer it is essential to transcend the framework of categories. It is the functions that command categorization, not vice versa. We must therefore stick with our functional approach and try to re-phrase the above enumeration of grammatical categories in functional terms. We must broaden our view from the category as the grammaticalized instance to include competing modes of expression that are, perhaps, less grammaticalized, less obligatory, yet convey more or less the same function. As an example, let us look at causativity in German. We find the following options:

(6) *Die Grossisten   manipulieren   die Ölpreise –*
the wholesalers   manipulate (V_1)   the oil prices
– *die Ölpreise   sinken*
the oil prices   fall (V_2):
two independent, yet closely connected full clauses with two different verbs V_1 and V_2.

(7) *Die Grossisten   machen,   daß die Ölpreise   sinken*
the wholesalers   make (V_1)   that the oil prices   fall (V_2):
a complex sentence with a semantically emptied main verb (V_1) and a semantically full subordinated verb (V_2).

(8) *Die Grossisten   lassen   die Ölpreise   sinken*
the wholesalers   let (AV)   the oil prices   fall (V):
a simple clause with an auxiliary (AV) and a full verb (V).

(9) *Die Grossisten   senken   die Ölpreise*
the wholesalers   sink:CAUS   the oil prices:
= let fall
a simple clause with a causative verb form, i.e. a grammaticalized representation of essentially the same correlation between cause and effect as in the foregoing and the following variants. Note that the process of grammaticalization by means of Umlaut: *sinken* 'to go down' vs. *senken* 'to make go down' is no longer productive in Modern Standard German.

(10) *Die Grossisten   dumpen   die Ölpreise*
the wholesalers   dump   the oil prices:
= let fall
a simple clause with a verb that is an English loan (colloquial) and serves as a lexical causative. This represents the maximally condensed and compact option while (6) represents the maximally explicit option.

We note that the versions (6) to (10), although differing in meaning, are nevertheless isofunctional in that they all represent the same correlation between cause and effect. We therefore want to have them all included in our consideration, and not just to concentrate on the grammaticalized peak. We further note that it is possible to order these and potential further options in a continuum of gradually increasing (i.e. going from (10) to (6)) vs. decreasing (i.e. going from (6) to

(10)) explicitness. Adjacent options, as, e.g., (7) and (8), share more properties than non-adjacent ones: the semantically emptied main verb *machen* is just one step away from the auxiliary *lassen*. There is a strong systematicity here which is a fact of that particular language, i.e. German, but which is paralleled by comparable facts in other languages, and which needs to be accounted for. The continuum in its bidirectionality: from maximal compactness and inherence to maximal explicitness, and vice versa — is the tangible, observable counterpart of a common functional denominator for which we shall use a distinct functional term: *causation* instead of *causative, causativity*, which is the categorical term. It is still the case that the grammaticalized, categorical version of (9) occupies a special position within the continuum. But it is hopefully clear by now that the category cannot be fully understood unless its place within the functionally commanded continuum is accounted for.

The facts as described in the above shall be embraced by the functional term of TECHNIQUE, the TECHNIQUE OF CAUSATION. The technique is constituted by a continuum. A more detailed analysis reveals that it is constituted by a bundle of several continua, yet, it is not possible to go into these details at this point. Causative formations such as Umlaut in German, or derivational affixes such as English *-en* in *black/black-en* or Turkish *-dür* in *öl-dür-* 'die-cause' = "kill" are the grammaticalized instantiation of the technique of causation.

Now, we are left with nine more grammatical categories enumerated in 3.1. We will say that they are the grammaticalized instantiations of corresponding techniques. The respective functional terms and their corresponding semantic, syntactic, and morphological counterparts are as in the following chart.

(S 3)

	functional	semantic	syntactic	morphological
1.	positing p'ation	thetic	AUX	clitics
2.	p'ants/p'atum distinction			noun/verb
3.	generally implied p'ants	verb classes	verb classes	
4.	specifically implied p'ants		valence	
5.	orientation	attention flow viewpoint	voice	active, passive
6.	transition	foregrounding/ backgrounding	transitivity/ intransitivity	transitive/ intransitive
7.	role assignment	roles	case marking	case marking
8.	introduction of p'ants		serial verb constructions	
9.	causation	cause and effect	causative constructions	causative formation
10.	complex p'ata		complex sentences	

[p'ants = participants; p'atum = participatum]

These are the techniques that constitute the dimension of participation. The ordering of these techniques will be exposed in a further section. We shall now briefly discuss the first two techniques and leave extensive treatment of the entire dimension to our book publication (Seiler and Premper (eds) 1991).

3.2.1 Positing participation

The functional purpose of this technique consists in a holistic representation of a situation, and this means: in a holistic representation of the relation between p'ant and p'atum, without specification of either of these partners in the relation. The linguistic expressions subsumed under this technique simply convey: a relation p'ant/p'atum exists. Identification of the respective partners is left to (metalinguistic) interpretation.

The linguistic expressions are highly context- and discourse-dependent. They predominantly result from metalinguistic operations. Their import is primarily pragmatic, where pragmatic is understood as the output of those mental operations which bear directly on language in the speech act.

In the different languages we find a great variety of options, where each of them does not stand by itself but is integrated in a continuum of isofunctional options. The technique, then, is a bundle of subcontinua. Here follows an overview:

1. Context-sensitivity: one-word utterances, meteorological expressions.
   (11) *Night. Rain. Silence.*

2. Thetic judgements:
   (12)   *There was a king*   vs   **A king was*
   (13)   *Arriva Fabrizio*   vs. *Fabrizio arriva*
   ITALIAN arrives Fabrizio   vs. Fabrizio arrives[2]

3. Copular
   3.1. Nominal clause; clitics act as a link:
   (14)   *Dan   hu   ha-more   seli   le-*
   HEBREW   D.   SUB.CLIT.3.SG.M   ART-teacher   my   to-
   matematica
   mathematics
            "D. (is) my mathematics teacher"
            (agreement also contributes to the linking function)

3.2. Nominal clause; rhyme as a link:
(15)   *nomen   omen*
LATIN name:nom.SG.NTR prognostic:NOM.SG.NTR
       "The name   (is) a prognostic"

3.3. Reference-worthiness: absolutive suffic in Uto-Aztecan:
(16) (i)   *húya   -l*
CAHUILLA straightening-ABS
          lit. "straightening is", i.e."(it is) an arrow"
     (ii) *ne   -húyʔa*
          1.SG -straightening
          lit.   "my straightening", i.e. "my arrow"

4. Metalinguistic operations: Expressions of TRUTH, APPLIES, IDENTITY, CLASS INCLUSION, EXISTENCE.
   Common structural criterion: selection restrictions not between auxiliary verb and noun: anything can be said to be TRUE, to EXIST, etc.; but between noun and noun; compare:
   (17)   (i) *Judy is a waitress*   (ii) **The house is a waitress*

We find a continuous transition here from pure positing, i.e. non-specification of p'ant and p'atum, respectively, toward increasingly suggestive identifications. Compare:

(18) *The evening star is the morning star*
(19) *This is a harpsichord*
(20) *Carl is a teacher* (i.e. *one who teaches*)
(21) *Carl is a student* (i.e. *Carl studies*)

We agree with S. Steele (1981) who claims that the auxiliary is the "head of the sentence". This ties in with the thetic, positing character of these expressions.

To sum up we would say that these options, some of which may occur in combination, are highly marked in their pragmatic aspect. On the other hand they exhibit a minimum of morpho-syntactic and semantic machinery. The relation p'ant/p'atum is unspecified, unmarked, minimally explicit, maximally inherent. As the morpho-syntactically and semantically unmarked technique it is the basis of the entire dimension. It is the filter for the subsequent techniques, the techniques, in sum, on which the subsequent ones build.

3.2.2 Participant/participatum distinction

The functional purpose of this technique is to introduce a first distinction of the terms of the relation of p'ant/p'atum. It seems safe to say that all languages provide means for distinguishing between a term (or terms) that is (are) referential, absolute, i.e. that can be referred to, and a term that is non-referential, unsaturated, i.e. involving participants. It is not the case, however, that in all languages the distinction is brought about by two distinct word classes called noun (N) and verb (V). Where such a distinction exists, as in German or Latin, we are presented with the grammaticalized instantiation of the technique called participant/participatum distinction.

As the works of H. Walter (1981) and J. Broschart (1987), both based on the UNITYP model, have shown, factual evidence both within one particular language and in cross-linguistic comparison points to a continuum of N/V distinction where N and V are two poles at either end of the continuum and where there is a gradual, continuous transition between noun and verb properties. This is reflected by the following geometrical representation:

(S 4)

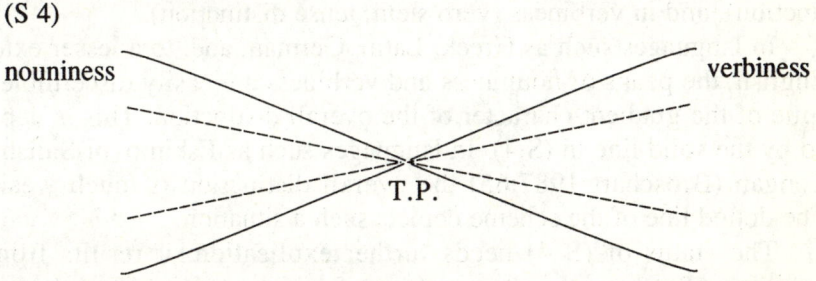

The curves say that as we move from N to V or in the other direction, the increase of one property is proportionally correlated with a decrease of the other. J. Ross (1972:316) has proposed the following "category squish" for N/V in English:

(S 5)

```
            Present       Perfect       Passive
Verb   >                >             >              >  Adjective
            Participle    Participle    Participle

Preposition (?)  >  "adjectival noun"  >  Noun
                     (e.g. fun, snap)
```

Here, the noun is exclusively negatively characterized, i.e. by the total absence of verbal properties. Ross failed to recognize the fundamentally correlative character of N and V: They are each positively characterized by opposite properties. As (S 5) shows, there is a point of inversion of the curves, called the turning point (T.P.), where properties of nouniness and of verbiness are about equal in performance and whereafter the direction of the curves changes. In the English series of (S 5) this point would be represented by the perfect or passive participle. The time-honoured grammatical term of "participle" — *participium*, literally "participation" created by the Greek and Roman grammarians — reflects their insight that the participles in Greek and Latin are entities that "partake" both in nouniness (gender and case distinction), and in verbiness (verb stem, tense distinction).

In languages such as Greek, Latin, German, and, to a lesser extent, English, the peaks of nouniness and verbiness are easily discernible, in spite of the gradient character of the overall distinction. This is depicted by the solid line in (S 4). In languages such as Eskimo, or Salish, or Tongan (Broschart 1987:65) the overall distinction is much weaker. The dotted line of the scheme depicts such a situation.

The status of (S 4) needs further explication: it results from a bundling of at least three parameters of variation that define the technique of N/V distinction. The *locus* of bundling is represented by the prototypical values of each parameter. The parameters and their prototypical values are as follows:

1. The parameter of relationality. It comprises the relational and absolute poles. Relational here means roughly "calling for participants". The optimal or prototypical verb is highly relational and minimally absolute. The prototypical noun is highly absolute and minimally relational.

2. The identity parameter with its referential and non-referential poles. Referential here means identifiable. The prototypical noun is highly referential, definite and specific; prototypical verbs are highly general and minimally referential.
3. The time-place parameter with its two poles of time vs. location. Prototypical verbs are maximally accessible to time differentiation, and minimally accessible to localization. Prototypical nouns show the opposite characteristics.

The verb-defining parameters would bundle in their respective prototypical instantiations as highly relational/highly general/highly time-specifiable. The noun-defining parameters meet in the instantiations of highly absolute/highly referential/highly localizable.

As we lower maximal values on one or several of these parameters, we get less prototypical instantiations of N and V, and, eventually, a weakly grammaticalized distinction between p'ants and p'atum. J. Broschart (1987:87ff) has shown how languages like Tongan or Salish behave in such a situation and how syntactic devices step in to determine the interpretation of basic lexical units.

3.3 The ordering of the techniques in the dimension

We have outlined two techniques and must leave the remaining seven for treatment elsewhere. But even with this small amount of exposed systematicity the principles of ordering the techniques in the dimension can now be discerned. The proposed ordering will first be presented in the following geometricized form (S 6, next page).

We have two converse gradients comparable to the ones depicting N/V distinction. The gradients correspond to two complementary functional principles that command the ordering. Their names are, respectively: INDICATIVITY vs. PREDICATIVITY. INDICATIVITY means: the cognitive content, which is in our case the relation p'ant(s)/p'atum, is linguistically represented by positing, by pointing out (indicative = pointing out). The relation is taken for granted, as inherently given. This is particularly evident in the second technique, i.e. its grammaticalized option, where the verb, in conformity with the parameter of relationality, inherently "calls for participants". The entire relation is CENTRALIZED in the participatum. While INDICATIVI-

(S 6) *The dimension of participation*

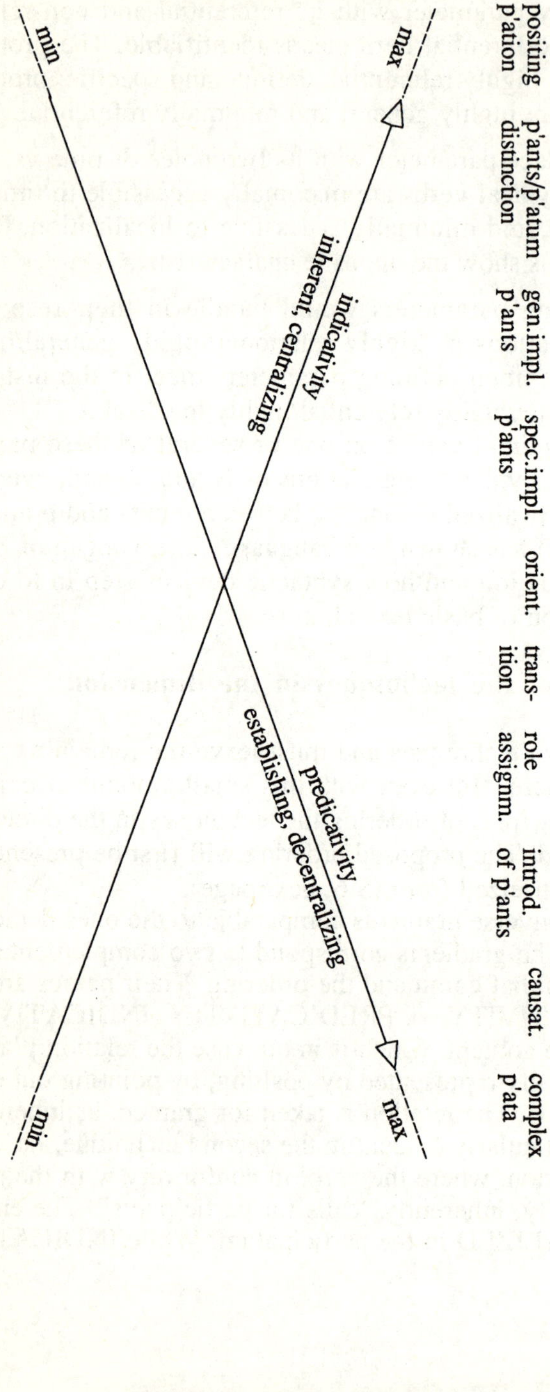

positing	p'ants/p'atum distinction
	gen.impl. p'ants
indicativity	spec.impl. p'ants
inherent, centralizing	orient. p'ants
	trans- ition
	role assignm.
predicativity	introd. of p'ants
establishing, decentralizing	causat.
	complex p'ata

min ← → max (indicativity, inherent, centralizing)
min ← → max (predicativity, establishing, decentralizing)

TY is the most general form of that particular functional principle which manifests itself in all the dimensions studied by UNITYP thus far, CENTRALIZING is its manifestation within the dimension of participation.

PREDICATIVITY means: the relation p'ants/p'atum is linguistically represented by gradual unfolding, i.e. by increasingly introducing morpho-syntactic machinery. PREDICATIVE here includes syntactic predication, but is larger in scope, and means to establish the relation by increasing specification. The relation is decreasingly inherent in the p'atum, it is increasingly DECENTRALIZED. DECENTRALIZATION, then, is the dimension-specific manifestation of the overall and, we should add, universal functional principle of PREDICATIVITY. The extreme pole of decentralization is reached with the technique of "complex participata", represented by complex sentences of different types. Here, too, as in the other techniques we have different subdimensions or parameters of variation. One of them, the "hierarchy of binding" parameter shows that the strength of the ties between main verb (p'atum) and subordinated clause varies for different types (Givón 1979:333ff).

There is a point of inversion of the two gradients located around the technique of transition. This is the point where several things change: It marks the syntactic transition from government (to the left of the T.P.) to modification (to the right of the T.P.). It also marks the shift from predominant "head marking" to predominant "dependent marking" (on these concepts and terms see J. Nichols 1986:56ff). It should be added that the techniques with predominant indicativity/centralization are characterized by a minus in morpho-syntactic complexity and are unmarked in this respect, but that they are also characterized by a plus in pragmatic complexity and are thus pragmatically marked. Techniques with predominant predicativity/decentralization are certainly not incompatible with pragmatic aspects. Yet the latter are not in any sense a necessary ingredient of those particular techniques.

3.4 Conclusion

What have we done in this exemplification? We have presented a dimension as a specimen of our model and of our current research. What is such a dimension good for? *First* of all it substantiates our claim in section 3.1 of an interface between cognitive content and the invariants of linguistic representation. *Second*, it enables us to show the connections between a multitude of linguistic phenomena differing from one another both in form and in meaning and to show that these connections hold both within one particular language and among the diversified languages of the world. *Third*, it introduces an order into this multi-faceted diversity. *Fourth*, it brings to the fore two universal-functional principles: indicativity vs. predicativity, which are the dynamic controllers of dimensional ordering. *Fifth*, it shows that these same forces determine ordering both within a dimension and within the subdimensions bundled together in a technique. *Sixth*, it constitutes the basis of comparison for typological statements: it represents the overall "menu" from which the different language types make their particular selection. *Seventh*, it is the *locus* for pointing out diachronic change: adjacent techniques that share more properties than non-adjacent ones tend to interact diachronically. The area around the turning-point is marked by structural instability and is thus particularly prone to diachronic change.

4   Basic notions

In our exposition of basic thoughts (section 2) there appeared the following notions: function, *repraesentandum*, *tertium comparationis*, universal, continuum, dimension, subdimension, invariant, variant.

In the exemplary presentation of a dimension (section 3) the following further notions were exposed: technique, bundle of subdimensions, prototype, grammaticalized instance, functional principles, indicativity, predicativity, participation, participant, participatum, centralization, decentralization.

While the content of these terms may be fairly well understood from their use, it is certainly not claimed that they have been exhaustively defined and fully operationalized — in the sense of "How do you recognize a dimension when you see one?" Here is a brief survey of the problems that the UNITYP linguist has to face in this respect,[3] and of the possible pathways toward a solution.

It was stated above (section 1) that the universal *repraesentanda* pertain to the cognitive conceptual domain. As such they transcend the domain of linguistics proper. Several disciplines are involved here: philosophy, logic, psychology, neurolinguistics, etc. It will take the joint efforts of an interdisciplinary research among these disciplines to fully explicate the theoretical status of universal *repraesentanda*.

A further problem concerns the logic of the interrelation between the various dimensions and between the subdimensions of a dimension. As for the latter, a first step toward a solution can be seen in our interpretation of the notion of prototype (section 3) as the point of bundling of subdimensions in a technique, and furthermore in our proposed ordering of techniques within a dimension, an ordering supported by internal structural coherence (see below S 7).

Ultimately, a full explication of these notions will come from a "recursive unfolding of the processual structure of thinking" (Hasenclever forthc.). It is quite likely that topology will be the appropriate domain to embrace function, invariant, and variation.

There is thus a certain deficit on the side of deduction and apriorism, with which we must live for a while. No algorithm is proposed. Intuition must help out where operationalized concepts would be needed.

On the side of inductive generalization we have the grammatical categories. Do we really "have" them? The record of their operationalization and definition is anything but brilliant. At least they are used, willy nilly, by the broad community of linguists. In section 3 we somewhat disrespectfully viewed them as "the rear entrance" toward the recognition of dimensions and subdimensions. They are useful, indispensable indeed, for the heuristics of inferring underlying continua. As categories *per se* and outside the continua they belong to, they will never tell us the full story; they are fraught with paradoxes such as: definable within one single language, but not cross-linguistically — and yet the same term applied to many/all languages (see the discussion about N/V, section 3). Further research will probably resolve the paradox by explicating the status of grammatical categories as the average grammaticalization on the relevant continua.

Beside their universal character the functional principles structuring dimensions and subdimensions manifest themselves in observable structural properties. Indicativity and predicativity were mentioned thus far. They are joined by a third principle, viz. ICONICITY. This is the representation by icon, i.e. based on relational similarity between *repraesentandum* and *repraesentans*. It may combine with any of the other principles; but as I have shown (Seiler 1988) its preferred peak is where the other two principles neutralize each other, i.e. at the turning point. For the dimension of participation this would be the area around the technique of transition. Iconicity appears here in the distribution of head- vs. dependent-marking: it is about even between participatum and participants.

The internal coherence structuring dimensions and subdimensions can be visualized in the following chart (S 7, next page). In chart (S 7) "etc." after "point of inversion" abbreviates "neutralization, similarity-based representation, polyvalence".

The chart highlights three points on the dimension or subdimension: maximally dominant indicativity, the turning point as the preferred peak of iconicity, and maximally dominant predicativity. The abbreviations on the left hand margin (Gram = grammar, Funct = function, Prag = Pragmatics, Comp = computer science, Peirce = C. S. Peirce) indicate that the properties are taken from different fields of linguistics and even from disciplines other than linguistics. The coherence of the dimension or subdimension is thus established by bundles of properties which translate into one another in different fields of disciplines.

5 The gradual unfolding of the model

There is a pronounced isomorphism between the unfolding of the processes of linguistic representation and the unfolding of the model that brings these processes to consciousness.

Our work began with an instantaneous, "indicative" recognition of a "Universalien-Konzept" (Seiler 1973:6ff): language as a problem solving system, centrality of the notion of function, representation of

(S 7)

	Indicativity	Iconicity	Predicativity
Gram	lexical absolute less regular less freedom of substitution less marked more grammaticalized more likely of suppletion		syntactic relational more regular more freedom of substitution more marked less grammaticalized less likely of suppletion
Funct	more cohesion less "new" information instant recognition		less cohesion more "new" information construed recognition
Prag	more open to pragmatics pragmatically complex metalanguage dominating		less open to pragmatics pragmatically simple object language dominating
Comp	immediate representation analog shorter search time expression/referent		mediated representation digital longer search time expression/referent
Peirce	index secondness	icon firstness	symbol thirdness
		point of inversion, etc. instability T.P.	

cognitive concepts, interdisciplinary approach. Subsequent research did not have to revise these basic characteristics but strived for greater explicitness, and important concepts were added. One of them is grammaticalization as recognized by C. Lehmann (1982, 1987). Another one is relationality — basic for participation — also introduced by Lehmann (1983, 1986). A number of dimensions and subdimensions were described in full detail: nomination (formerly called descriptivity) (Seiler 1975); determination (Seiler 1978, 1985); possession (Seiler 1983); apprehension (Seiler and Lehmann 1982, Seiler and Stachowiak 1982, Seiler 1986); participation (Seiler 1984, and *akup* publications mentioned above, section 3). The internal coherence of these dimensions and the explanatory potential emanating from it testifies to the usefulness of this construct.

The necessity for positing language-independent *tertia comparationis* as the repraesentanda in the language process was recognized (Seiler 1984, 1985a:9ff), and a clear distinction was proposed (Seiler 1986:1ff) between the invariant, resulting from inductive generalization, and the universal, pertaining to deduction. At the present stage the concept of universal appears as emanating from deduction and reaching down into language-specific manifestations. Compared to this it seems significant that in such a monumental publication as the four-volume "Universals of Human Language" (Greenberg et al. (eds) 1978) no definition of the concept of universal is offered, except by one author who was not a member of the Stanford group (Lieb 1978: 157ff) (compare also Seiler 1980:827ff).

In its present-day aspect the UNITYP model is still a model, i.e. a simulation rather than a full-grown theory. Yet it is striving for a theory, a theory of language, that is, and not a theory of grammar. As one can judge from the foregoing, there is still a certain reliance on iconic representation manifesting itself in graphs and in a number of metaphors.

However, as the growing number of linguists working with this model shows, and as the scope and interest of the numerous publications underscores, it seems to be a framework one can work with and produce significant results. Dimensionality enables us to better understand many linguistic phenomena which, in isolation, presented unsolvable riddles to the practising linguist. Moreover, it is the framework which makes predictions possible: typological predictions (Seiler 1986: 157ff, 1987:259ff), and predictions regarding language change.

6 H. Lieb's principles of new structuralism

Lieb's plea for a new structuralism is to be welcomed in more than one respect: it makes allowance for a pluralism of theories, models, and methods, yet, instead of presenting them in additive fashion it tries to bring to the fore the common denominators. It takes up some threads of classical structuralism but goes far beyond, both in scope and in interest.

Lieb considers his new structuralism "as a means to close the gap between practical work and theoretical persuasion in linguistics" (1990: 2.1, and Principle 1). This is precisely what UNITYP tries to achieve. Full agreement also regarding "the question of how mental objects are related to extramental ones" (1990: 2.1): it matches the UNITYP question of how cognitive concepts are related to linguistic structure (see S 1).

"Traditional structuralism" (Principle 8) is, of course, a cover term that embraces several rather divergent trends. Lieb distinguishes elsewhere between American and European structuralism. One of the major features dividing the two is the nearly total absence of interest in dynamicity, processuality, teleonomy, and language history in the American varieties, and a vivid interest in these very problems that characterizes most of European structuralism. UNITYP here finds itself decidedly on the latter's side (see sections 2 to 4).

Regarding Lieb's principal tenet as to the opposition between the mental and the extra-mental, if I may be allowed to paraphrase it in simpler words, I would say that it is illegitimate to identify linguistic structures — including their meaning — with cognitive content, and cognitive content — or linguistic structures — with mental states, events, or mechanisms. In agreement with this, UNITYP makes a sharp distinction between "the mind" and the meaning of linguistic structures; however, it would add: distinction — yes, separation — no. As the graphic representation of the model (S 1) suggests, conceptual *repraesentanda* are connected with linguistic structures. This is also what Lieb seems to convey (Principle 2). An exemplary case of an, illicit, identification between "mind" and language is G. Lakoff's treatment of (numeral) classifiers (Lakoff 1986:13; 1987:91ff). He speculates on the coherence of classes including "women, fire, and dangerous things", overlooking that classifiers are in the first place not classes of things, but classes of nouns. "Classifiers as a reflection of mind" is another of Lakoff's suggestive titles (1986:13), and an entire edifice called "the ecological aspect of mind" (op. cit. 49) is construed along these lines. Surely, classifiers are a reflection of mind, but in the almost trivial sense in which all of language is a reflection of mind. It is also a near-truism that the reflection is never direct, always mediated.[4]

Notes

[1] Research in this group has been and is being funded by the German Research Council (Deutsche Forschungsgemeinschaft), which is herewith gratefully acknowledged.

[2] On this topic, see H. Sasse (1987:511ff).

[3] I am indebted to Mr. Dirk Hasenclever for a very stringent formulation of these problems (Hasenclever forthc.).

[4] See the discussion in Seiler (1989:23).

References

A complete bibliography of earlier UNITYP publications (1973-1983) is found in Seiler and Brettschneider (1985:63-66).

Abbreviations:

akup stands for *Arbeiten des Kölner Universalienprojekts*, edited by Hansjakob Seiler. Köln: Institut für Sprachwissenschaft der Universität.

LUS stands for *Language Universals Series*, edited by Hansjakob Seiler. Tübingen: Gunter Narr Verlag.

Broschart, Jürgen. 1987. *Noun, Verb, and Participation*. (*akup* 67).
Craig, Colette (ed.). 1986. *Noun Classes and Categorization: Proceedings of a Symposium on Categorization and Noun Classification, Eugene, Oregon, October 1983*. Amsterdam: Benjamins. (TSL 7).
Foley, William. A., and Robert D. Van Valin Jr. 1984. *Functional Syntax and Universal Grammar*. Cambridge: Cambridge University Press.
Givón, Talmy. 1979. *On Understanding Grammar*. New York: Academic Press.
Greenberg, Joseph H., Ferguson, Charles A., and Edith A. Moravcsik (eds). 1978. *Universals of Human Language*. Volumes 1 - 4. Stanford: Stanford University Press.
Hasenclever, Dirk. forthc. "Trialektische Variation als basale Struktur autopoietischen Denkens: Ein philosophisches Modell und sein Bezug zu UNITYP". Paper prepared for the Internationales Kolloquium "Sprache und Denken". Lenzburg/Switzerland, 17-19 May 1989. MS.
Heger, Klaus. 1983. "Zum Verhältnis von Semantik und Noematik". In: Stimm and Raible (eds) 1983. 40-44.
—. 1985. "Concepts and Noemes". In: Seiler and Brettschneider (eds) 1985. 97-101.
Lakoff, George. 1986. "Classifiers as a reflection of mind". In: Craig (ed.) 1986. 13-51.
—. 1987. *Women, Fire, and Dangerous Things: What Categories Reveal about the Mind*. Chicago: University of Chicago Press.
Lehmann, Christian. 1982. *Thoughts on Grammaticalization*. A Programmatic Sketch. Vol. I. (*akup* 48).
—. 1983. "Rektion und syntaktische Relationen". *Fol* 17.339-378.
—. 1986. "Relationality and the grammatical operation". (*akup* 64). 47-63.
—. 1987. "Theoretical implications of processes of grammaticalization". Wenner-Gren Foundation for Anthropological Research. Paper prepared in advance for participants in the conference, no. 105.
Lieb, Hans-Heinrich. 1978. "Universals and linguistic explanation". In: Greenberg, Ferguson and Moravcsik (eds) 1978. Vol. 1. 155-202.
—. 1990. "Rundtisch/Round Table 12. Prospects for a New Structuralism". In: W. Bahner, J. Schildt, and D. Viehweger (eds). *Pro-*

ceedings of the Fourteenth International Congress of Linguists, Berlin/GDR, August 10 – August 15, 1987. Vol. I. Berlin: Akademie-Verlag. 325-328.

Nichols, Johanna. 1986. "Head-marking and dependent-marking grammar". *Language* 62.56-119.

Ross, John R. 1972. "The category squish: Endstation Hauptwort". In: Paul M. Peranteau, Judith N. Levi, Gloria C. Phares (eds). *Papers from the Eigth Regional Meeting of the Chicago Linguistic Society.* Chicago, Ill.: Chicago Linguistic Society. 316-328.

Sasse, Hans-Jürgen. 1987. "The thetic/categorical distinction revisited". *Linguistics* 25.511-580.

Schlerath, Bernfried, and Veronica Rittner (eds). 1985. *Grammatische Kategorien*. Funktion und Geschichte. Wiesbaden: Dr. Ludwig Reichert Verlag.

Seiler, Hansjakob (ed.). (1973-1981). *Structura* 1-13. München: Fink Verlag.

—. (ed.). 1978. *Language Universals*. Papers from the Conference held at Gummersbach/Cologne, October 1976. Tübingen: Gunter Narr Verlag. (Tübinger Beiträge zur Linguistik 111).

—. (ed.). 1982. *Language Universals Series* [= *LUS*] 1-6. Tübingen: Gunter Narr Verlag.

—. 1973. "Das Universalienkonzept". In: H. Seiler (ed.). *Linguistic Workshop I*. Vorarbeiten zu einem Universalienkonzept. München: Fink Verlag. (Stuctura 4). 6-19.

—. 1975. "Die Prinzipien der deskriptiven und der etikettierenden Benennung". In: H. Seiler (ed.). *Linguistic Workshop III*. Arbeiten des Kölner Universalienprojekts 1974. München: Fink Verlag. (Structura 9). 2-57.

—. 1978. "Determination. A functional dimension for interlanguage comparison". In: H. Seiler (ed.). *Language Universals*. Papers from the Conference held at Gummersbach/Cologne, October 1976. Tübingen: Gunter Narr Verlag. (Tübinger Beiträge zur Linguistik 111). 301-328.

—. 1983. *Possession as an Operational Dimension of Language*. Tübingen: Gunter Narr Verlag. (*LUS* 2).

—. 1984. *Die Dimension der Partizipation*. (Valenz, Diathese, Transitivität, Kasusmarkierung, usw.). Vorlesung im WS 1983/84. Bear-

beitet von: Michael Kurzidim und Thomas Müller-Bardey. Köln: Institut für Sprachwissenschaft. MS.
—. 1985. "Kategorien als fokale Instanzen von Kontinua: gezeigt am Beispiel der nominalen Determination". In: Schlerath and Rittner (eds). 1985. 435-448.
—. 1985a. "Diversity, unity, and their connection". In: Seiler and Brettschneider (eds). 1985. 9-13.
—. 1986. *Apprehension: Language, Object, and Order.* Part III: *The Universal Dimension of Apprehension.* Tübingen: Gunter Narr Verlag. (LUS 1/III).
—. 1987. "Language typology in the UNITYP model". *XIVth International Congress of Linguists, Berlin, 10-15 August, 1987.* Preprints of the Plenary Session Papers. Berlin: Editorial Committee. 250-271.
—. 1988. *L'iconicité en perspective fonctionelle.* Köln: Institut für Sprachwissenschaft der Universität. (*akup* 73).
—. 1989. *A Functional View on Prototypes.* Linguistic Agency University of Duisburg. Series A. Paper No. 248. Duisburg: L.A.U.D.
—, and Christian Lehmann (eds). 1982. *Apprehension.* Das sprachliche Erfassen von Gegenständen. Teil I. Bereich und Ordnung der Phänomene. Tübingen: Gunter Narr Verlag. (*LUS* 1/I).
—, and Franz-Josef Stachowiak (eds). 1982. *Apprehension.* Das sprachliche Erfassen von Gegenständen. Teil II. Die Techniken und der Zusammenhang in Einzelsprachen. Tübingen: Gunter Narr Verlag. (*LUS* 1/II).
—, and Gunter Brettschneider (eds). 1985. *Language Invariants and Mental Operations.* International Interdisciplinary Conference held at Gummersbach/Cologne, Germany, September 18-23, 1983. Tübingen: Gunter Narr Verlag. (*LUS* 5).
—, and Waldfried Premper (eds). 1991. *Partizipation.* Das sprachliche Erfassen von Sachverhalten. Tübingen: Gunter Narr Verlag. (*LUS* 6).
Steele, Susan. 1978. "The category AUX as a language universal". In: Greenberg et al. (eds). 1978. Vol. 3. 7-45.
Stimm, Helmut, and Wolfgang Raible (eds). 1983. *Zur Semantik des Französischen.* Beiträge zum Regensburger Romanistentag. Wiesba-

den: Steiner. (*Zeitschrift für französische Sprache und Literatur.* Beiheft 9).

Walter, Heribert. 1981. *Studien zur Nomen-Verb-Distinktion aus typologischer Sicht.* München: Fink Verlag. (*Structura* 13).

Integrational Linguistics: Outline of a Theory of Language

Hans-Heinrich Lieb
Freie Universität Berlin

Contents

0 Introduction
   0.1   Aim and method
   0.2   Integrational Linguistics

1 Background
   1.1   Languages, varieties, idiolects
   1.2   Systems
   1.3   Integrational grammars
   1.4   Language and speech

2 Phonology
   2.1   Introduction and overview
   2.2   Base forms and features
   2.3   Units, categories, and structures
   2.4   Functions

3 Morphology
   3.1   Introduction
   3.2   Base forms and units
   3.3   Categories
   3.4   Structures
   3.5   Functions

4 Syntax
   4.1   Introduction
   4.2   Base forms, units, and categories

    4.3 Structures
    4.4 Functions
5 Lexical semantics (morphosemantics)
    5.1 Introduction
    5.2 Basic idea for lexical meanings
    5.3 Meanings as concepts
    5.4 Lexical meaning composition
6 Syntactic semantics (sentential semantics)
    6.1 Introduction
    6.2 Syntactic meanings
    6.3 Syntactic meaning composition
    6.4 Remarks on syntactic meaning composition

0 Introduction

0.1 Aim and method

It is the aim of this paper to characterize a recent approach to linguistics, Integrational Linguistics (IL), by presenting in rough outline its theory of language, or rather, a major part that deals with the system aspect of languages. (Integrational Linguistics shares its name only with an approach advocated by Harris, e.g. in 1981.) The general orientation of Integrational Linguistics may indeed be characterized by the Nine Principles of New Structuralism although they were formulated, as it were, after the event; Integrational Linguistics was not developed to revindicate structuralism, be it in a traditional or a modern form.

    Conformity of Integrational Linguistics to the Nine Principles may be most striking if its theory of language is simply presented, however informally, rather than related to the principles explicitly. This, then, is the method I choose, simple presentation. Due to this decision I also refrain from drawing comparisons with theories currently proposed in other frameworks; I trust that the reader will recognize the more important similarities and differences. (It is for this reason, then, that few authors outside IL will actually be mentioned.)

    The theory of language, in particular its system part, will be presented in the form it has currently taken in my own work, in Lieb

(1983) and subsequent research. In the main body of this paper (Secs 2 to 6), relevant references will as a rule be given at the end of each introductory subsection (Secs 2.1 etc.), by way of 'further reading' lists. In a few places the theory will be developed beyond its current state. (For example, there is the problem of morphs being 'resyllabified' when occurring in phonological words. As a solution, 'open morphs' are introduced in Sec. 3.2. In morphology, affixes as 'heads' and stems as 'complements' may cause notorious problems. As a solution, scope functions rather than complement and head functions are assigned a fundamental role in affixation, see Sec. 3.5.)

In presenting the theory I will try to bring out its conceptual structure — the 'conceptual net' it throws on reality — more so than its propositional content. Thus, the entities postulated by the theory, and the theoretical concepts embodied in its definitions, are at the centre of attention rather than the assumptions explicitly made in the theory.

The integrational theory of language has been developed far enough clearly to exhibit its axiomatic structure. I will not, however, follow its structure in presenting the theory. Rather, I choose the traditional disciplines of phonology, morphology, syntax and semantics for overall organization, characterizing the theory's relevant parts in each of these fields. Presentation itself will be by extended examples rather than general statements. In short, presentation is as informal as I could make it for a formal theory. (Knowledge of naïve set theory is presupposed.)

0.2 Integrational Linguistics

Historically, IL has arisen mainly from work done by Lieb since roughly 1965. From 1972 to 1982, a Berlin research group founded and directed by Lieb worked on problems of general syntax, with applications to German. The most comprehensive presentation of IL to date is Lieb (1983), which also contains a bibliography of relevant literature up to 1983, and is to be followed by further volumes (in prep.). As with most approaches growing over a sufficient period of time, there have been some divergent developments. Eisenberg (^{2}1989) is fairly close to Lieb (1983) in theoretical outlook (Eisenberg continues in syntax the original direction of the Berlin research group, which was rather rigorously oriented towards syntactic form; Lieb assigns a larger role to word meaning also in syntax). More distantly, IL is one of the sources of Lutzeier (1991), which has a similar orientation in syntax (though not in sentential semantics) and adopts some important notions from IL in construing syntactic structures.

There has been a large number of papers and articles by Lieb and others. Book-size studies by authors other than Lieb, either published or in preparation, may here be listed: Eisenberg (1976), on the syntax and semantics of the German adjective; Fischer (1981), a monograph on the syntax and semantics of German conditionals; Lutzeier (1981), on the notion of lexical field; Eisenberg (^{2}1989), a reference grammar of Modern German; Richter (1988), a study of linguistic indexicality within the framework of Integrational Semantics (Lieb 1983); Peters (forthc.), a critical evaluation of current conceptions of language universals; Peters (in prep.), an intentionalist theory of the very early stages of first language acquisition; Kendzia (in prep.), a study of syntactic accents in Modern German; Budde (in prep.), a theory of word order; Hoepfner (in prep.), a study of indirect speech acts using Integrational Semantics; and Falkenberg (in prep.), a reconsideration of the Integrational theory of linguistic grammars; see also Choi (in press).

"Integrational" in the *name* of the approach is meant to be programmatic. IL may claim to be *integrative* in several respects. First, it takes a broad view of the range of linguistics, which is to deal with all aspects of natural languages that are directly or indirectly relevant to their use. Second, linguistics is construed as a well-defined discipline in its own right but at the same time placed within a system of interrelated disciplines that include biology, psychology, and sociology. Third, IL proposes both a theory of language and a theory of linguistic grammars that presupposes the theory of language. Fourth, the theory of language — which is to cover more than the system aspect of languages — is to cover the system aspect in its entirety; thus, the theory has a phonological, a morphological, a syntactic, and a semantic part.

IL is *integrative* also in a more technical sense: it proposes a way of integrating theories of different types, both linguistic — say, a general syntactic and a general semantic theory — and linguistic and non-linguistic — say, a syntactic theory and a psychological theory of learning. In particular, theories of language and individual grammars are interconnected; grammars may actually be *formulated in terms of a theory of language*.

The main body of this paper (Secs. 2 to 6) is devoted to the system part of the IL theory of language. Integrational Linguistics takes language variability — both within and between languages — as a fundamental rather than a peripheral fact. Therefore, the system part of the theory of language can be properly understood only when the theory's treatment of language variability has been explained. The theory of linguistic grammars that is based on the theory of language should also be briefly considered for the way in which it accounts for language variability. Finally, it is emphasized in IL that linguistic 'systems' are 'systems for speech', and this emphasis is reflected in the system part of the theory of language. The topics of variability, grammar writing, and speech are taken up in Sec. 1.

1 Background

1.1 Languages, varieties, idiolects

A language in the IL sense may be either a complete historical language through time, such as English from its beginnings to its end some time in the future; or a historical period of such a language, e.g. Modern English. (Being a language is to be independent of any political requirements either on the language or the language community.)

It is a traditional assumption that languages in such a sense — at least languages that are historical periods — are 'systems'. There are two problems with this view.

First, the view implies a dichotomy between a language (a system) and the 'speech' by which a language is 'realized' — a set of utterances. But this dichotomy leaves no place for the (abstract) sentences that underlie the utterances and can each be uttered an indefinite number of times. We are here confronted with a Saussurean conundrum that led Buyssens (1943) to postulate *discours* as intermediate between *langue* and *parole*. Given the notion of *discours*, the concept of language may apply at the level of *discours*, to constructs based on abstract sentences (which is also Chomsky's conception in his earlier work); rather than *being* systems, languages *have* systems (see also Heger 1992, on these questions). I adopted this idea early on; it is basic to the outline of a theory of language presented in Lieb (1970).

Second, languages as 'systems' are hard to reconcile with language-internal variability: any 'historical language through time', or historical period of such, has a number of varieties of different types — regional dialects, sociolects, registers (language styles), and the like. The difficulty is more easily overcome by a conception that applies the notion of language at the level of abstract sentences.

In the IL theory of language we proceed as follows. We start from individual speakers and their 'idiolects'; a *language* is a set of idiolects, and each *variety* of a language is a subset of the language. An *idiolect* is a certain set of abstract sentences (form-meaning pairs); this set is simultaneously an element of a certain regional or interregional variety, of a certain sociolect, register etc., depending on which types of varieties are present in the language. A speaker's total share of a language — a *personal variety* — is not an idiolect but a *set* of idiolects (it may of course be a unit set).

The *varieties* of a language are given through its *variety structure*: a classification system (a set of classifications) whose source is the language itself. The varieties are the classes that are elements of classifications in the variety structure. The classes in each classification are simultaneously determined by, on the one hand, *external criteria*, related to properties of speakers or utterances such as speaker residence, social class etc., or utterance situation; and by *system-based criteria* on the other, related to properties of 'idiolect systems'.

1.2 Systems

We assume that each idiolect has a *system* — a system *of* the idiolect — that specifies which form-meaning pairs are elements of the idiolect. Formally, an idiolect system is construed as an ordered sixtuple:

(1.1) Let "S" stand for any idiolect system. S is an ordered sixtuple.
    a. *The phonetic-phonological subsystem* or *sound subsystem* of S (if S is a system of a 'spoken' idiolect) = the pair consisting of the first and second components of S.

b. *The graphetic-graphemic subsystem* of S (if S is a system of a 'written' idiolect) = the pair consisting of the first and second components of S.
c. *The morphosyntactic subsystem* of S = the pair consisting of the third and fourth components of S.
d. *The semantic subsystem* of S = the pair consisting of the fifth and sixth components of S.

Thus, there are three *subsystems* and six *parts* of an idiolect system: the *phonetic* (*graphetic*), *phonological* (*graphemic*), *morphological*, *syntactic*, *morphosemantic*, and *syntactic-semantic* (or *sentence semantics*) parts.

No *pragmatic* subsystem is assumed, mainly for two reasons. (i) It is not at the level of the idiolect system that language variability is accounted for. (ii) Right from the start the system aspect of 'language' is conceived — especially in the area of meaning (see Secs 5f) — as subservient to the 'speech' aspect (see Sec. 1.3). Thus, essentially nothing is left to motivate a 'pragmatic' subsystem.

The six parts of an idiolect system must of course each have an internal structure. Indeed, each can be construed as an n-tuple, for some n. The IL theory of language is not yet advanced far enough to specify for each part of an idiolect system the tuple with which it may be identified. This means that idiolect systems themselves have not been completely determined formally.

Generally, the components of a part of an idiolect system (components of an n-tuple) are to be the most complex entities that must be distinguished. Therefore, units, categories, structures etc. as characterized in the main body of this paper are not yet components — in the set-theoretic sense of "component" — of parts of an idiolect system; rather, the *set* of unit/structure pairs in a given part might count as a component of that part. However, even where the theory of language has already established most components of a part of an idiolect system, I will as a rule discuss only the entities of which a component *consists*, and not formally identify the component itself.

Different idiolect systems may have shared properties. Given a *set* of idiolects, such as a language or language variety, we conceive a *system for* the set as a *construct from* properties that are shared by the systems of all idiolects in the set. Consider a *stage* (a certain subset) of a language or language variety. A chain of increasingly abstract systems may be associated with the stage; the more abstract systems are also systems for increasingly larger temporal sections of the language.

This, then, is the way in which the IL theory of language deals with internal variability of historical languages. The conception, worked out in Lieb (1970) and subsequently modified (Lieb 1982, 1983), is opposed to the view, held by generativists and some non-generativists alike, that the pretheoretic notion of a historical language is not worth explicating (Chomsky 1981, Hudson 1980: Ch. 2, Carr 1989, 1990). Indeed, the variability conception can be further developed into a theory (Lieb forthc. b) that accounts not only for related conceptions like Coseriu's (1981/1988) but also for seemingly different approaches to language variability like Chomsky's (1981, 1986) 'Principles and Parameters' framework. The theory is easily extended to include variation among languages and thus, to do justice to typological work and universality research (whose status has been a major metatheoretical concern in IL, see Lieb 1975, Peters forthc.).

The integrational theory of linguistic *grammars* is based on the IL theory of *language* and is, in particular, affected by the way in which the theory of language accounts for language variability. It is mainly from this point of view that the theory of grammars will be briefly discussed in the present context (see also Lieb 1989). Also, questions concerning grammar format or the status of grammar rules would eventually be clarified in the theory of grammars not the theory of language; hence, they do not figure at all in the main body of this paper where the system part of the theory of *language* is characterized.

1.3 Integrational grammars

A grammar is construed as a theory. The object of the theory is, or contains, a pair whose first component is either an idiolect or a set of idiolects (a variety, stage, or even an entire language), and whose second component is a system of or for the first. Correspondingly, we may have idiolect grammars, variety grammars etc. Idiolect grammars are not only about an idiolect and idiolect system but also about a speaker and his or her utterances. Variety grammars are ultimately related to specific speakers and utterances by being used as a basis for idiolect grammars.

Normally, linguists are concerned not with grammars of idiolects but with grammars of idiolect sets, i.e. grammars whose object is a pair consisting of a set of idiolects and a system for the set. The following stipulations are made in IL for such grammars:

(1.2) *Grammars of idiolect sets (language varieties etc.)*
 a. Each grammar is an axiomatic theory.
 b. Descriptive constants used in the grammar — other than names of the idiolect set and its system, which may be the only 'axiomatic constants' of the grammar itself — are as a rule provided by a presupposed theory of language.
 c. Axioms and theorems of the grammar are typically formulated as universal implications over the idiolects in the idiolect set and their systems.

(c) is motivated by the fact that any system *for* a set of idiolects is conceived as a construct from shared properties of all systems *of* all idiolects in the set. (c) is therefore a way of describing the system that is part of the grammar's object.

Features (b) and (c) may be exemplified as follows. Suppose **D** is a certain variety of German, i.e. a certain set of idiolects C that are elements of German. Assume a theory of language that contains "Phoneme" as a binary relational constant: "p is a Phoneme of S", where "S" stands for any system of any idiolect (in arbitrary languages), and "p" for any 'sound' in any idiolect system. Define, for any binary relation R and any y: "$R(-,y) = \{x| (x,y) \in R\}$", where "$R(-,y)$" may be read as "R of y". Thus, $Phon(-,S) = \{p| (p,S) \in Phon[eme]\}$, i.e. Phon$(-,S)$ = Phoneme of S = the set of phonemes of S. A grammar of (**D**, σ) — where σ is a system for **D** — may then contain an axiom or theorem of the following type:

(1.3) For any C ∈ **D** and any system S of C: Phon$(-,S) = \{$/b/, /p/, ...$\}$.

In (1.3), "**D**" is an axiomatic constant of the grammar, and "Phon" is a non-logical relational constant from the presupposed theory of language. "Phon$(-,S)$" is a complex term used in (1.3) to refer to the set of phonemes of any system S of any idiolect in **D**, i.e. to a certain *category* of S. Thus, reference to such categories requires only constants from the presupposed theory of language; this is an example of what it means to say that the grammar is *formulated in terms of* such a theory. The remaining constants "/b/", "/p/" etc. may or may not be from the presupposed theory of language, depending on how they are defined.

On purely formal grounds (1.3) is not a definition of anything (certainly not of the term "Phon"); it is an axiom or theorem of the grammar that identifies, for any system of any idiolect in **D**, the set of phonemes of the system; as an identification claim, it may be true or false. In order to understand the claim the term "Phoneme" must already be understood. It is a question concerning the presupposed theory of language not the grammar how to interpret the term "Phoneme".

The example, whose force does not of course depend on phonemes being allowed as theoretical constructs, is simple but still characterizes a grammar's key sentences, whether in phonology, morphology, syntax or semantics. Typically, these are identity claims or else, have the form of equivalences, to be characterized in a strictly analogous form. Such identity claims or equivalences may form groups that have the formal structure (though not the theoretical status) of systems of simultaneous recursive definitions. So-called 'rules of grammar' (descriptive expressions formulated in the language of a grammar) may be identified either with some of the identity claims or equivalences or with parts that appear on their right-hand sides (right of the identity or equivalence signs).

The expression on the left-hand side is based on a relational predicate (such as "Phon" in (1.3)) or a function name that are, as a rule, axiomatic constants not of the grammar but of a presupposed theory of language. These constants are to be understood in the same sense in arbitrary grammars formulated in terms of the presupposed theory. This allows, in a natural way, for grammars that are comparative or contrastive, and even for typological theories.

On the integrational conception it is idiolect systems that are of prime importance both to grammars and to the integrational theory of language. In particular, the theory of language takes idiolect systems as a starting-point for relating 'language' and 'speech'.

1.4 Language and speech

Consider the following sentence from some spoken English idiolect:

(1.4) *Come here*!

The sentence is to be a pair consisting of a 'phonetic form' (here denoted, rather vaguely, by an orthographic name) and some normal 'meaning' of this form (left unspecified in (1.4)).

Among the properties of *Come here*!, there is

(1.5) the property of being a sentence that has [k] as the first sound of its phonetic form.

Come here! can be uttered an indefinite number of times. For any sound event to be an utterance of this sentence, a certain relation must hold between the event and the speaker who produces it:

(1.6) the relation between any sound event and person such that: the event has an initial part that 'realizes' [k] with respect to the person.

(If an articulatory conception of sounds is adopted and "[k]" is understood in the usual sense, the initial part of the sound event would have to be produced by the person in a specific way: by using the dorsum of the tongue to form an occlusion against the back part of the roof of the mouth, etc.)

Property (1.5) is a property of abstract sentences that *Come here*! happens to have. Relation (1.6) connects sound events and persons and must relate any sound event and its speaker if the event is to be a (successful) utterance of *Come here*!

Now take any system of the presupposed English idiolect to which *Come here*! belongs. It is due to the system that (1.5) and (1.6) are combined; more generally:

(1.7) Any system of a 'spoken' idiolect determines a set of property/relation pairs such that, for any such pair: if a sentence in the idiolect has the property, then a sound event produced by a person is a *successful utterance of the sentence by the person with respect to the idiolect system* only if sound event and person are related by the relation.

A sound event is a *successful* utterance if it is an utterance that results from a successful speech action, i.e. a speech action where the articulatory movement satisfies the content of the intention-in-action, see Lieb (Section I, above: Sec. 4). Satisfying the content may imply that a complex relation of *correspondence* holds between the sound event and the 'phonetic form' that is the first component of the sentence; cf. the relation of *Entsprechung* in Lieb 1988: Sec. 4.2. (The notion of a *successful* utterance replaces the concept of 'normal' utterance as found in my earlier work.)

The set of property/relation pairs determined by a given idiolect system may be called *the speech value of the system*. Intuitively, the speech value of a system of an idiolect specifies necessary conditions for successful utterances of the idiolect's sentences. On the IL view, a linguist engaged in describing a language is concerned mainly with determining the speech value of systems of idiolects that belong to the language. This view places linguistics on a firm intentionalist footing at least as far as the system aspect of languages is concerned.

Presupposing the background that has now been provided, I characterize the system part of the IL theory of language, concentrating on its conceptual structure and ontological aspects. For each part of an idiolect system — the phonetic, phonological, morphological, syntactic, morphosemantic, and semantic parts — I characterize the linguistic entities that IL postulates as 'building-blocks' of the components of the given part (itself a tuple of components that as a rule will not be identified). The relevant parts of the theory of language are given their traditional names of phonology (to be treated only briefly; Sec. 2), morphology (excluding morphosemantics; Sec. 3), syntax (Sec. 4), and semantics (lexical semantics, in particular, morphosemantics: Sec. 5; syntactic semantics, in particular, sentential semantics: Sec. 6).

2 Phonology

2.1 Introduction and overview

I continue to use "S" as a variable for arbitrary idiolect systems. In discussing examples, I may use "**S**" as an ambiguous constant, i.e. as the name of a certain system that remains unspecified. (Generally, bold face is used for such constants: for names of certain entities that are not fully identified. Ambiguous constants may name different entities in different contexts.) Formulations such as "let S be an English idiolect system [a system of an idiolect that is an element of English]" serve to restrict discussion to certain systems; they do not reinterpret the variable. Relevant terms — like "the phonetic part", "sound", etc. — are from now on to be understood as relativized to idiolect systems S (or a certain system **S**) — "the phonetic part of S", ".. is a sound of S" — even when there is no explicit reference to S (or **S**).

Only systems of 'spoken' idiolects will be considered in this Section. A section on 'written' idiolects would have to be largely analogous, adding a part on how systems of 'written' idiolects are related to systems of 'spoken' ones.

An idiolect is to be a set of sentences, understood as abstract form/meaning pairs. Suppose S is a system of a given idiolect. We may then identify the idiolect with *the set of phonetic sentences determined by S*. Each phonetic sentence determined by S is a form/meaning pair whose first component — a *phonetic sentence form* — is a 'structured unit' of the phonetic part of S.

We postulate, it will be remembered, a two-part sound system of S consisting of *the phonetic part of S* and *the phonological part of S*. The two parts are largely analogous. Each comprises features, base forms, units, categories, structures, and relations, in particular, functions.

Phonetic base forms are *phonetic sounds* on the one hand and suprasegmental entities like *phonetic pitches* or *phonetic lengths* on the other. Not only pitches but also sounds are understood in auditive (perceptual) rather than articulatory terms, and not only sounds but also pitches are construed as sets of *phonetic features*.

All *phonetic units* are sequences of phonetic sounds, more specifically:

(2.1)   The phonetic units are:
   a. the unit sequences of phonetic base forms;
   b. certain consonantal and vocalic groups that play a role in the subdivision of phonetic syllables (onset, nucleus, coda);

    c. those sequences of sounds which may be identified with the phonetic syllables of S (understood as units of S rather than parts of sound sequences);
    d. the sound sequences of phonetic words;
    e. the sound sequences of *phonetic sentence forms*, i.e. of first components of phonetic sentences.

(Both phonetic words and phonetic sentence forms are unit/structure pairs, or 'structured units', see below.)

Phonetic categories are sets of phonetic units, such as the set of vocalic units or the set of vocalic groups.

A *phonetic structure* of a unit is a pair consisting of a *phonetic constituent structure* that determines, in particular, the syllables (if any) *of the unit*, and a *suprasegmental structure* of the unit.

Among the *relations* of the phonetic part of S there is the *phonetic structure assignment* of S, a set of unit/structure pairs whose domain is the set of phonetic units, and whose counterdomain is the set of phonetic structures of S. The elements of the structure assignment are called *structured phonetic units* of S.

A *phonetic function* takes triples consisting of a phonetic unit of an idiolect system and one of it structures (i.e. a structured unit) and of the system itself and assigns to each triple a set of tuples whose components are, typically, constituents of the unit. Equivalently, a phonetic function takes pairs consisting of (i) a structured phonetic unit of S and (ii) S itself, and assigns to each pair a set as just described. For example, the phonetic nucleus function may take a pair consisting of a phonetic word (a sound sequence plus a structure) and a system and assign to it the set of pairs that each consist of the nucleus of some constituent and the constituent itself. *Phonetic accents* may also be construed as such functions.

The phonological part of S is quite analogous to the phonetic part (simply replace "phonetic" by "phonological" in preceding formulations).

There are also *correspondence relations* (typically, many-many relations between phonetic and phonological base forms, phonetic and phonological units etc., and conversely). For example, on a classical structuralist model — not adopted in IL — the allophone relation in S would be such a relation.

The theoretical status of correspondence relations has not yet been sufficiently clarified in IL. Since the relations involve entities from both the phonetic and the phonological parts of S, they are not easily assigned to either. Some of these relations may have to be independently specified, giving rise to an additional part of the sound system itself. Alternatively, we might propose that correspondence relations be taken as basic, defining the phonetic and phonological parts of S in terms of correspondence relations. Either way (1.1a) would have to be revised.

What the phonetic and phonological parts of S *agree* in is this: they both represent *basic form properties* of (spoken) sound events, i.e. properties that directly relate to either the production, the perception or the physical shape of sound events (on the IL view, perception takes precedence).

The two parts are distinguished by a criterion that may be formulated roughly as follows: the *phonological part* represents those basic form properties of sound events which figure in the morphosyntactic or semantic subsystems of S; the *phonetic part* represents all basic form properties — over and beyond the 'phonological' ones — that make a speech event 'sound right' if it is a successful utterance of some phonetic sentence determined by S. Thus, phonological entities are as a rule more abstract than corresponding phonetic ones.

Because of the many parallelisms between the phonetic and phonological parts, both parts may frequently be covered by a single statement; the terms "phonetic" and "phonological" may then be dropped. The entities that make up the two parts will now be considered in somewhat greater detail. (Integrational Phonology was developed piecemeal, and continues to be the most incomplete part of the integrational theory of language: cf. Lieb 1979, 1980a, 1985b, 1988. Recently, Eisenberg, from a related though different point of view, has been studying written varieties in their own right, also contributing to phonology; see, in particular, Eisenberg 1985, 1988, forthc. a, forthc. b, Eisenberg and Butt 1990.)

2.2 Base forms and features

Base forms, and sounds in particular, are construed as sets of features; their nature therefore depends on how features are understood.

In present-day linguistics notions of feature have come to play a larger role beyond their traditional domain in the sound system and, to some extent, the analysis of meanings. The formal status of features, be it in phonology, morphology, syntax or semantics, is, however, hardly clear in the literature. Differently from other approaches, IL allows features only in the sound system.

Articulatory and auditive features are construed on the pattern of the following example ("V_1" here stands for any person with a normal speech apparatus):

(2.2) *Definition.* Nasal relative to V_1 [Nasal(V_1)] = the property of being a sound event produced by V_1 through use of V_1's speech apparatus with air escaping only through V_1's nose.

Nasal as defined in (2.2) exemplifies the formal status of all *articulatory* and *auditive* features: any such feature is a function that assigns to any suitable person a person-relative property of sound events. *Acoustic* features are simply properties of sound events; persons are not involved.

The articulatory feature Nasal in the sense of (2.2) must be distinguished from Nasal in the sense of *Nasality*: this may be understood as a function whose arguments are numbers, say 1 and 0, or symbols like "+" and "–", and whose values are two functions, Nasal in (2.2) and 'Non-Nasal' defined by inserting "not" in front of "only" in (2.2). If the term "feature" is reserved for functions like Nasality, then Nasal in (2.2) is not a feature but is a feature *value*, i.e. Nasal = Nasality(+), mostly written "+Nasality". The term "dimension" is occasionally used for functions like Nasality; it appears to be more appropriate than "feature".

Nasal in (2.2) is an *articulatory feature* because its values are properties defined in terms of articulation; analogously, there are *auditive* (perceptual) and *acoustic* (physical) *features*. IL takes the position that not only suprasegmental base forms but also sounds must be construed as sets of *auditive* not articulatory or acoustic features because hearing is the most important controlling factor in all normal speech production.

Even so, a set of articulatory features may serve as a 'basis' for a sound: if a sound event is produced in conformity to these features, then the event 'sounds right' to the speaker, i.e. the sound event has all the perceptual properties determined by the auditive features that are elements of the sound. More informally, being produced right is sufficient for sounding right. Given this assumption, we may use traditional notations for sets of *articulatory* features as a basis for denoting sounds that are sets of *auditive* features; for example ("φ" stands for any function that assigns sound event properties to persons):

(2.3) a. [n] = {Nasal, Alveolar, ...}
b. [n]' = the set of auditive features φ such that for any person V_1 and any sound event, if the sound event has all the [articulatory] properties associated with V_1 by functions in [n], then the event also has the [auditive] property associated with V_1 by φ.

Differently from sounds, *pitches* and other suprasegmental base forms are easier to describe directly in auditive terms than by reference to their articulatory basis.

2.3 Units, categories, and structures

Explanations will be based on an example. Consider the following structured phonological unit — unit together with a structure — of a specific Modern English idiolect system **S**, left unidentified (using traditional phoneme notation we do not commit ourselves to traditional phoneme conceptions; furthermore, all phonemic symbols should be understood on the pattern of (2.3b) not (2.3a), i.e. should be supplemented by a prime symbol (') to denote a set of auditive not articulatory features; a superscripted "p" is a reminder of "phonetic/phonological"):

(2.4)

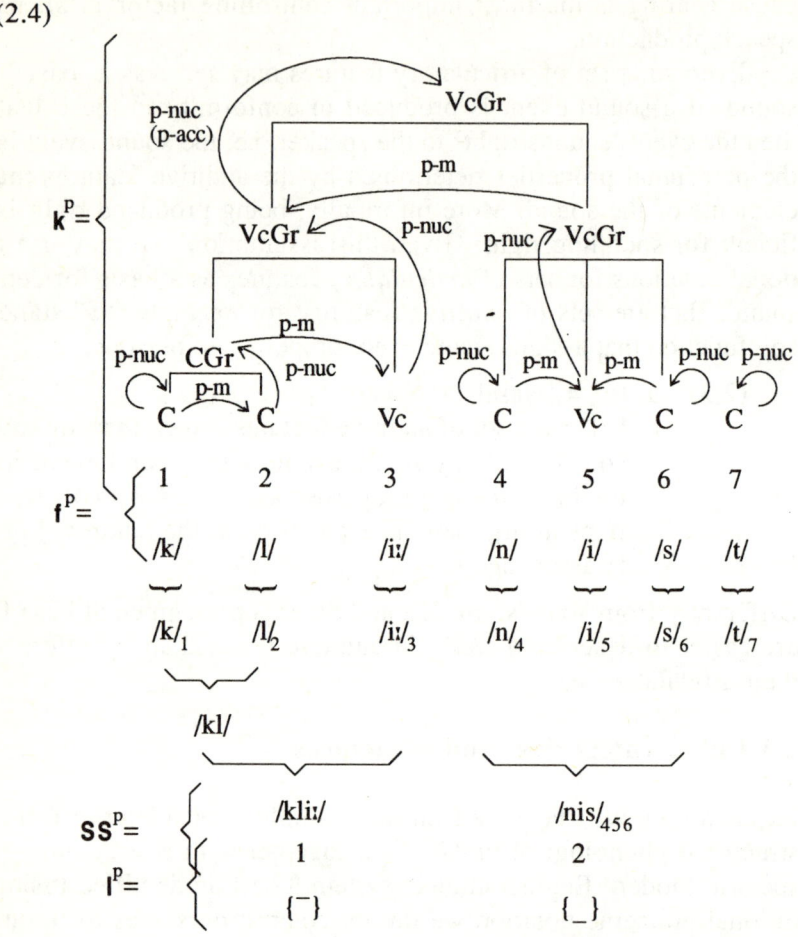

($/kl/ = /kl/_{12} = \{(1, /k/), (2, /l/)\}$, etc.). The structured unit is

(2.5)   *cleanest* = $(f^P, s^P) = (f^P, k^P, l^P)$, where $s^P = (k^P, l^P)$ and

a. f^P = $\{(1, /k/), (2, /l/), ...\}$, a sequence of phonological sounds of **S**;

b. k^P = $\{(\{1\}, C(-,\mathbf{S})), (\{1,2\}, CGr(-,\mathbf{S})), ...\}$, a certain relation between sets of integers and phonological categories (constituent categories) of **S** (for notation, see § 1.3);

c. $/k/_1 = \{(1, /k/)\}$; $/l/_2 = \{(2, /l/)\}$; ...
d. $\mathbf{SS} = \{(1, /\text{kli:}/), (2, /\text{nis}/_{456})\}$;
e. $\mathbf{I^p} = \{(1, \{^-\mathbf{S}\}), (2, \{\_\mathbf{S}\})\}$.

$\mathbf{f^p}$ is *the sound sequence* of *cleanest*. $\mathbf{k^p}$ is its *constituent structure*; C (-,**S**) etc. are the sets of consonantal units, vocalic units, consonantal groups, and vocalic groups of **S**. $/k/_1$ etc. and $\mathbf{f^p}$ are the *constituents* of *cleanest*; in particular, /kli:/ and $/\text{nis}/_{456}$ are its *syllables* (more precisely, the syllables of the word's sound sequence), and **SS** is its *syllable sequence*. $\mathbf{I^p}$ is the *suprasegmental* or *intonation structure* of *cleanest*. Only pitches — High in **S** and Low in **S** — happen to be involved in the intonation structure; the sets that are members of an intonation structure may, in principle, also contain suprasegmental base forms other than pitches. The interrelations between entities (a) to (e) should be intuitively clear from (2.4) and (2.5).

cleanest is an *open phonological word*, i.e. a phonological word with a *weak* constituent structure (whose 'tree name' lacks a 'root', see (2.4)). Separation of $/t/_7$ in (2.4) accounts for the fact that in a *phonological sentence form*, $/t/_7$ may combine with the first syllable of the next word to form a syllable of the sentence form (cf. *the cleanest⌣ economic solution ...* — phonological sentence forms are the 'representations', at the phonological level, of phonetic sentence forms). A *closed phonological word* — such as *enjoy* — has a *strong* constituent structure and no such part.

For any word we may consider its *closure*: the closure of a closed word is the word itself; the closure of an open word is the result of replacing its weak constituent structure by an appropriate *strong* one (whose 'tree name' has a 'root'). Phonological words are usually identified with word closures but this causes syllabification problems when phonological sentences are considered.

2.4 Functions

The arrows in (2.4) indicate the values of two phonetic functions — *phonological nucleus* (p-nuc) and *phonological modifier* (p-m) — for the ordered pair (*cleanest*, **S**) as argument:

(2.6) a. p-nuc(*cleanest*, **S**) =
 $\{(/k/_1, /k/_1), (/l/_2, /kl/), (/iː/_3, /kliː/), ..., (/kliː/, /kliːnis/)\}$.
b. p-m(*cleanest*, **S**) = $\{(/k/_1, /l/_2), ...\}$.

(a) means that $/k/_1$ is a nucleus of itself in *cleanest* and **S**, and $/l/_2$ a nucleus of /kl/, etc.; analogously, (b).

Traditional notions relating to syllables, like syllable nucleus, periphery, coda etc., are reconstructed by functions that are partly defined by means of either p-nuc or p-m. For example, the function *syllable nucleus* (s-nuc) assigns to a structured-unit/system pair a certain subset (possibly empty) of the value of p-nuc: the set of pairs (of constituents of the unit's sound sequence) such that the second component is a syllable of the unit (of its sound sequence) and the first component is the nucleus of the second; e.g.,

(2.7) s-nuc(*cleanest*, **S**) = $\{(/iː/_3, /kliː/), (/i/_5, /nis/_{456})\}$.

Even the notion of (*having*) *phonological accent* is reconstructed in this way: the function of phonological accent (p-acc) assigns to a word/system pair the set of pairs such that the first component of each pair is a syllable of the word and is a nucleus of (a largest constituent of) the word's sound sequence and 'is accented' (this depends on the intonation structure of the word), e.g.,

(2.8) p-acc(*cleanest*, **S**) = $\{(/kliː/, /kliːnis/)\}$.

The concept of p-acc covers the traditional notion of (primary) *word accent* at the phonological level. Degrees of accentuation (or degrees of 'heaviness') may also be accounted for by appropriate functions.

The details of our structure/function example (2.4) cannot here be justified. This would require, among other things, reference to 'sonority scales'.

3 Morphology

3.1 Introduction

Morphology in a traditional sense deals with both the formal and the semantic structure of 'words'. Morphological structure 'builds on' phonological structure but excludes whatever belongs to phonology proper. Morphology in the IL sense is restricted to questions of form; semantic structure is assigned to morphosemantics. Naturally, morphology and morphosemantics are closely linked.

At the same time morphology is interrelated with syntax, which also builds on phonology and is itself interconnected with sentential semantics. Morphology and syntax are jointly opposed to, and interrelated with, morphosemantics and sentential semantics. Idiolect systems are construed accordingly: the morphological and syntactic parts form the morphosyntactic subsystem, and the morphosemantic and sentence semantics parts form the semantic subsystem. Morphology in the IL sense, then, is essentially concerned with the morphological parts of idiolect systems, taken within this larger framework.

Morphological entities are ultimately constructed from phonological ones, and types of morphological entities are largely analogous to types of entities in the sound system: there are *morphological base forms, units, categories, structures*, and *relations*, in particular, *functions*. There are no 'morphological features', though. (IL does not extend the notion of feature beyond the study of the sound system to morphology and syntax.)

In addition, there are two types of morphological entities that have no counterpart in the sound system: *morphological paradigms* and *lexemes*, construed as pairs of a paradigm and a concept that is a meaning of the paradigm. Even where counterparts in the sound system do exist, morphological entities may be rather different from their counterparts.

(For the development of Integrational Morphology, see Lieb 1978, 1983. Even Lieb 1983: Part C, which is the most complete version to date, is still sketchy. The following account contains three improvements: introduction of open morphs (Sec. 3.2); of functions (m-nuc^n) to account for 'multiple nuclei'; and of the function of morphological qualification (m-qual) (Sec. 3.4).)

3.2 Base forms and units

Morphological base forms, or *morphs*, are entities of the same formal type as structured phonological units, i.e. base forms are pairs consisting each of a sequence of phonological sounds ('phonemes') and a phonological structure of the sequence, which in turn consists of a constituent structure and a suprasegmental structure. It may indeed be suggested that morphs *are* structured phonological units: certain units — phonological words — are syntactic base forms, certain other units — morphs — are morphological ones.

Continuing example (2.4), we may propose:

(3.1)

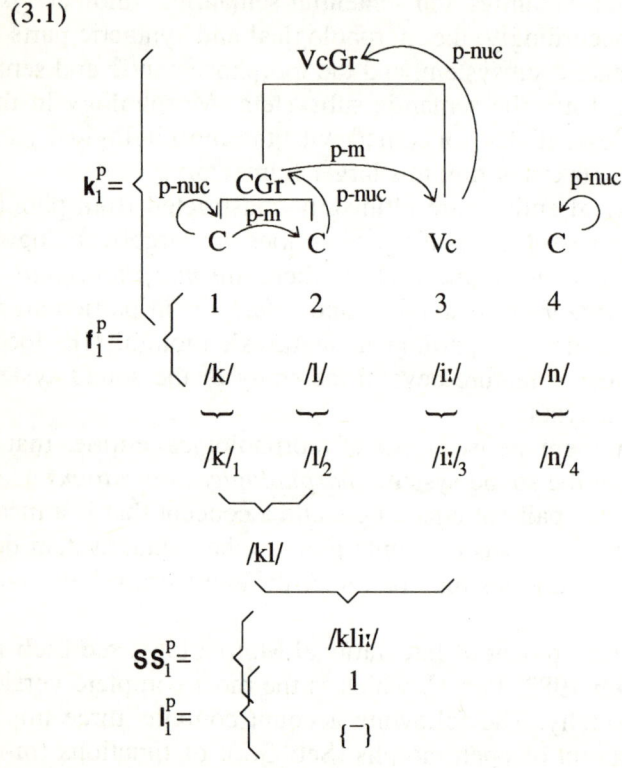

The morph is

(3.2) $clean = (f_1^P, s_1^P) = (f_1^P, k_1^P, l_1^P),$

where the various entities are understood on the pattern of (2.5) and are, accordingly, the sound sequence of *clean* (f_1^P), etc. (In the case of *non*-syllabic morphs both the syllable sequence and the intonation structure are empty.)

Morphs, again, may be either *open* (e.g., *clean* in (3.1), with a weak constituent structure and a separable part, cf. /n/$_4$ in (3.1) and /t/$_7$ in (2.4)) or *closed* (such as the morphs *see* or *s*). The *closure* of a closed morph is the morph itself; the closure of an open morph is obtained by introducing a suitable 'strong' constituent structure. For example, the closure of *clean* in (3.2) is the triple obtained from *clean* by replacing k_1^p with

(3.3)

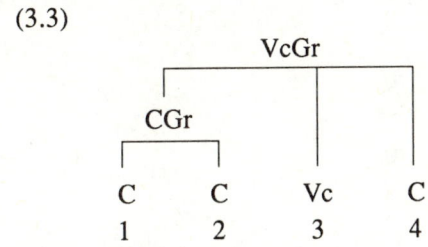

Morphological units are sequences of morphs. More precisely, this is true of *pure* morphological units, in contradistinction to *mixed* ones, which also contain *syntactic* base forms (complete phonological words): *tage* ("days") as part of German *fünf-tage-woche* ("five day week") is not to be analysed morphologically. Morphological units are either stem forms, affix forms, or stem groups; 'morphological words', i.e. morphological units that correspond to phonological words, are either stem forms or stem groups.

For example,

(3.4) the unit sequence of $clean = clean^1 = \{(1, clean)\}$

is a morphological unit (of **S**). Or again,

(3.5) $clean\ est = \{(1, clean)\}, (2, est)\}$

is a morphological unit, where

(3.6) $est = (f_2^p, s_2^p) = (f_2^p, k_2^p, l_2^p)$

is the morph defined in

(3.7)

$$k_2^p = \begin{cases} \text{p-nuc} \nearrow \text{VcGr} \\ \begin{array}{ccc} \text{p-m} & \text{p-nuc} & \text{p-nuc} \\ \text{Vc} & \text{C} & \text{C} \\ 1 & 2 & 3 \end{array} \\ /i/ /s/ /t/ \end{cases}$$

$$f_2^p = \begin{cases} /i/_1 /s/_2 /t/_3 \end{cases}$$

$$ss_2^p = \{ \; /is/ \;$$

$$l_2^p = \{ \; \{\_\} \;$$

Compare the phonological word *cleanest* in (2.4) — a single structured phonological unit — and the morphological unit *clean est* in (3.5), the sequence of the two open morphs defined in (3.1) and (3.7) — a sequence of *two* structured phonological units. There is an obvious way of obtaining either *cleanest* from *clean est* or else *clean est* from *cleanest* that, if generalized, specifies the interrelation of morphological units and structured phonological ones.

3.3 Categories

In phonology, there is only one type of category. In morphology there are two types: *type 1* or *unit categories* (as in phonology) and *type 2* or *lexeme categories*.

   Unit categories are sets of morphological units. These are the three constituent categories *Stem form* (Sf) (non-empty for any idiolect system), *Affix form* (Af), and *Stem Group* (SGr), and, possibly, subcategories of Sf. (Phenomena like thematic vowels in Latin may require a fourth constituent category unless covered by Affix form or treated as stem form alternation.) Stem form is the set of morphological units that are *stems of* 'syntactic word forms' (see below, Sec. 4.2), and Stem form is also the set of morphological units that are *forms of* 'stem paradigms'. (So far only *word stem* paradigms have been allowed in Integrational Morphology. A good case can be made for also admitting paradigms of *inflectional stems*.) Similarly, Affix form is the set of morphological units that are *forms of* 'affix paradigms'. Stem and affix paradigms are the two types of 'morphological paradigms'. Stem groups are, in particular, all forms that result from inflexion by means of affixes.

Each *morphological paradigm* is a set of pairs (a two-place relation). In each pair the first component may be an element of Stem form, and the second component a set of categories that are proper or improper subsets of Stem form. Each subset contains the first component as an element; the first component is thus 'categorized' as, say, Preterite stem (stem of a Preterite form of a verb), etc. In this case the paradigm is a *stem paradigm* (and may be either a 'word stem' paradigm or an 'inflectional stem' paradigm). Or else, the first component in each pair is an element of Affix form, and the second component is {Affix form}. In this case the paradigm is an *affix paradigm*. Such paradigms are *improper* ones: there is a type 1 category (Affix form) such that the second component of each pair in the paradigm is the unit set of this category. — The *forms of* a paradigm are the first components of its elements.

Morphological paradigms combine with concepts to form 'lexemes': a *lexeme* is a pair consisting of a morphological paradigm and a concept (possibly, the 'empty concept') that is a meaning of both the paradigm and each of its forms. The *forms* of a lexeme are the forms of its paradigm.

Depending on the nature of the paradigm, the lexeme is a *stem lexeme* or an *affix lexeme* (thus, the traditional use of "lexeme" is extended). All affix lexemes have the empty concept as their second component.

STEM (LEXEME) and AFFIX (LEXEME) are examples of lexeme categories (capitals indicate sets of paradigm/concept pairs). Traditional distinctions like prefix vs. suffix or derivational vs. inflectional affix are reconstructed by lexeme categories not unit categories.

Generally, the set of lexemes is *the morphological lexicon* of S, and the lexeme categories are obtained through a system of classifications on the morphological lexicon.

For an example of a lexeme, suppose that *cle(a)n* is the morph whose sound sequence is /klen/ (cf. *cleanly*); Unm_A (i.e., $\text{Unm}_A(-,S)$) is the set of 'unmarked stem forms of adjectives'; and Der_A the set of 'derivational stem forms of adjectives' (i.e. stem forms that are used only in derivation). We may assume that

(3.7) $clean\text{-}_1^P = \{(clean^1, \{\text{Unm}_A\}), (cle(a)n^1, \{\text{Der}_A\})\}$

is a morphological paradigm;

(3.8) $clean\text{-}_1 = (clean\text{-}_1^P, \cdot clean\cdot)$

is a stem lexeme ($\cdot clean\cdot$ is the concept of being clean); and

(3.9) $clean\text{-}_1 \in \text{POS-ST}$,

where POS-ST is the set of stem lexemes of positive adjectives.

3.4 Structures

Diagram (3.10) (next page), to be explained immediately, exemplifies both morphological structures and morphological functions.

First, **k** is a morphological constituent structure of **f**:

(3.11) a. $\mathfrak{f} = clean\ est = \{(1, clean), (2, est)\}$.
       b. $\mathbf{k} = \{(\{1\}, \text{Sf}(-,S)), (\{2\}, \text{Af}(-,S)), (\{1,2\}, \text{Sf}(-,S))\}$.

Constituent structures of morphological units are analogous to constituent structures of phonological ones: they are relations between sets of integers and morphological (instead of phonological) constituent categories. The constituents of $\mathfrak{f}$ in **k** are not given in (3.10); obviously, there are just three, $clean_1$, est_2, and $\mathfrak{f}$ itself.

Morphological units and their constituents also have *marking structures*. (Lack of marking structures in phonology is due to absence of paradigms; in the sound system, the role of paradigms is, in a sense,

(3.10)

$$k = \begin{cases} \quad\quad\quad \text{m-nuc}^1 \\ \quad\quad\quad\quad\quad\quad\quad \text{Sf} \\ \quad\quad\quad\quad\quad \text{m-qual} \\ \text{Sf} \quad\quad\quad\quad\quad\quad \text{Af} \end{cases}$$

$$f = \begin{cases} 1 & 2 \\ \textit{clean} & \textit{est} \end{cases}$$

$$e = \begin{cases} \cdot\text{clean}\cdot & b^0 \\ 1 & 2 \end{cases}$$

$$m = \begin{cases} \{\text{Unm}_A\}\ \{\text{POS-ST},...\} & \{\text{Af}\}\ \{\text{POS/SUP},...\} \\ \{\text{Non-Der}_A\}\ \{\text{SUP-ST},...\} \\ 1 & 2 \end{cases}$$

$$l = \begin{cases} \{^-\}^1 & \{\_\}^1 \end{cases}$$

taken over by the feature composition of base forms, in particular, sounds.) For example:

(3.12) a. m = {({1}, {Unm$_A$(–,S)}, {POS-ST(–,S), ...}),
({2}, {Af(–,S)}, {POS/SUP(–,S), ...}),
({1,2}, {Non-Der$_A$(–,S)}, {SUP-ST(–,S), ...})},
where

b. Non-Der$_A$(–,S) = the set of non-derivational stems of adjective forms of S,

c. POS/SUP(–,S) = the set of affixes of S that 'derive superlatives from positives',

d. SUP-ST(–,S) = the set of stem lexemes of superlatives.

m is a marking structure of f relative to k, and the unit sets of the first two triples are, respectively, marking structures of the constituents $clean_1$ and est_2 relative to f and k.

Generally, a marking structure of a morphological unit relates all appropriate constituents of the unit to forms of lexemes, their categorizations, and to categories to which the lexemes belong. Thus, constituent $clean_1$ of unit f is related (i) to $clean_1$, a form of the lexeme $clean-_1$, see (3.8) (actually, $clean_1$ = {(1, $clean$)} = $clean^1$; as a rule, constituent and form are different); (ii) to {Unm$_A$} as a categorization of $clean^1$; and (iii) to the set {POS-ST, ...} of categories to which the lexeme $clean-_1$ belongs. It is not the constituents themselves (e.g., $clean_1$) that figure in the marking structures but only their domains, i.e. certain sets of integers (e.g., {1}).

Formally, a marking structure is a set of triples that each consist of a set of integers, a set of unit categories, and a set of lexeme categories, cf. m in (3.12).

Suprasegmental or *intonation structures* of morphological units are construed as in

(3.13) l = {(1, {$^-$S}^{1}), (2, {_S}^{1})}, where {$^-$S}^{1} = {(1, {$^-$S})}
= the unit sequence of {$^-$S}.

l is an intonation structure of *clean est*. l is simply the *sequence* of the phonological intonation structures of the two morphs. More generally morph intonation structures may also be *modified*, in various ways, before entering an intonation structure of a morphological unit. If a *morph* intonation structure is empty, it may still be a member of an intonation structure of a morphological *unit* (which, therefore, has a non-empty intonation structure).

Finally, complete *morphological structures* of morphological units are triples consisting of a constituent structure, marking structure, and intonation structure; thus,

(3.14) **s** = (k,m,l) is a morphological structure of *clean est* in **S**.

As in phonology, the set of unit/structure pairs or structured units — *the morphological structure assignment* — forms a component of the morphological part, in any idiolect system.

3.5 Functions

As explained in Sec. 2.3, phonological functions like p-nuc and p-m take pairs of a structured phonological unit (e.g., a phonological word) and an idiolect system as arguments (equivalently, take triples consisting of a sound sequence, a phonological structure, and an idiolect system) and assign to each pair a set of pairs of constituents of the unit, i.e. a relation between constituents; the relation holds between the constituents *given the structured unit and the idiolect system.*

Morphological functions like one-place *morphological nucleus* (m-nuc^1) are analogous to phonological functions, with two qualifications. First, morphological structures are richer, also containing a marking structure. Second, there are reasons to take into consideration not only structures but also lexical meanings in determining the values of morphological functions like m-nuc^1. This is achieved by including 'morphosemantic interpretations' — meaning assignments — in the arguments of a morphological function, for example, **e** in (3.10), i.e.

(3.15) **e** = {($clean_1$, ·clean·), (est_2, b^0)}. (b^0 = the empty concept)

As demonstrated by **e**, a *morphosemantic interpretation* of a morphological unit relative to a structure and an idiolect system is a function that assigns to each primitive constituent of the unit a concept that is the meaning of an appropriate lexeme; in (3.10), the lexemes are the stem lexeme *clean*–$_1$ and the affix (lexeme) -*est* = (-est^P, b^0), where -est^P = {(est^1, {Af})}.

The 'm-nuc¹ arrow' in (3.10) indicates the value of m-nuc¹ for f and s (f = *clean est*, s = (k,m,l)):

(3.16) $\text{m-nuc}^1(\text{f,s,e,S}) = \{(clean_1, \text{f})\}$.

I.e. the relation of one-place morphological nucleus on f given s, e, and S = $\{(clean_1, \text{f})\}$ ($clean_1$, and only $clean_1$, is a nucleus of anything relative to f, s, e, and S.) "One-place" and the index "1" refer to the number of constituents that may be nuclei of a given constituent; in (3.16), f is the only constituent of f to have a nucleus, and f has just one nucleus. However, a number of simultaneous nuclei has to be admitted for 'copulative compounds' (e.g., the German colours are *schwarz-rot-gold*, "black-red-gold"). More generally we must therefore allow functions m-nuc^n, for n > 0, whose values are sets of (n+1)-tuples such that in each tuple, the first n components are simultaneous nuclei (and form a nuclei n-tuple, for n > 1) of the last component.

There is a second function whose value for f and s is indicated in (3.10): morphological qualification (m-qual). The values of m-qual are sets of triples:

(3.17) $\text{m-qual}(\text{f,s,e,S}) = \{(est_2, clean_1, clean_1)\}$.

I.e. the relation of morphological qualification on f given s, e, and S = $\{(est_2, clean_1, clean_1)\}$ — est_2, $clean_1$, and $clean_1$ are the only constituents of f such that the first 'qualifies' the second with respect to the third.

m-qual is a *scope function* similar to negation in syntax, or to syntactic qualification (see Sec. 4.4, below). $clean_1$ is both the *domain* and the *scope* of the qualifier est_2. Domain and scope need not coincide, e.g. in *letter writ ing*, we would have *letter writ* as the domain of ing_3 and $writ_2$ as its scope. All sorts of suffixation, including *inflexion* ((3.10) does not represent inflection but derivation) is dealt with by means of the scope function m-qual. Such a treatment can be shown to be vastly superior to current analyses in terms of the function of nucleus ('head'), also adhered to in Lieb (1983).

In addition, the functions of *morphological complement* (m-comp¹; possibly, m-comp^n for n > 1) and *morphological modifier* (m-mod) must be allowed, too: *letter* is a complement of $writ_2$ in *letter writ ing*, and *dis* a modifier of $continue_2$ in *dis continue*).

Finally, there is *morphological accent* (m-acc), again construed as a function but of a somewhat different type (for details, see Lieb 1983: Sec. 12.5). Morphological accent does not, however, correspond to word accent in a traditional sense, which is reconstructed by accent in phonology (p-acc, see above, (2.8)).

The morphological subsystem is similar to the syntactic, as appears from the following sketch of Integrational Syntax. (Historically, it was syntax not morphology that was developed first in IL.)

4 Syntax

4.1 Introduction

Integrational Syntax is a surface syntax. This means, very roughly, that it constructs all complex syntactic entities from base forms that are phonological in nature and from lexical meanings, establishing a relationship between syntactic and phonological sentence forms by which order in the latter is retained in the former. (A *syntactic sentence form* represents a phonological one, which in turn represents the first component — the form component — of a phonetic sentence.) The requirement of surface syntax implies, in particular, that there are no 'empty' units or categories (though the empty set is allowed a role in connection with syntactic functions), and no 'deep structures' of any kind.

Integrational Syntax is also a *syntax as a basis for semantics*. This means, very roughly, that the meanings of complex syntactic units are obtained on the basis of their structures from the meanings of their parts, starting from an assignment of lexical meanings to a given unit. While the principle of meaning composition is widely accepted in present-day syntax and semantics, both the IL conception of non-lexical meanings and the actual form of the composition principle are quite unorthodox. (Integrational Morphology also represents a 'surface morphology as a basis for semantics', a point that was not emphasized in Sec. 3.)

From a formal point of view, even more so than from a semantic one, the morphological and syntactic parts of an idiolect system are generally analogous. In the syntactic part, too, there are base forms;

units; paradigms; lexical words that correspond to lexemes; type 1 and type 2 categories; structures that each consist of a constituent structure, marking structure, and intonation structure; and functions. Moreover, analogous entities in the morphological and syntactic parts are of exactly the same formal type. Formal explanations given for morphology need therefore not be repeated in our syntactic sketch.

Syntactic entities may, however, be more varied and complex than analogous morphological ones; also, there are certain subtypes of syntactic entities, such as types of syntactic functions, that have no morphological counterpart. Even where counterparts do exist, there may be important differences of detail. I doubt that any attempt to construe morphology simply as a 'syntax of words' has a chance to succeed. (The following outline of syntax is based on Lieb 1983: Part B, and the modifications made in Lieb forthc. a; it presupposes the view of paradigms in Lieb forthc. c.)

4.2 Base forms, units, and categories

The *syntactic base forms* are exactly the phonological words, such as *cleanest* in Sec. 2.3, allowing for non-syllabic ones; for example, *it's* would be a sequence of two phonological words, with non-syllabic *s*. (If a single phonological word is assumed in such cases, syntactic base forms and phonological words do *not* coincide).

Pure syntactic units are, once again, non-empty sequences of syntactic base forms (*mixed* syntactic units include morphs among their members, as in German *ver und zerstören*, equivalent to *verstören und zerstören*, "derange and destroy"). For instance, the following are syntactic units:

(4.1)   a. *cleanest^1* = {(1, *cleanest*)}
          b. *the cleanest = the$_1$ cleanest$_2$* = {(1, *the*), (2, *cleanest*)}
          c. *the former manager had foreseen that the company will not prevail*

Just as in the morphological case, *syntactic type 1 categories*, or *unit categories*, are non-empty sets of syntactic units. There are major and minor unit categories. *Major unit categories* are the *constituent categories*, which in turn are either *basic* or *derived*. Basic constituent categories in English idiolect systems are just the three sets of *noun forms* (sets of forms of words that are nouns in the broad sense, including not only substantives), *verb forms,* and *particle forms*; derived constituent categories are *noun group* (traditionally, noun phrase), *verb group*, and *particle group*. Traditional 'sentences' (syntactic sentence forms) are distributed over the categories of verb group and particle group (e.g., two 'sentences' conjoined by *but* are a particle group whose nucleus or head is the *but* occurrence).

There are no further subclassifications on derived constituent categories but there may be such classifications on basic ones, resulting in *minor unit categories*; in English, these are ultimately categories like the tenses, verb genders, or noun numbers. For example, if S is an English idiolect system, Pres(–,S), or Pres for short, is the set of present tense forms of verbs of S.

Syntactic paradigms are relations between syntactic units and sets of minor unit categories. Since the minor categories are sets of forms of lexical words (e.g., nouns, verbs, particles), it follows that all syntactic paradigms are *word paradigms*. Each syntactic paradigm is a set of pairs such that the first component of each pair is a syntactic unit (a sequence of base forms whose length may be greater than 1 — cf. *is running*) and the second component is a set of minor unit categories (\{3P, Sg, Pres, Ind, Progressive, Non-Negative, Act\}). The syntactic unit that is the first component is an element of each of these categories; the set of categories is a *categorization* of the unit. All first components of pairs in a paradigm share a lexical meaning (possibly, the empty concept); this, then, is a meaning of the paradigm. For example, a good case could be made for the following set as a noun paradigm of S:

(4.2) $company^P =$
$\{(company^1, \{Sg, Unm_d\}),$
$(the\ company, \{Sg, Def\}),$
$(a\ company, \{Sg, Indef\}),$
$(companies^1, \{Pl, Indef\}),$
$(the\ companies, \{Pl, Def\})\}$

where $Unm_d = Unm_d(-,S) =$ the set of syntactic units of S that are 'unmarked for definiteness', etc.

Once again, the *forms* of a paradigm are the first components of its elements; there are *proper* paradigms ($company^P$) and *improper* ones (in English idiolect systems, all particle paradigms). There may also be *idiom paradigms*, i.e. paradigms that have only forms whose length is greater than one (such paradigms may also occur in the morphological part of an idiolect system).

Lexical words correspond to lexemes; they are pairs of a syntactic paradigm and one of its meanings, e.g.

(4.3) $company_1^W = (company^P, \cdot company_1 \cdot)$,

where $\cdot company_1 \cdot$ is the concept of, roughly, 'a body of persons combined for a common commercial object'. The *forms* of a lexical word are the forms of its paradigm.

The set of lexical words is *the word lexicon* of an idiolect system. *Syntactic type 2 categories* or *word categories* are sets of lexical words that result from classifications on (subsets of) the word lexicon. Again, there are *major word categories*. These include at least the *major word classes* (traditional 'parts of speech'). *Minor word categories* are obtained through classifications on (subsets of) major ones; of special importance are *government* (or '*valence*') *categories* ($company_1^W$ is a noun that does not 'govern' anything: its forms occur without complements; $company_1^W$ is therefore a noun whose valency — not: valence — is zero).

4.3 Structures

Syntactic structures are, once again, triples consisting of a constituent structure, marking structure, and intonation structure. Diagram (4.4) (next page) incompletely specifies (i) a syntactic structure (k,m,l) for unit f = (4.1c), and (ii) the values of syntactic functions for the 'syntactic quadruple' (f,s,e,S) (e a lexical interpretation; symbols "k" etc., but not "S", are redefined from (3.10)).

The diagram is to be interpreted on the pattern of (3.10). Categories are denoted in the usual way: Nf = Nf(−,S) = the set of forms of nouns of S. New symbols are to be understood as follows:

(4.5) a. [*Constituent categories*]
    Vf: verb form
    Nf: noun form
    Pf: particle form

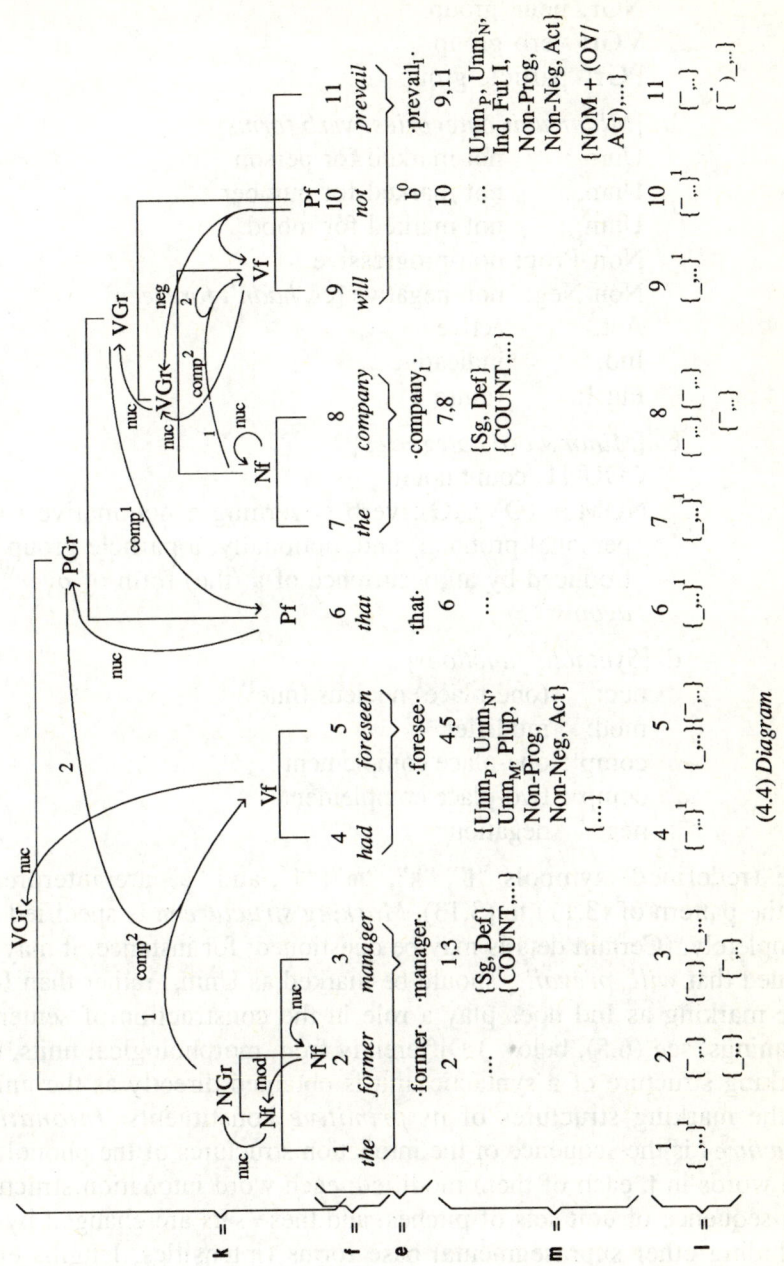

(4.4) *Diagram*

NGr: noun group
VGr: verb group
PGr: particle group

b. [*Minor unit categories: verb forms*]
Unm_P: not marked for person
Unm_N: not marked for number
Unm_M: not marked for mood
Non-Prog: non-progressive
Non-Neg: non-negative [cf. *hadn'̃t foreseen*]
Act: active
Ind: indicative
Fut I: future I

c. [*Minor word categories*]
COUNT: count noun
NOM + (OV/AG): verb governing a nominative (of a personal pronoun) and, optionally, a particle group introduced by an occurrence of a (the) form of *over*^{W} or *against*^{W}.

d. [*Syntactic functions*]
nuc: (one-place) nucleus (nuc^1)
mod: modifier
$comp^1$: one-place complement
$comp^2$: two-place complement
neg: negation

The (redefined) symbols "f", "k", "m", "l", and "e" are interpreted on the pattern of (3.11) to (3.13). *Marking structure* m is specified incompletely. (Certain details may be questioned; for instance, it may be argued that $will_9\ prevail_{11}$ should be marked as Unm_M rather than Ind. The marking as Ind does play a role in the construction of sentence meanings, see (6.5), below.) Differently from morphological units, the marking structure of a syntactic unit is obtained directly as the union of the marking structures of its *primitive* constituents. *Intonation structure* l is the sequence of the intonation structures of the phonological words in f, each of them modified: each word intonation structure is a sequence of unit sets of pitches, and these sets are changed by (i) including other suprasegmental base forms (intensities, lengths etc.)

and possibly (ii) choosing a different pitch. (Note that the 'pitch contour' of l is quite stylized, allowing for two levels only.) e is a *lexical* not a morphosemantic *interpretation* of f.

In analogy to (3.14),

(4.6)   s = (k,m,l) is a syntactic structure of f in (4.1c).

In any idiolect system, the set of unit/structure pairs, or *syntactic structure assignment*, forms a component of the syntactic part of the system. For each syntactic sentence form there is an indefinite number of syntactic structures which differ only in their intonation structure components. (Syntactic structures are also determined for concatenations of syntactic units that are not syntactic units themselves.)

4.4 Functions

The functions whose values are indicated in (4.4) are of the same formal type as morphological functions: they are *component functions*, i.e. functions whose arguments are *syntactic quadruples* of a syntactic unit (or concatenation of units), syntactic structure, lexical interpretation, and idiolect system and whose values are n-place relations between parts of the unit, as a rule, constituents. The following values of syntactic functions are identified by arrows in diagram (4.4):

(4.7) a. $\text{nuc}(f,s,e,S)$ = {$(former_2, former_2)$,
$(the_7\ company_8, the_7\ company_8)$,
$(the_1\ manager_3, the\ former\ manager)$,
$(will_9\ prevail_{11}, the_7\ company_8\ will_9\ prevail_{11})$,
$(the_7\ company_8\ will_9\ prevail_{11}, the_7 \ldots not_{10}\ prevail_{11})$,
$(that_6, that_6 \ldots prevail_{11})$,
$(had_4\ foreseen_5, f)$}

b. $\text{mod}(f,s,e,S)$ = {$(former_2, the_1\ manager_3)$}
c. $\text{comp}^1(f,s,e,S)$ = {$(the_7 \ldots prevail_{11}, that_6)$}
d. $\text{comp}^2(f,s,e,S)$ = {$(the\ former\ manager, that_6 \ldots prevail_{11}, had_4\ foreseen_5)$,
$(the_7\ company_8, f^0, will_9\ prevail_{11})$}

e. $neg(f,s,e,S)$ = $\{(not_{10}, the_7\ company_8\ will_9\ prevail_{11}, will_9\ prevail_{11})\}$

This is not the place to justify the details of (4.7) from the point of view of English. Note that $comp^1$ takes (1+1)-place relations as values, and $comp^2$ (2+1)-place relations; generally, $comp^n$ has (n+1)-place relations as its values. f^0 in (d) is the empty set. f^0 is neither a unit nor a constituent but is still allowed as a complement, to account for 'optionality of complements'. Complementation depends on government categories, as appears from the marking structure of $will_9\ prevail_{11}$.

The functions nuc, mod, and $comp^n$ on the one hand and neg on the other belong to different types of constituent functions: the former are *grammatical functions*, the latter is a *scope function*: not_{10} (the negator) negates $the_7\ company_8\ will_9\ prevail_{11}$ (the domain) with respect to $will_9\ prevail_{11}$ (the scope). Generally, IL allows for the types of syntactic functions listed in diagram (4.8).

(4.8)

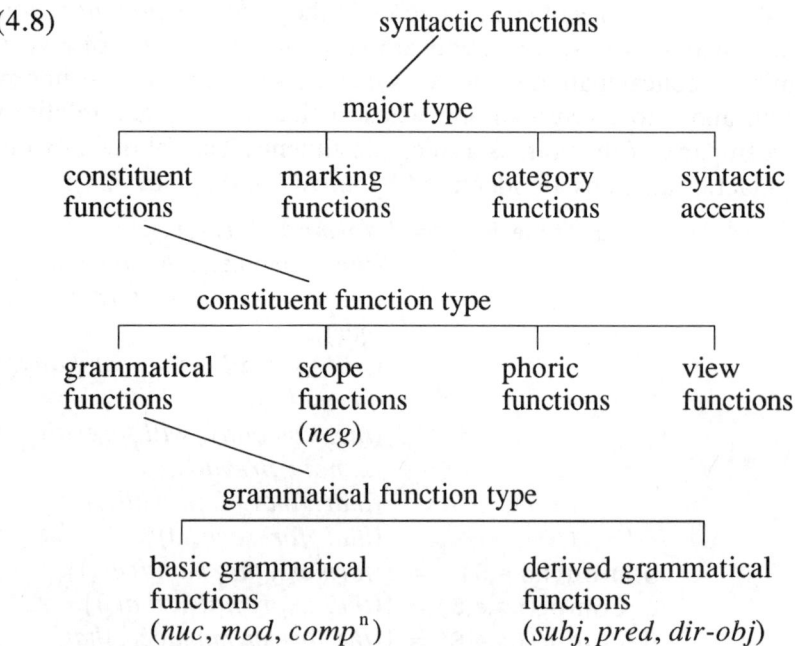

Marking functions take care of agreement phenomena (such as number agreement between subject and predicate constituents). *Cate-*

gory functions are the formal basis for a component of sentence meanings that determines the speech act type of utterances. *Syntactic accents* are functions whose arguments are triples obtained from syntactic quadruples by dropping lexical interpretations; they determine, largely on the basis of syntactic intonation structures, accented constituents, accent places, and accent domains (there is just one occurrence of a syntactic accent in (4.4); accent place is on the syllable *vail*).

Phoric (anaphoric, cataphoric) *functions* account for phenomena of 'binding' in pronoun use. *View functions* are the formal basis for semantic or 'pragmatic' topic/comment phenomena in languages where these are directly represented in syntactic structure.

Derived grammatical functions are the traditional 'grammatical relations' insofar as these can be defined, in one way or another, through the basic grammatical functions. Differently from what is usually assumed, it is the basic not the derived functions that figure in the composition process by which sentence meanings are constructed from lexical meanings.

5 Lexical semantics (morphosemantics)

5.1 Introduction

There are at least two fundamental questions that must be answered in any general semantic theory: (i) Meanings — what are they? (ii) How are 'complex' meanings of linguistic entities obtained from 'simpler' ones, in particular, how are meanings of complex linguistic entities obtained from meanings of their parts? Question (i) — asking for the type or types of entities that meanings belong to — formulates *the ontological problem* for meanings, and question (ii) *the composition problem*.

Integrational Semantics solves the ontological problem differently for meanings in morphology and the lexicon on the one hand, and meanings in syntax on the other. For this reason meaning composition, too, is construed differently for lexical and for syntactic meanings.

Lexical meanings, which are the only ones to figure in morphology and the lexicon, are conceived as *potential concepts* in a sense that takes up the psychological tradition in semantics and combines it with the realist. *Lexical meaning composition*, the only semantic composition process to occur in morphosemantics, is achieved by *concept functions*, i.e. functions that take potential concepts, or n-tuples of such, as arguments and assign to each argument a potential concept; assignment depends on the 'intension' of the original concept or concepts. Concept functions are associated with morphological functions and operate on the basis of *application conditions* that may be either morphological or semantic in nature. (The following sketch is based on Lieb 1983: Part D; see also Lieb 1980b, 1985a, 1992a for further elaboration and comments, and the relevant parts of Richter 1988.)

5.2 Basic idea for lexical meanings

Any lexical meaning is a potential concept in a psychological sense (the converse does not hold).

We start from *perceptions* (certain mental events) and *conceptions* (mental states) of individual persons. Both a perception and a conception have a *content*. In the case of a *perception*, this is a non-empty set of *attributes* of perceivable entities, which may be individual real-world entities or n-tuples of such. In the first case, the attribute is *one-place*, hence, a *property*; in the second case, the attribute is an *n-place intensional relation* (n > 1). The content of a perception is the set of attributes such that the perception is the assumption that there is some perceivable entity that has all the attributes. Very roughly, if something is being perceived, then the content of the perception is the set of attributes that are attributed to whatever is perceived.

In the case of a *conception*, the content again is a non-empty set of n-place (n > 0) attributes of real-world entities. The entities need not be perceivable, though, and may be more abstract than perceivable entities (e.g., may be properties of properties of perceivable entities).

In speaking of 'real-world entities', we mean 'real-world from the point of view of the person who has the perception'; there is no independent ontological commitment by the theorist to the 'reality' of such entities, hence, of their attributes. We are, however, committed to people and their mental states and events as construed from the theorist's point of view. Thus, there are two types of entities: the ones that must be assumed 'from people's point of view' and the ones to be assumed 'from the theorist's point of view'; mental states and events must be allowed in either category.

Naturally, entities from the theorist's point of view may also have properties. In particular, different perceptions or conceptions, which are entities from the theorist's point of view, may have shared properties, and such properties may be *content*-related: more specifically, there may be a set M^n ($n > 0$) of n-place attributes (of entities from *people's* point of view) such that the content of each of the perceptions or conceptions contains M^n as a subset. In this case, the different perceptions or conceptions all share the following property (of entities from the *theorist's* point of view): *the property of being a perception or conception whose content* (a set of attributes of entities from people's point of view) *contains M^n as a subset*. This property then is a *potential concept*.

5.3 Meanings as concepts

To begin with, let *the empty concept* (b^0) be the property of being a perception or conception whose content is empty. (There is no such perception or conception, which makes b^0 analogous to the empty set in set theory.) Let "V_1" stand for any object in space-time and "z" for any mental state or event (from the theorist's point of view); "b", "b_1", ... for any property of entities z; "x", "x_1", ... for any (individual) real-world entity (from people's point of view); and "M^n" for any set of n-place attributes either of entities x (if $n = 1$) or n-tuples (x_1, ..., x_n) (if $n > 1$).

(5.1) *Definition*. b is a *potential concept* if and only if (a) or (b):
a. $b = b^0$.
b. There is exactly one n ($n > 0$) and non-empty M^n such that b = the property of being a perception or conception z of some V_1 such that $M^n \subseteq$ the content of z.

b is a *concept of* V_1 if b is a potential concept that V_1 actually 'has'.

The following notions are easily defined for potential concepts. Potential concept b is *n-place* if either $b = b^0$ and $n = 0$, or $b \neq b^0$ and n = the number determined by (5.1b). For any n-place potential concept b, $n \neq 0$: *the (n-place) intension of* b (^{ni}b) = the M^n determined by (5.1b); *the (n-place) extension of* b (^{ne}b) = the set of entities that each have every attribute in ^{ni}b (i.e., a set of entities x, for n =1; of n-tuples $(x_1, .., x_n)$, for n > 1).

Define, for example,

(5.2) $\cdot prevail_1 \cdot =_{df}$ the property of being a perception or conception z of some V_1 such that $\{PREVAIL_1\} \subseteq$ the content of z, where

$PREVAIL_1 =_{df}$ the attribute of being a triple (x_1, x_2, x_3) s. t.
a. x_1 is a process of 'prevailing over something or somebody',
b. x_2 is an agent of x_1,
c. x_3 is an affected object of x_1.

The formulation in (a) in inverted commas abbreviates a more detailed characterization. $\cdot prevail_1 \cdot$ can of course be a property only of conceptions not of perceptions. $PREVAIL_1$ is a three-place intensional relation.

It follows from (5.2) and previous definitions that (i) $\cdot prevail_1 \cdot$ is a potential concept; (ii) $\cdot prevail_1 \cdot$ is three-place; (iii) $^{3i}\cdot prevail_1 \cdot = \{PREVAIL_1\}$; (iv) $^{3e}\cdot prevail_1 \cdot =$ the set of all (x_1, x_2, x_3) such that (x_1, x_2, x_3) has $PREVAIL_1$, i.e. such that x_1, x_2, and x_3 are related by $PREVAIL_1$.

(5.2) is a definition; it makes no claim on anything, certainly not on anything linguistic: $\cdot prevail_1 \cdot$, a property of conceptions, is no linguistic entity. It is only the following assumption, which relates $\cdot prevail_1 \cdot$ to lexical entities of English idiolect systems, that makes an empirical claim:

(5.3) For any Modern English idiolect system S, $\cdot prevail_1 \cdot$ is a meaning of *prevail–* in S.

(*prevail–* is a stem lexeme.) Assumption (5.3) may be wrong on factual grounds, which makes the assumption empirical.

We may certainly assume that there are Modern English idiolect systems. Hence, (5.3) yields as a corollary that $\cdot prevail_1 \cdot$ is a *concept* not just a potential concept: each speaker of S (there are such speakers) must 'have' $\cdot prevail_1 \cdot$.

It is postulated quite generally in Integrational Semantics that the meanings of any meaningful morphological or lexical item in an idiolect system are potential concepts (possibly empty) in the sense of (5.1).

5.4 Lexical meaning composition

Consider the structured morphological unit given by diagram (5.4) (symbols "f" etc., but not "S", are redefined from both (3.10) and (4.4)).

(5.4)

$$k = \begin{cases} \text{m-nuc}^1 \\ \quad\quad\quad \text{Sf} \\ \quad\quad \text{m-qual} \end{cases}$$

$$f = \begin{cases} \begin{array}{ll} \text{Sf} & \text{Af} \\ 1 & 2 \\ \textit{prevail} & \textit{ing} \end{array} \end{cases}$$

$$e = \begin{cases} \cdot\textit{prevail}_1\cdot \quad\quad\quad b^0 \end{cases}$$

$$m = \begin{cases} \begin{array}{ll} 1 & 2 \\ \{\text{Unm}_V\}\;\{\text{VST}_i,...\} & \{\text{Af}\}\;\{\text{VST}/\text{SST}_j,...\} \\ & 1, 2 \\ \{\text{Unm}_{SSt}\}\;\{\text{SST}_j,...\} \end{array} \end{cases}$$

$$l = \begin{cases} \begin{array}{ll} 1 & 2 \\ \{\_\}\{\bar{}\} & \{\_\}^1 \end{array} \end{cases}$$

Unm_V [= $\text{Unm}_V(-,S)$] = the set of unmarked word stems of forms of verbs; VST_i: a certain (i-th) class of verb stem lexemes; SST_j: a certain (j-th) class of substantive stem lexemes; VST/SST_j = the set of affixes (affix lexemes) that 'derive elements of SST_j from elements of VST, the set of verb stem lexemes'; Unm_{SSt} = the set of unmarked word stems of forms of substantives.

f = *prevail ing* is a (the) word stem of forms of the lexical word *prevailing*$_1^W$ (as in *the prevailing of john over jim*). The meaning of the word stem *prevail ing* (hence, of the word *prevailing*$_1^W$) is obtained from b^0 and ·prevail$_1$· by means of a *concept function*, to be called "ing$_1^{0;3}$" and defined as a special case of the following definition schema:

(5.5) *Definition*. Let $b_1 = b^0$ and b_2 an n-place 'verbal' potential concept.

ing$_1^{0;n}(b_1, b_2)$ =$_{df}$ the property of being a perception or conception z of some V_1 such that $\{\text{ING}_1^n(b_2)\} \subseteq$ the content of z, where

$\text{ING}_1^n(b_2)$ =$_{df}$ the property of being an x_1 such that for some $x_2, ..., x_n$, $(x_1, ..., x_n) \in {}^{ne}b_2$.

A potential concept b is *verbal* if, roughly, it qualifies as a meaning of verb paradigms in *some* idiolect system. It is a defensible assumption that all verbal potential concepts are at least two-place (·prevail$_1$· is three-place).

The name of concept function ing$_1^{0;n}$ ("ing-1-0-n") is motivated as follows. "ing" recalls the affix with which the function typically associates in English. "0;n" indicates that the function's arguments are pairs of a zero-place and an n-place (n > 1) potential concept. The subscript "1" allows for other *-ing*-associated functions. Intuitively, function ing$_1^{0;n}$ assigns to a given argument (b_1, b_2) the potential concept 'of being the first component (the process etc.) in an n-tuple that is an element of the extension of b_2'; thus, the empty concept b_1 is, as a matter of fact, disregarded.

Strictly speaking, ing$_1^{0;n}$ is to be associated not with affix *-ing* itself but with the morphological function m-qual (morphological qualification). We proceed as follows.

Consider *the restriction of m-qual to* **S**, or m-qual[**S**], i.e. that subfunction of m-qual whose arguments — syntactic quadruples — have **S** as their last component. We form all triples (m-qual[**S**], ing$_1^{0;n}$, c_n), for n > 1 (and possibly smaller than some fixed number), where c_n is an *application condition* for concept function ing$_1^{0;n}$. The idea is that

$ing_1^{0;n}$ *may be applied whenever there is an 'occurrence' of m-qual*[S] *and* c_n *is satisfied.*

For example

(5.6) $(ing_2, prevail_1, prevail_1) \in$ m-qual(f,s,e,S),

i.e. $(ing_2, prevail_1, prevail_1)$ is an occurrence of m-qual[S]. For m-qual as a scope function see Sec. 3.5: $prevail_1$ is both the 'domain' and the 'scope' of ing_2.

Condition c_3 *for* $ing_1^{0;3}$ *is satisfied*: roughly, ing_2 is an occurrence of a form of affix -*ing*; b^0 is a 'constituent meaning' of ing_2 relative to f, s, e, and S, and ·$prevail_1$· is a meaning of $prevail_1$, the domain of ing_2; both constituent meanings are, as a matter of fact, supplied by the morphosemantic interpretation e. Finally, ·$prevail_1$· is a three-place verbal concept; b^0 and ·$prevail_1$· are therefore as required by the definition schema (5.5) for the function $ing_1^{0;3}$.

We may therefore *apply* $ing_1^{0;3}$ to $(b^0, ·prevail_1·)$ to obtain a meaning of *prevail ing*, i.e. we formulate the following empirical assumption:

(5.7) $ing_1^{0;3}(b^0, ·prevail_1·)$ is a morphological constituent meaning of $ing_2 \cup prevail_1$ (= *prevail ing*) relative to f, s, e, and S,

where

(5.8) $ing_1^{0;3}(b^0, ·prevail_1·)$ = the property of being a perception or conception z of some V_1 such that $\{ING_1^3(·prevail_1·)\} \subseteq$ the content of z, where

$ING_1^3(·prevail_1·)$ = the property of being an x_1 such that for some x_2 and x_3, $(x_1, x_2, x_3) \in {}^{3e}·prevail_1·$.

Defining

(5.9) ·the prevailing· $=_{df} ing_1^{0;3}(b^0, ·prevail_1·)$,

we obtain from (5.7) that

(5.10) ·the prevailing· is a morphological constituent meaning of *prevail ing* relative to f, s, e, and S.

This, of course, does not add anything to (5.7).

The example is meant to clarify *the essential idea for lexical meaning composition* in morphosemantics: for a given idiolect system S we take the restrictions to S of appropriate morphological functions and associate with each restriction pairs consisting of a concept function (or a set of such functions) and an application condition for the concept function; we thus obtain a set of triples each consisting of a function restriction, concept function, and application condition. This set is — disregarding some complications — *the morphological function interpretation of* S. Given an 'occurrence' of the restriction of the morphological function such that the application condition for the concept function is satisfied, a meaning of the *union* of relevant constituents is obtained by applying the concept function to meanings of the *constituents*.

6 Syntactic semantics (sentential semantics)

6.1 Introduction

Syntactic meanings — i.e. meanings of syntactic units, or of concatenations of units, or of constituents of units or concatenations — are conceived so that sentence meanings, the most important type of syntactic meanings, satisfy the following requirement: for any syntactic unit or concatenation that has a sentence meaning, the meanings of the unit or concatenation jointly represent a necessary condition for successful utterances of the unit or concatenation, a condition based on speaker intention and speaker belief. *Ontologically*, a sentence meaning is an (intensional) relation between potential utterances and potential speakers. Meanings of *constituents* may be of the same type as sentence meanings, or they may consist of a potential concept and an utterance-related component.

This conception of syntactic meanings combines the meaning-as-use tradition in semantics with elements from the psychological and realist traditions. The conception, which would be a 'pragmatic conception of meanings' on some accounts of 'pragmatics', is a major reason why no pragmatic subsystems of idiolect systems are assumed in IL: what would be pragmatic in some frameworks is covered already by semantics.

Just as lexical meaning composition, *syntactic meaning composition* is achieved by functions that map meanings into meanings but are, of course, rather different from concept functions (these do play a limited role in sentential semantics, too). Similarly to morphosemantics, semantic composition functions may be associated with syntactic functions of most types, see (4.8). Differently from morphosemantics, semantic composition functions may also be directly associated with syntactic categories, i.e. unit categories like tenses, verb genders, or noun categories of definiteness. Composition functions once again operate on the basis of application conditions, which may be either syntactic or semantic in nature.

It appears, then, that Integrational Semantics in its entirety draws on nearly all major traditions in semantics; it may be the first approach to apply meaning composition, a hallmark of the realist approach, to meanings conceived in the psychological and meaning-as-use traditions. (The following sections are based on Lieb 1983: Parts E and F; see also Lieb 1992a,b and Richter 1988 for further developments.)

6.2 Syntactic meanings

The paramount case of syntactic meanings are sentence meanings. Disregarding potential differences between spoken and written idiolects, sentence meanings may be construed as relations-in-intension u between sound events and persons such that for a relevant syntactic unit (or concatenation of units: this should be added here and elsewhere) one of these relations must hold between speech event V and speaker V_1 in any successful utterance of the unit: the speaker must have certain intentions concerning any hearer, must refer to certain entities (direct the hearer's attention to them), must have certain beliefs etc.

Each 'simple' sentence meaning u has at least the following *components*, from which the meaning is obtained by formal operations.

(6.1) a. *The referential part of* u: a set (possibly empty) of relations-in-intension u_1 that, in an appropriate syntactic unit, are meanings of referential expressions of the unit (the set must contain exactly one meaning per referential expression).

b. *The propositional part of* u: a pair consisting of a hearer-oriented propositional attitude assignable to speakers — *the directive part of* u — and its content, a relation u_1 that represents a state of affairs and is *the proposition of* u.
c. *The propositional background of* u, a set of attitude/content pairs where the attitudes are doxastic attitudes assignable to speakers.

The referential part represents conditions on what a speaker may refer to in an utterance of a syntactic form with meaning u. The directive part roughly determines how the speaker wants his utterance to be understood, i.e. it determines the speech act type of the utterance. The proposition determines what the utterance is about, and the propositional background, what additional beliefs etc. the speaker expresses, beliefs related in some way or other to the state of affairs represented by the proposition.

Non-simple sentence meanings make allowance for, in particular, subordinate clauses of all types and for coordination.

Generally, sentence meanings are relative to syntactic quadruples (a syntactic unit or concatenation of units, syntactic structure, lexical interpretation, and idiolect system), and may have to be relativized further. Thus, understanding "f", "s", and "e" as in (4.4) and (4.6) (f = *the former manager had foreseen that the company will not prevail*), a (non-simple) sentence meaning of f would be identified by a statement of the following form:

(6.2) (u,f) ∈ sent(f,s,e,S) (u is a sentence meaning of f relative to f, s, e, and S).

Having f appear twice in (6.2) allows for cases where a proper constituent of a syntactic unit, or concatenation of units, itself has a sentence meaning.

So far, only simple sentence meanings have been studied in Integrational Semantics. In particular, the semantic aspect of most types of clauses have not yet been investigated in any detail (the semantic treatment of conditionals in Fischer 1981 uses a framework different from IS). We may have to introduce a separate concept of *clause meaning*, allowing clause meanings as an additional type of 'intermediate syntactic meanings' (such meanings are associated in IS with syntactic constituents in the process of meaning composition).

A complete specification of a sentence meaning for sentence f in (4.4) would be both cumbersome and partly ad hoc because of problems not yet solved in Integrational Semantics. For this reason I formulate only one component u_1 of a clause meaning of $the_7\ company_8\ will_9\ not_{10}\ prevail_{11}$ in f: the component that corresponds to the proposition of a simple sentence meaning that could be assigned to the unit (not: the constituent) *the company will not prevail*:

(6.3) u_1 = the relation-in-intension between any V and V_1 such that: for any x_2, if V_1 refers by $the_7\ company_8$ in V to x_2, then it is not the case that, for some x_1 and for some x_3, $(x_1, x_2, x_3) \in {}^{3u}\cdot prevail_1\cdot$ and $(x_1, x_2, x_3) \in$ the reference basis for $will_9\ prevail_{11}$, V, V_1, and $\cdot prevail_1\cdot$, and ...

where the dots indicate a part that accounts for the semantic effect of the tense category Fut I.

The *reference basis* for the four entities is the set of triples (x_1, x_2, x_3) determined roughly as follows: V_1, in producing the $will_9\ prevail_{11}$-part of utterance V, is willing either to assume that (x_1, x_2, x_3) is in the extension of $\cdot prevail_1\cdot$, or to assume that it is not. The reference basis provides, among other things, entities for reference (in particular, 'cases' x_1 of 'prevailing'); hence its name.

6.3 Syntactic meaning composition

A sentence meaning is determined in two steps: (i) the components of the meaning are established, (ii) the meaning is obtained by formal operations on the components. (i) if not (ii) also holds of clause meanings (which may, however, have fewer types of components) and will here be outlined for u_1 in (6.3). (In describing the various composition steps, we may occasionally refer to the *names* of meaning components rather than to components themselves; this is meant only as a kind of suggestive shorthand.)

Consider, once again, diagram (4.4) for the part connected with $the_7\ company_8\ will_9\ not_{10}\ prevail_{11}$. u_1 is obtained in seven steps.

As a first step in determining u_1, we form a *basic syntactic meaning* of $will_9\, prevail_{11}$ on the basis of ·$prevail_1$·, i.e. of the concept associated with $will_9\, prevail_{11}$ by the lexical interpretation **e**. The basic meaning is a pair whose second component is ·$prevail_1$· and whose first component is the set of all quintuples (x_1, y, x_3, V, V_1) such that $(x_1, y, x_3) \in$ the reference basis for $will_9\, prevail_{11}$, V, V_1, and ·$prevail_1$·. ("y" stands for entities of the same type as "x", "x_1", etc. do: real-world entities 'from people's point of view'. "y" replaces "x_2" in (6.3) for technical reasons.)

As a second step, we apply to $will_9\, prevail_{11}$ a semantic function associated with the syntactic category Fut I.

As a third step, we combine 'the referring by means of $the_7\, company_8$' with the 'conjunction' of the results of the first two steps, applying 'existential quantification' to the conjunction; i.e. we form a pair whose first component is 'the referring by means of $the_7\, company_8$' and whose second component is

(6.4) the set of all (x_1, y) such that, for some x_3, $(x_1, y, x_3) \in {}^{3u}$·$prevail_1$· and $(x_1, y, x_3) \in$ the reference basis for $will_9\, prevail_{11}$, V, V_1, and ·$prevail_1$·, and ... [beginning with "for some x_3", this is the same as the second part of (6.3), with "y" for "x_2"].

Forming this pair is licensed by the fact that $(the_7\, company_8, f^0)$ is a complement pair for $will_9\, prevail_{11}$ (see (4.7d)), and is effected by a semantic function associated with $comp^2[S]$, the restriction to **S** of the syntactic function $comp^2$; existential quantification ("for some x_3") is due to the fact that the second complement of $will_9\, prevail_{11}$ is empty (f^0). (If "x_3" is left as a free variable in (6.4) rather than bound by existential quantification, the clause meaning of $the_7 \ldots prevail_{11}$ — and eventually the sentence meaning of **f** — will be a relation not between V and V_1 but among x_3, V, and V_1. This corresponds to the case where in an utterance of **f** the 'prevailed-over' entity is considered to be retrievable from utterance context.)

As a fourth step, we apply — metalinguistically speaking — existential quantification to "x_1" in (6.4), obtaining

(6.5) the set of all y such that, for some x_1 and for some x_3, ... [as in (6.4)].

This is licensed by the fact that $will_9\,prevail_{11}$ is a nucleus of $the_7\,company_8\,will_9\,prevail_{11}$ and is marked as an indicative non-negative verb form, see (4.3); and is effected by a semantic function associated with nuc[**S**].

As a fifth step, we apply negation in (6.5), obtaining

(6.6) the set of all y such that it is not the case that, for some x_1 ... [as in (6.5)].

This is licensed by the fact that not_{10} negates $the_7\,company_8\,will_9\,prevail_{11}$ with respect to $will_9\,prevail_{11}$, which is the *scope* of not_{10}. (Note the placement of "it is not the case that" in (6.3), which leaves the antecedent of the implication — "V_1 refers by $the_7\,company_8$ in V to x_2" — outside the scope of "it is not the case that".) The step is effected by a semantic function of negation associated with neg[**S**].

As a sixth step, we form a universal implication on the basis of (6.6) and the referring by means of $the_7\,company_8$ (see above, third step):

(6.7) for any x_2, if V_1 refers by $the_7\,company_8$ in V to x_2, then $x_2 \in$ (6.6), i.e. $x_2 \in$ the set of all y such that, for some x_1 and x_3, $(x_1, y, x_3) \in {}^{3u}\cdot prevail_1\cdot$ and $(x_1, y, x_3) \in$ the reference basis for $will_9\,prevail_{11}$, V, V_1, and $\cdot prevail_1\cdot$, and ...,

which is equivalent to the relevant part of (6.3). This step is licensed by the fact that $the_7\,company_8\,will_9\,prevail_{11}$ is both the domain of not_{10} and the nucleus of $the_7\,company_8\,will_9\,not_{10}\,prevail_{11}$, and is effected by a semantic 'closure' function associated with nuc[**S**].

Finally, a formulation equivalent to the right-hand side of (6.3), the definiens for "u_1", is obtained from (6.7) by using a 'relation forming operator' (actually, the λ-operator) to bind the two remaining free variables "V" and "V_1" in (6.7).

6.4 Remarks on syntactic meaning composition

As appears from the example in Sec. 6.3, the 'semantic' functions associated with syntactic functions and categories that are responsible for syntactic meaning composition are *logical* functions except where reference by speakers is involved or time is brought in (as in 'interpreting' the syntactic category Fut I).

True, for some of these functions to work properly in meaning composition, the order of real-world entities in tuples that belong to verb meaning extensions — "$(x_1, y, x_3) \in {}^{3u} \cdot \text{prevail}_1 \cdot$" — must be fixed in one way rather than another but this does not affect the logical nature of the composition functions. Again, order of entities may be partly determined by real-world 'role-relations' like 'is an actor of', but no way must semantic composition functions be confused with such relations, or with linguistic constructs like 'semantic cases' or 'theta-roles', which do not figure in meaning composition and do not, in my opinion, serve any useful purpose at all. We do require correlation statements for predicate complements and the places in role relations that referents of the complements may occupy but such statements should be derivable from (i) syntactic statements on the complements and (ii) assumptions on the concept that is assigned to the predicate constituent as its lexical meaning.

Syntactic functions were classified into types in (4.8). In deriving u_1 as the proposition of a clause meaning, only constituent functions of two kinds had to be used: basic grammatical functions (nuc, comp^n) and scope functions (neg). It is indeed a *plausible hypothesis* that (i) derivation of proposition-type meaning components is based on basic grammatical functions, scope functions, and phoric functions (the role of syntactic accents is not entirely clear); (ii) determination of directive parts is based on category functions; (iii) propositional background is determined on the basis of syntactic accents, scope functions, and view functions; and (iv) syntactic categories may contribute to the determination of proposition-type components, directive parts, or rhematic background in (i) to (iii) either *directly* through their interpretations, or *indirectly* by entering into application conditions for semantic functions that are associated with syntactic function restrictions.

References

Titles that do not belong to Integrational Linguistics are preceded by an asterisk.

*Albrecht, Jörn (ed.). 1988. *Schriften von Eugenio Coseriu 1965-1987*. Tübingen: Narr. [= Vol. I of Albrecht, Jörn; Lüdtke, Jens; and Harald Thun (eds). 1988. *Energeia und Ergon*. Studia in honorem Eugenio Coseriu. 3. vols. Tübingen: Narr. (TBL 300)].

Budde, Monika. in prep. *Wortstellungsmuster*. Ein Beitrag zur Allgemeinen Syntax.

*Buyssens, Eric. 1943. *Les langages et le discours*. Essai de linguistique fonctionelle dans le cadre de la sémiologie. Brussels.

*Carr, Philip. 1989. "Autonomism, realism, and linguistic change". *Folia Linguistica Historica* IX/2.13-31.

*—. 1990. *Linguistic Realities*. An Autonomist Metatheory for the Generative Enterprise. Cambridge etc.: Cambridge University Press. (Cambridge Studies in Linguistics 53).

Choi, Kyu-Ryun. in press. *Das Passiv im Deutschen und Koreanischen — Syntax und Semantik*. Trier: WVT Wissenschaftlicher Verlag Trier. (Fokus).

*Chomsky, Noam 1981. *Lectures on Government and Binding*. Dordrecht: Foris.

*—. 1986. *Knowledge of Language: Its Nature, Origin, and Use*. New York etc.: Praeger. (Convergence).

*Coseriu, Eugenio. 1981/1988. "Die Begriffe 'Dialekt', 'Niveau' und 'Sprachstil' und der eigentliche Sinn der Dialektologie". In: Albrecht et al. (eds). 1988. 15-43. [Spanish, 1981].

Eisenberg, Peter. 1976. *Oberflächenstruktur und logische Struktur*. Untersuchungen zur Syntax und Semantik des deutschen Prädikatadjektivs. Tübingen: Niemeyer. (Linguistische Arbeiten 36).

—. 1985. "Graphemtheorie und phonologisches Prinzip. Vom Sinn eines autonomen Graphembegriffs". In: Georg Augst (ed.). *Graphematik und Orthographie*. Frankfurt/M.: Lang. 122-128.

—. 1988. "Über die Autonomie der graphematischen Analyse". In: Dieter Nerius and Georg Augst (eds). *Probleme der geschriebenen Sprache*. Berlin. 25-35.

—. ²1989. *Grundriß der deutschen Grammatik*. Stuttgart: Metzler. [Revised. 1st ed. 1986].

—. forthc. a. "Syllabische Struktur und Wortakzent. Prinzipien der Prosodik deutscher Wörter". *Zeitschrift für Sprachwissenschaft* 10 (1991).

—. forthc. b "Suffixreanalyse und Syllabierung. Zum Verhältnis phonologischer und morphologischer Syllabierung". In: Werner Abraham (ed.). *Proceedings of the 11th Groningen Grammar Talks, Groningen, 1990*.

Eisenberg, Peter, and Mathias Butt. 1990. "Schreibsilbe und Sprechsilbe". In: Christian Stetter (ed.). *Zu einer Theorie der Orthographie. Interdisziplinäre Aspekte gegenwärtiger Schrift- und Orthographieforschung*. Tübingen. 33-64.

Falkenberg, Thomas. in prep. *Untersuchungen zur Theorie der Integrativen Grammatiken*.

Fischer, Bernd-Jürgen. 1981. *Satzstruktur und Satzbedeutung. Plädoyer für eine semantikfundierende Oberflächengrammatik; am Beispiel der Bedingungssätze des Deutschen*. Tübingen: Narr. (Ergebnisse und Methoden moderner Sprachwissenschaft 12).

*Harris, Roy. 1981. *The language myth*. London: Duckworth.

*Heger, Klaus. 1992. "Langue und parole". In: Vilmos Ágel and Regina Hessky (eds). *Offene Fragen – offene Antworten in der Sprachgermanistik*. Tübingen: Niemeyer. (RGL 128). 1-13.

Hoepfner, Birgit. in prep. *Indirekte Sprechakte*.

*Hudson, Richard A. 1980. *Sociolinguistics*. Cambridge etc.: Cambridge University Press. (Cambridge Textbooks in Linguistics).

Kendzia, Stephan. in prep. *Untersuchungen zu den syntaktischen Akzenten im Deutschen*.

Lieb, Hans-Heinrich. 1970. *Sprachstadium und Sprachsystem. Umrisse einer Sprachtheorie*. Stuttgart etc.: Kohlhammer.

—. 1975. "Universals of language: quandaries and prospects". *Foundations of Language* 12.471-511.

—. 1978. "Morphological structure and morphological meaning". In: Wolfgang Dressler and Wolfgang Meid (eds). *Proceedings of the Twelfth International Congress of Linguists, Vienna, 1977*. Innsbruck: Universität Innsbruck. (Innsbrucker Beiträge zur Sprachwissenschaft). 204-208.

—. 1979. "Some basic concepts of Trubetzkoy's phonology". *Forum Linguisticum* IV,1.1-25.
—. 1980a. "Segment und Intonation: Zur phonologischen Basis von Syntax und Morphologie". In: Hans-Heinrich Lieb (ed.). *Oberflächensyntax und Semantik*. Tübingen: Niemeyer. (Linguistische Arbeiten 93). 134-150.
—. 1980b. "Wortbedeutung: Argumente für eine psychologische Konzeption". *Lingua* 52.151-182.
—. 1982. "Language systems and the problem of abstraction". *Zeitschrift für Sprachwissenschaft* 1.242-250.
—. 1983. *Integrational Linguistics*. Vol. 1: *General Outline*. Amsterdam: Benjamins. (CILT 17).
—. 1985a. "Conceptual meaning in natural languages". *Semiotica* 57.1-12.
—. 1985b. "Zum Begriff des Wortakzents". In: Thomas T. Ballmer and Roland Posner (eds). *Nach-Chomskysche Linguistik. Neuere Arbeiten von Berliner Linguisten*. Berlin/New York: de Gruyter. 275-283.
—. 1988. "Auditives Segmentieren: Eine sprachtheoretische Grundlegung". In: Hans-Heinrich Lieb (ed.). *BEVATON – Berliner Verfahren zur auditiven Tonhöhenanalyse*. Tübingen: Niemeyer. (Linguistische Arbeiten 205). 147-192.
—. 1989. "Integrational grammars: an integrative view of grammar writing". In: Gottfried Graustein and Gerhard Leitner (eds). *Reference grammars and modern linguistic theory*. Tübingen: Niemeyer. (Linguistische Arbeiten 226). 205-228.
—. 1992a. "Integrational Semantics: an integrative view of linguistic meaning". In: Maxim Stamenov (ed.). *Current Advances in Semantic Theory*. Amsterdam/Philadelphia: Benjamins. (CILT 73). 239-268.
—. 1992b. "Die Polyfunktionalität des deutschen Vorgangspassivs". *Zeitschrift für Phonetik, Sprachwissenschaft und Kommunikationsforschung* 45,2.178-188.
—. forthc. a. "Integrational Linguistics". In: Joachim Jacobs et al. (eds). *Syntax. Ein Handbuch internationaler Forschung*. Berlin/New York: de Gruyter. (Handbücher zur Sprach- und Kommunikationsforschung).

—. forthc b. *Linguistic variables*. Towards a unified theory of linguistic variation, with special reference to syntax.

—. forthc. c. "Paradigma und Klassifikation: Explikation des Paradigmenbegriffs". *Zeitschrift für Sprachwissenschaft* (1992).

Lutzeier, Peter Rolf. 1981. *Wort und Feld*. Wortsemantische Fragestellungen unter besonderer Berücksichtigung des Wortfeldbegriffes. Tübingen: Niemeyer. (Linguistische Arbeiten 103).

*—. 1991. *Major Pillars of German Syntax*. An Introduction to CRMS theory. Tübingen: Niemeyer. (Linguistische Arbeiten 258).

Peters, Jörg. forthc. *Was sind sprachliche Universalien?* Die Überwindung des Essentialismus in der Sprachuniversalienforschung.

—. in prep. *Artikulatorische Handlungsabsichten und die stimmliche Entwicklung des Kindes.*

Richter, Heide. 1988. *Indexikalität: Ihre Behandlung in Philosophie und Sprachwissenschaft.* Tübingen: Niemeyer. (Linguistische Arbeiten 217).

III. AREAS

A New Structuralism in Phonology

Jerzy Bańczerowski, Jerzy Pogonowski,
Tadeusz Zgółka
Adam Mickiewicz University, Poznań

0 Introductory Remarks

Our paper is divided into two distinct parts. The main goal of the first, introductory part (Secs 1 to 3) is briefly to present a general philosophical and methodological framework for characterizing the phenomenon called 'linguistic structuralism'. Our very method of presentation is 'structuralist': i.e. we aim to bring out fundamental oppositions between categories of linguistic theories such as subjectivism vs. objectivism, descriptivism vs. nomologism, etc. These categories, as here understood, are in a sense analogous to language categories determined by properties, features, or oppositions, used in structural descriptions of languages to define the so-called system of a language. In characterizing linguistic structuralism we thus use an approach that is technically close to, if not identical with, structuralism.

In the second part of our paper (Secs 4 to 6) the following thesis will be argued: the ideas of classical structural phonology, despite undergoing certain changes, have persisted during the whole postclassical period up to the present day. After some concluding remarks (Sec. 7) the Nine Principles of New Structuralism will be discussed in an Appendix.

No attempt will be made in arguing the above thesis to draw a comprehensive picture of postclassical phonology, desirable no doubt but unfeasible within the limits of this paper. Instead, we restrict ourselves to a selection of phonological theories or theory fragments.

1 Philosophical properties of linguistic theories

There are certain binary oppositions in the class of linguistic theories that are established by the theories' philosophical properties. On the basis of these oppositions, linguistic theories can be grouped together as indicated by the following diagram:

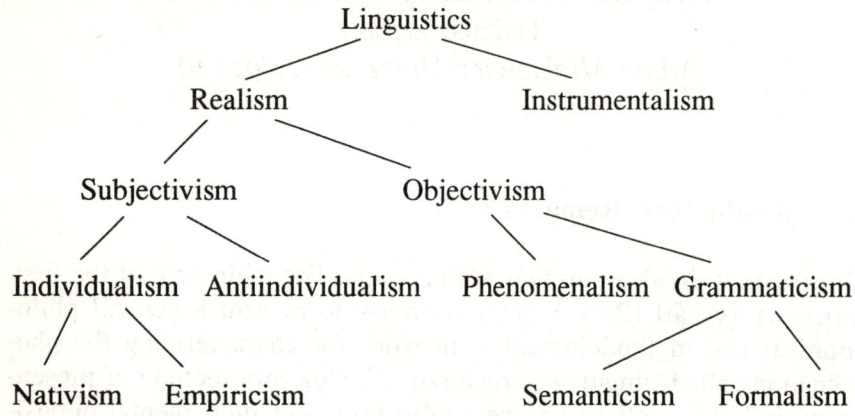

The first opposition — between realism and instrumentalism — is methodological rather than strictly philosophical. The main difference holding between realist and instrumentalist positions concerns the relation between a theory and reality (Kmita 1974). In realist approaches three levels of scientific cognition are postulated:

(i) the language of a theory (viewed as a sequence of theorems that form a subset of the set of all sentences that can be formulated in the given language),
(ii) a semantic model correlated with the language as its interpretation, and
(iii) reality itself.

The semantic model is construed as a kind of image of reality (Wójcicki 1982). The model may be tied to reality by a category such as praxis. Instrumentalist approaches are actually restricted to the first two levels: the language of the theory and its semantic interpretation (model), and reality is treated as an irrelevant category. While reality may be the most important category for philosophy, metaphysics etc., it is of course not directly accessible to the empirical sciences including linguistics.

The second opposition — between subjectivism and objectivism — appears to be restricted to the humanities, i.e. the study of human beings. Approaches of the subjective type may be understood as humanistic in a narrow sense. This means that the object of scientific inquiry in the humanities consists of specifically human phenomena such as doings or actions that require a background of consciousness, are relative, to a mind, consciousness, a soul (psyche), a brain, etc. Objectivist approaches treat phenomena that are considered as free from such relativizations (Giedymin 1964).

There are two ways to achieve subjective relativizations:

(i) by reference to an individual consciousness,
(ii) by reference to a social consciousness.

In the first case, a theory is concerned with a mind (a soul, or even a brain) considered individually. Adherents of this conception recommend using psychological terms, hypotheses, or premises throughout humanistic research, where the presupposed version of psychology may be associational, cognitive or behavioural. In the second case, subjectivism acquires an antiindividualistic status. Although it makes use of the concept of consciousness, subjectivism is understood in an extramental sense, i.e. consciousness finds its interpretation at the social level. The notion of *langue* in a Saussurean sense, i.e. as a special kind of 'social fact' (Saussure 1916), may be regarded as an example of this way of thinking.

Within the individualistic approach two different philosophical positions may be distinguished depending on where the consciousness (or 'tacit knowledge') possessed by an individual actor (human being, acting person, especially speaker-hearer) is to arise from. Traditional philosophical thinking offers two fundamentally different answers: Either the source of knowledge inheres in experience, and only there, a philosophical assumption accepted, for example, in theories based on the concept of behaviour. Or else, there are theories in the rationalist tradition, where it is claimed that all knowledge possessed and used by actors has its source in the mind. As a version of a rationalist perspective, a version of special interest, we have the nativist hypothesis.

Returning to the opposition of subjective vs. objective, we now deal with its second member. As previously mentioned, an objective perspective consists in disregarding subjective relativizations of facts that are of interest in the humanities. This approach, which again allows for two different interpretations, will here be considered only with respect to linguistics. The opposition which then suggests itself is phenomenalism vs. grammaticism. The former demands that grammarians should occupy themselves with concrete utterances, or more specifically, with speaking treated as a physical phenomenon, i.e. with portions of speech understood as acoustic sound events. Phenomenalism guarantees that the phenomena studied are accessible to methods of scientific analysis and exact description such as segmentation and classification (cf. Harris 1951). As for grammaticism, remember mathematical linguistics, in particular, the automata-theoretical approach to language, whose main goal is to construct grammars as abstract devices by which given sets of sentences may be generated.

There are two versions of grammaticism, formalism and semanticism, distinguished by the role assigned to the semantic component within a grammar. We either demand that the devices called grammars are purely formal, i.e. involve only syntactic properties of language entities. The rules for generating and transforming sentences determine properties of expressions such as their potential complexity, but this does not allow to distinguish meaningful from meaningless syntactic constructions among the ones that are generated. Semanticism, on the other hand, claims that the semantic component is basic to any grammar. The syntax of a language is a kind of mapping which mirrors the syntax of the world. Consequently, such categories as nouns, verbs, predicates, numerals, etc., which result from linguistic classifications, are only shadows of the corresponding ontological categories such as objects, properties, processes, numbers, etc. (Gardies 1985).

The difference between formalism and semanticism also underlies the controversy in the sixties and seventies between Chomskyan generative grammar and generative semantics, which was not new but deeply rooted in medieval philosophical disputes, including the problems of universals.

2 Methodological properties of linguistic theories

The following diagram, which illustrates the oppositions between linguistic theories form the point of view of their methodological properties, will be helpful in discussing some of the methodological problems connected with the structure of linguistic theories and, in particular, with the ways in which they may be constructed:

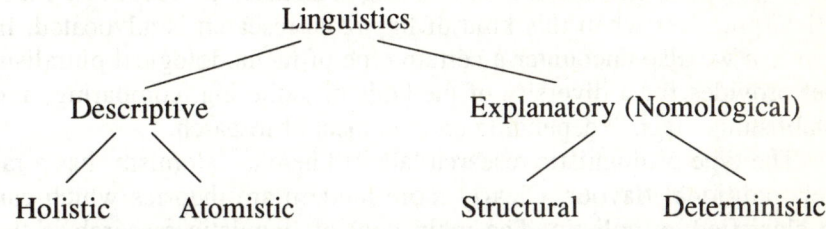

There are two kinds of procedures that may be employed in linguistics: purely descriptive and explanatory ones. This leads to the distinction of descriptive vs. explanatory linguistics. Descriptive procedures are uncontroversial in the humanities since almost any inquiry in this area has a descriptive component. The status of explanatory procedures is more doubtful. Generally, the problem reduces to the status of two kinds of questions, what-questions and why-questions. A conception by which linguistics is restricted to what-questions adopts the descriptive point of view. If why-questions are also allowed, then linguistics is assigned the status of a nomological discipline.

The distinction between descriptivism and nomologism is quite old and is rooted in philosophy. It entered linguistics via the conception of scientific linguistics as part of the neogrammarian doctrine. Claiming the status of a science for linguistics appears to be closely related to assigning nomological status to linguistics: linguistics, on this view, is a scientific discipline only if it is nomological whereas any linguistics limited to descriptive procedures does not satisfy the requirements for scientific theories (Paul 1880; Jankowsky 1972).

The Neogrammarian requirements did not prevent the pursuit of a purely descriptive linguistics, an approach actually followed in various structuralist theories. Thus grammatical reconstructions of particular natural languages undertaken within a grammaticist framework have a purely descriptive character. In our view there are two kinds of descriptive theories characteristic of contemporary linguistics. One of them, sometimes called material linguistics, will here be referred to as atomistic. An 'atomistic' orientation has proved productive both for diachronic and synchronic research; following atomism, the researcher should pursue a single aim, collection of as many facts as possible. Frequently, we also meet with a strong reluctance to adopt any theoretical premises when this kind of linguistic research is advocated. In atomism we also encounter a certain type of methodological pluralism that provides for a diversity of methods of gathering, comparing, and establishing "facts", depending on the object of research.

The type of linguistic research labelled here as 'atomism' has a rather traditional flavour. Clearly more modern are theories which can be classified as holistic. The main goal of linguistic research is the same as in atomism, description, but additional requirements are imposed: descriptions should be complete, if at all possible, and multidimensional, in a word holistic, should consider each object of description in its entirety. As an example take the theory of speech acts, half linguistic, half philosophical, which emphasizes the necessity to take into account all factors, properties, parameters, etc. relevant to the act of speaking. Communication should thus be described as a whole (Sadock 1974); restriction to selected functions, channels, or parameters is far from satisfactory. It is a clear manifestation of this trend toward more complete linguistic descriptions that the concept of language competence may be replaced by more comprehensive concepts, such as communicative competence which includes not only strictly grammatical rules but also pragmatical, situational, and sociolinguistic ones (Hymes 1972).

Returning to nomological linguistics, we point out, once again, that corresponding theories are not purely descriptive but also explanatory. Explanatory procedures presuppose lists of scientific (linguistic) laws. Such laws have the form of implications by which it is claimed that a certain type of connection holds between the antecedent (reason, cause) and the consequent (result). Depending on the kind of connection, different types of explanation may be distinguished. We are going to concentrate on only two such types: functional explanation and cause-result deterministic explanation. The former is characteristic of structuralist theories of language, the latter was adopted in neo-grammarian doctrine.

3 Change and persistence of structuralist ideas

Instead of summarizing Secs 1 and 2 we formulate a few remarks that should be relevant to a proper understanding of the second part of our paper.

(i) Our categorization of linguistic theories can be used to determine the place of structuralism among these theories. For the entire field of linguistics to be divided into just two parts, structuralist and non-structuralist linguistics, we must be able to state the specific properties of at least the former.

(ii) Contemporary structuralism is not a homogeneous theory of language. Rather, it is a complex of theories which apply both specific and shared principles, a complex that is strongly differentiated internally. It should be no surprise then that two theories constructed within the structuralist domain may exhibit mutually exclusive properties, for instance, one may follow realist and the other instrumentalist principles. The most striking example for such diversity is provided by the American vs. the European versions of structuralism. While the former may be considered as a purely descriptive theory, the latter version (especially in the Prague School) stresses the importance of functional explanation, thus reaching nomological status. Or again, let us consider key terms such as 'structure', 'system' etc. They may be related to reality in two ways. Either we assume that reality is structured in advance and the task of the researcher consists in revealing its structure, or else we assume that reality is an unordered chaos, and it is only when structuralists make use of their instruments and structural nets that order is imposed on it. This by the way clarifies the difference between a realist and an instrumentalist approach.

(iii) Structuralism appears to stand out clearly from both neogrammarianism and generativism. Neogrammarianism adopted deterministic explanation, while the Prague structuralists preferred functional explanation. And whereas American structuralists were empiricists (trying to reduce linguistics to a theory of verbal behaviour or verbal habits), generativism revived the nativist hypothesis.

(iv) In our opinion, the structuralist stage in the development of linguistics is anything but a thing of the past. It is an open question whether generativism is a continuation of, rather than a successor to structuralism. To be sure, generativism waged war against so-called taxonomic linguistics, but its relationship to Prague School theories is obviously more complex. We feel inclined to claim that structuralist ideas persist in generativism in a changed form; without the structuralist stage generativism presumably could not have arisen, or, more strongly, it may appear as a direct consequence of structuralism.

(v) The second part of our paper largely argues the thesis that there is both change and persistence of classical structuralist ideas in the postclassical period of phonology. This will be argued by demonstrating:

(a) the viability of the theory of phonological oppositions,
(b) various possibilities for a logical reconstruction of classical structuralist phonological theories,
(c) the reducibility of generative phonology to traditional structuralist theory.

4 A contribution to the theory of phonological oppositions

In this part we aim at a logical reconstruction of some fundamental phonological concepts introduced in Trubetzkoy's classical monograph *Grundzüge der Phonologie*. Our main result will be formulation of a *minimal* mathematical conceptual apparatus sufficient for describing the notion of opposition and concepts related to it.

We restrict our attention to oppositions understood as binary relations between phonological entities. These relations are based on a comparison of the phonetic content of phones and phonemes.

From the very beginning it should be understood that the concept of opposition as discussed below concerns only one aspect of the theory of oppositions. We omit, among others, problems of alternative descriptions (say, oppositions as *primary* phonological objects and entities such as phones and phonemes as *derived* objects, e.g. "bundles of oppositions", an approach that might well be considered, using, for example, category theory).

For Trubetzkoy, phonological units (phonemes) are bundles of co-occurrent (i.e. combinable) features that have articulatory and acoustic character. In order to establish all elements of a given phonological system, one must also take into account their distributional properties, i.e. admissible contexts (neighbourhoods) of particular phonological units. Trubetzkoy proposes a list of rules determining the phonetic content of phonemes (i.e. the relation of combinability of phonetic features) as well as providing criteria necessary for distinguishing phonemes and variants (allophones). These (and other) rules may all be formulated in a precise way, cf. for instance Batóg (1967).

Let us now try to reconstruct Trubetzkoy's classifications of phonological oppositions.

DEFINITION 1.   We start with a system
$$\langle \text{OBJ}, \text{FTR}, \textbf{haf}, \text{PRM}, \text{WRD}, \text{CNT}, \textbf{adm}, \textbf{syn} \rangle$$
where:

- OBJ   is the set of phonological units (either phones or phonemes, depending on some further assumptions)
- FTR   is the set of phonetic features
- **haf**   is a relation with the domain OBJ and counterdomain FTR (*Interpretation*: x **haf** α means that x has the feature α.)
- PRM   is a non-trivial partition of FTR satisfying the following conditions:
  (i)   each member of PRM has at least two elements
  (ii) for every x in OBJ and $\mathfrak{A}$ in PRM there is exactly one α in $\mathfrak{A}$ such that x **haf** α
  (iii) for every $\mathfrak{A}$ in PRM the union of all sets of the form $\{x \in \text{OBJ}: x \text{ \textbf{haf} } \alpha\}$, for $\alpha \in \mathfrak{A}$, equals OBJ

(*Interpretation*: each member of the partition PRM is a set of homogeneous phonetic features, i.e. features of the same sort.)

Elements of PRM are called *phonetic parameters*.

WRD is a subset of the free semigroup generated by OBJ

(*Interpretation*: WRD is the set of phonetic representations of word-forms.)

CNT is the set of all WRD-contexts, i.e.

CNT = $\{(u,v)$: there is an x in OBJ such that the concatenation uxv belongs to WRD$\}$

(*Interpretation*: CNT is the family of all admissible contexts (= neighbourhoods) of elements of OBJ.)

adm is a relation with the domain OBJ and the counterdomain CNT such that for all x in OBJ and all (u,v) in CNT:

x **adm** (u,v) iff uxv belongs to WRD

(*Interpretation*: if x **adm** (u,v), then the context (u,v) is admissible for x.)

syn is a binary relation on WRD

(*Interpretation*: **syn** is the identity of meaning of word-forms.)

This system can be further characterized by suitable postulates, some of them already contained (implicitly) in Trubetzkoy's monograph. As an example, take the following one:

(*) $\forall x \in$ OBJ $\forall y \in$ OBJ $[\exists (u,v) \in$ CNT $(x$ **adm** (u,v) & y **adm** (u,v) & $\neg(uxv$ **syn** $uyv)) \Rightarrow \exists \alpha \in$ FTR $(\alpha \in$ **haf**$^\wedge x \div$ **haf**$^\wedge y)]$

(If two phonological units distinguish word-forms which convey different meanings, then they have different phonetic content; where $\div$ denotes symmetric difference of sets and **haf**$^\wedge x$ is the set of all **haf**-successors of x.)

We are not going to specify all the axioms here, a task to be postponed to a later paper.

Obviously, not all of the concepts introduced in Definition 1 are primitive concepts. As a matter of fact, the system can be based on only two primitive concepts: those of phonetic parameter and the relation of identity of meaning.

A NEW STRUCTURALISM IN PHONOLOGY

DEFINITION 2. Let us define two binary relations on the set OBJ:

x **op** y iff $\exists (u,v) \in$ CNT $[x$ **adm** (u,v) & y **adm** (u,v) & $\neg(uxv$ **syn** $uyv)]$
x **ops** y iff x **op** y & **haf**$^\wedge x \cap$ **haf**$^\wedge y \neq \varnothing$

The relation **op** holds between those phonological entities which distinguish word-forms that convey different meanings. For two phonological entities to stand in relation **ops** they must not only distinguish meanings but must also have some phonetic features in common. Each pair (x,y) such that x **ops** y is called an *opposition pair*. The relation **ops** is called *phonological opposition*.

Note that the following trivial proposition holds:

PROPOSITION. Assume that **syn** is an equivalence. Then:

(i) the relations **op** and **ops** are both irreflexive and symmetric.
(ii) If x **op** y then **haf**$^\wedge x \div$ **haf**$^\wedge y \neq \varnothing$.
(The same holds of **ops**.)

In what follows we restrict ourselves to providing exact definitions of the following classifications of oppositions given by Trubetzkoy:

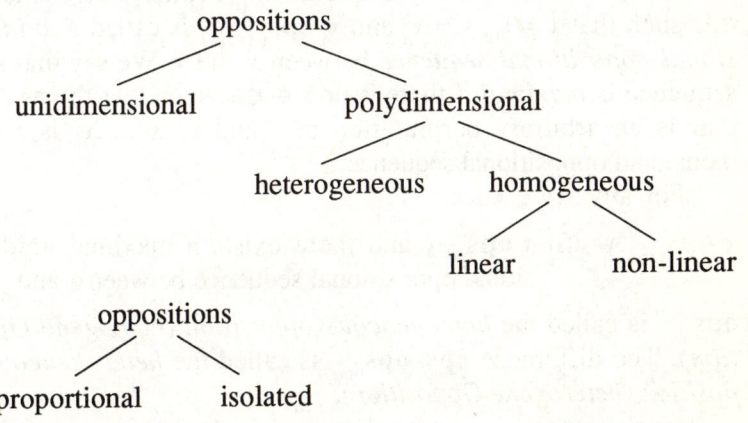

We will also provide formal definitions of correlations and bundles of correlations. The distinctions between private, gradual and equipollent oppositions need not here be discussed. All oppositions to be considered are construed as privative (cf. Pogonowski 1985 for a formal decription of gradual oppositions); Trubetzkoy's original terminology will be retained.

DEFINITION 3. Define the following binary relations on OBJ:

x **ops**$_{ud}$ y iff x **ops** y & $\neg \exists x_1 \exists y_1 [x_1, y_1 \in$ OBJ & $x_1 = y_1$ &
x_1 **ops** y_1 & **haf**$^\wedge x \cap$ **haf**$^\wedge y =$ **haf**$^\wedge x_1 \cap$ **haf**$^\wedge y_1]$

The relation **ops**$_{ud}$ is called the *unidimensional opposition* (*eindimensionale Opposition*).

x **ops**$_{pd}$ y iff x **ops** y & $\exists x_1 \exists y_1 [x_1, y_1 \in$ OBJ & $x \neq x_1$ &
$y \neq y_1$ & x_1 **ops** y_1 & **haf**$^\wedge x \cap$ **haf**$^\wedge y =$ **haf**$^\wedge x_1 \cap$ **haf**$^\wedge y_1]$

The relation **ops**$_{pd}$ is called the *polydimensional opposition* (*mehrdimensionale Opposition*).

EXAMPLE 1.

German: t **ops**$_{ud}$ d   French: d **ops**$_{ud}$ n
German: d **ops**$_{pd}$ b

DEFINITION 4.

If $x,y \in$ OBJ, then any sequence $(x_0, x_1, ..., x_n)$ of elements of OBJ such that $x = x_0$, $y = x_n$ and x_i **ops**$_{ud}$ x_{i+1} is called a *unidimensional oppositional sequence* between x and y. We say that such a sequence is *maximal* if there is no $z \in$ OBJ such that the n+2-tuple that is an arbitrary permutation of z and $x_0, x_1, ..., x_n$ is a unidimensional oppositional sequence.

For any $x,y \in$ OBJ:

x **ops**$_{hmg}$ y iff x **ops**$_{pd}$ y and there exists a maximal unidimensional oppositional sequence between x and y.

ops$_{hmg}$ is called the *homogeneous opposition* (*homogene Opposition*). The difference **ops**–**ops**$_{hmg}$ is called the *heterogeneous opposition* (*heterogene Opposition*).

EXAMPLE 2.

German: x **ops**$_{hmg}$ ŋ   p **ops**–**ops**$_{hmg}$ t

The sequence (u,o,ö,e) is a maximal unidimensional oppositional sequence between u and e in German.

DEFINITION 5. For any x,y in OBJ:

x **ops**$_{ln}$ y iff there exists exactly one maximal unidimensional oppositional sequence between x and y.

x **ops**$_{nln}$ y iff there exists more than one maximal unidimensional oppositional sequence between x and y.

The relation **ops**$_{ln}$ (resp. **ops**$_{nln}$) is called the *linear* (resp. *non-linear*) *opposition* (in Trubetzkoy's terminology: *geradlinige und ungeradlinige Oppositionen*).

EXAMPLE 3.

German:

x **ops**$_{ln}$ ŋ (because (x,k,g,ŋ) is the only maximal unidimensional oppositional sequence beween x and ŋ)

u **ops**$_{nln}$ e (examples of maximal unidimensional oppositional sequences between u and e are: (u,o,ö,e), (u,ü,ö,e)).

DEFINITION 6. Define the following opposition relations on OBJ:

x **ops**$_{pr}$ y iff there are $x_1, y_1 \in$ OBJ such that $x = x_1, y = y_1$ and **haf**$^\wedge x \div$ **haf**$^\wedge y =$ **haf**$^\wedge x_1 \div$ **haf**$^\wedge y_1$.

The relation **ops**$_{pr}$ is called the proportional opposition (*proportionale Opposition*).

x **ops**$_{is}$ y iff there are no $x_1, y_1 \in$ OBJ such that $x_1 \neq x, y_1 \neq y$ and **haf**$^\wedge x \div$ **haf**$^\wedge y =$ **haf**$^\wedge x_1 \div$ **haf**$^\wedge y_1$.

The relation **ops**$_{is}$ is called the *isolated opposition* (*isolierte Opposition*).

EXAMPLE 4.

German: p **ops**$_{pr}$ b   r **ops**$_{is}$ l

It is a common tendency among linguists to speak of oppositions as specific pairs of phonological units (phonemes). Such an approach may be called *local* while definitions 3 to 6 introduce opposition relations in a *global* sense. Both approaches are of course compatible.

The next definition introduces concepts reflecting, with slight modifications, Trubetzkoy's notion of correlation (*Korrelation*).

DEFINITION 7.

(i) For any $\mathfrak{A} \in$ PRM and $x,y \in$ OBJ:
x **crl**$_\mathfrak{A}$ y iff x **ops**$_{ud}$ y & x **ops**$_{pr}$ y & $\exists \alpha \in \mathfrak{A}$ ($\alpha \in$ haf$^\wedge x \div$ haf$^\wedge y$).

If x **crl**$_\mathfrak{A}$ y then we say that x and y form a *correlation pair with respect to the parameter* $\mathfrak{A}$. The relation **crl**$_\mathfrak{A}$ is called the $\mathfrak{A}$-*correlation*.

(ii) For any $x \in$ OBJ:
EVEN(x) iff $\exists \mathfrak{A} \in$ PRM $\exists y \in$ OBJ [x **crl**$_\mathfrak{A}$ y]
ODD(x) iff $\neg$ EVEN(x)

(iii) For $\mathfrak{A}, \mathfrak{B} \in$ PRM:
$\mathfrak{A}$ **sm** $\mathfrak{B}$ iff $\exists x,y,z \in$ OBJ [x **crl**$_\mathfrak{A}$ y & y **crl**$_\mathfrak{B}$ z].

If $\mathfrak{A}$ **sm** $\mathfrak{B}$ then we say that $\mathfrak{A}$ and $\mathfrak{B}$ are *related*. The relation **sm** is reflexive and symmetric. Let **sm**^{tr} denote the transitive closure of **sm** (i.e. the smallest transitive relation containing **sm**). Of course, **sm**^{tr} is an equivalence. If $\mathfrak{A}$ **sm**^{tr} $\mathfrak{B}$ then we say that $\mathfrak{A}$ and $\mathfrak{B}$ are *weakly related*.

(iv) For any $x,y \in$ OBJ and $\mathfrak{A} \in$ PRM:
x **Crl**$_\mathfrak{A}$ y iff $\exists \mathfrak{B} \in$ PRM [x **crl**$_\mathfrak{B}$ y & $\mathfrak{A}$ **sm**^{tr} $\mathfrak{B}$]
BDL(x) = {$y \in$ OBJ: $\exists \mathfrak{A} \in$ PRM [x **Crl**$_\mathfrak{A}$ y]}

The set BDL(x) is called the *correlation bundle* of x.

EXAMPLE 5.

German: (d,t),(b,p),(g,k) $\in$ **crl**$_{\text{Voice}}$

German: Voice **sm** Aspiration (understood as dichotomic parameters)

Ancient Greek: BDL(π) = {π,β,ϕ}, BDL(κ) = {κ,γ,χ}

DEFINITION 8. For any $x,y \in$ OBJ and $(u,v) \in$ CNT:

x **ntr**$_{(u,v)}$ y iff x **ops** y & $\neg$ [$uxv, uyv \in$ WRD]

If x **ntr**$_{(u,v)}$ y then we say that the opposition between x and y is *neutralized* in the context (u,v).

In concluding this part we point out that three primitive notions OBJ, FTR, and **haf** may be replaced by the following two:

FTR   interpreted as before
cmb   a binary relation on FTR (combinability of features; we assume that **cmb** is a similarity relation, i.e. a reflexive and symmetric relation).

The set OBJ can then be identified with the family of all maximal **cmb**-coherent sets (i.e. each phonological object is a bundle of combinable features). The relation **haf** is now defined as follows:

x **haf** α iff $\alpha \in x$

For a completely different attempt at a logical reconstruction of Trubetzkoy's system see Lieb (1979).

5   Some aspects of the logical reconstruction of structuralist theories

New structuralism in phonology is characterized by an attempt to perfect its methodology. Correspondingly, the formulation of phonological theories has become much more precise, and these theories have been lifted to a much more sophisticated level, a level where logico-mathematical methods can be applied.

No comprehensive account of the methods of structuralist phonology is possible within the limits of this paper. We shall confine ourselves to the most perfect of all formal methods, namely the axiomatic method, since we are convinced that this is the most interesting method for any theory-oriented study. We shall pass over all set-theoretic approaches that are not explicitly axiomatic.

Because of its relatively simple domain, phonology invites axiomatization. No wonder then that attempts at axiomatization have a relatively long history in phonology. One of the first scholars to make serious efforts in this direction was Bloomfield (1926), partly under the influence of logical positivist philosophers of the Vienna Circle. In the early twenties positivism was fashionable again due to the enormous amount of work done on the foundations of logic promising to provide the appropriate formal apparatus for the formulation of scientific theories. The axiomatic method then prevailing in logic and mathematics must have fascinated Bloomfield too, who endeavoured to transfer it to linguistic science. Bloomfield's ideas were taken up by Bloch in theoretical phonology (1948). Neither Bloomfield's nor Bloch's attempts were free of flaws and errors. Subsequently, there has been a growing number of attempts to apply logico-mathematical means and the axiomatic method by authors such as Revzin (e.g., 1977), Marcus (1963, 1967), Nebeský (1966a,b), Šreider (1972), Mulder (1968, 1989), Brainerd (1971, 1974), Vennemann (1972, 1980), and others who have contributed a great deal to making phonology more precise.

However, the most important step towards an axiomatic phonology was taken by Batóg in his work *The axiomatic method in phonology* (1967), which represents a fully adequate and explicit logical reconstruction of a specific phonological theory, namely the one developed by Harris. There are also two attempst at a logical reconstruction of Trubetzkoy's phonological theory that we know of, one by Zgółka (1976), the other by Lieb (1979) (Qvarnström 1979 was not accessible). Both were made independently and both are limited to fragments of Trubetzkoy's theory that include its most basic concepts. Bańczerowski's (1982) theory is also incomplete; it combines certain aspects of American and Praguian structuralism.

We are now going to compare essential features of Batóg's, Zgółka's and Lieb's approaches; this way we wish to demonstrate the advantages of an axiomatic approach for the logical reconstruction of informal phonological theories. An axiomatic theory allows one to distinguish between primitive and defined terms, and to draw a clear distinction between axioms and their consequences. Axioms are initial theorems which cannot be proved in terms of a given theory and which generate all the other theorems of this theory through application of the rules of logical deduction. Axiomatization cuts down on ambiguities and vaguenesses in informal phonological theories, which are thus more easily compared. In our case it will also allow us to demonstrate that generative phonology is simply a consequence of structuralist phonology.

The three axiomatizations by Batóg, Zgółka and Lieb differ in many important respects, especially in their approach to fundamental phonological notions, as will appear from the following comparison.

First, consider phonetic features, which play a basic role in each of the three theories. Batóg and Zgółka treat features extensionally. Batóg identifies them with certain sets of elementary segments, Zgółka with certain sets of utterances (that exhibit these features in certain positions). In his reconstruction of Trubetzkoy, Lieb prefers an intensional treatment of phonetic features, taking them to be properties of individual sound-events. Consequently, the concepts of sound and phoneme and of phonetic and phonological representation differ in the three approaches.

Batóg defines a sound as a class of phonetically equivalent unit-length segments, whereas Zgółka and Lieb identify a sound with a class of phonetic features. Batóg's phoneme is a class of sounds that are in free variation or complementary distribution, and are phonetically not too distant from one another. Thus, in order to group sounds into phonemes Batóg draws upon distributional information. On the other hand, Zgółka's and Lieb's phonemes are classes of distinctive features of sound-events. In Zgółka's case a sound is contained in a corresponding phoneme (due to the extensional treatment of features), in Lieb's a phoneme is contained in a corresponding sound. Still, phonemes in Zgółka's and Lieb's theories are not identified independently of the distribution of sounds. Distinctive features presuppose distinctive oppositions, which presuppose phonetic representations of words (minimal pairs). Such representations carry distributional information on sounds, i.e. they allow one to define concepts such as neighbourhood of a sound and generally, various distributional relations.

Batóg distinguishes relevant and distinctive features on the basis of prior definitions of sound and phoneme. A relevant feature is to be any phonetic feature exhibited by all sounds that are elements of the same phoneme. A distinctive feature is a relevant feature of sounds of a given phoneme that is opposed to some other phoneme by the presence versus the absence of this feature (cf. Batóg 1967:110-111, 1978: 59). The notion of distinctive feature is thus based on the notion of phoneme. In Zgółka's and Lieb's theories it is the other way around:

identification of distinctive features precedes identification of phonemes. Distinctive features are based not on phonemes but on distinctive oppositions.

A term such as 'distinctive opposition' is not found either among Batóg's primitive or his defined terms. He still makes use of the concept by way of a postulate of differentiation, which requires different phonological representations for two words that have different sets of potential meanings. Thus, it is not quite correct then to reproach Batóg for omitting the concept of distinctive opposition from his theory (cf. Lieb 1979:20).

Comparison of the three phonological theories could be extended to reveal further similarities and differences among them, but may here be concluded by some general observations. By axiomatizing phonological theories, we do not necessarily cut down on the number of interpretations for specific phonological terms. Fundamental phonological terms such as phonetic feature, sound, phoneme, and phonetic or phonological representation may each denote different entities in different axiomatic theories. Within a single theory, however, the meaning of each term is fixed, and this, of course, saves discussion.

A single informal phonological theory may be axiomatized in different ways, depending on the way in which its ambiguities and inconsistencies are to be resolved. Thus, different axiomatic theories may result from a single informal one, each emphasizing specific features inherent in the informal theory.

In what follows we would like to present Vennemann's formal system in Bartsch and Vennemann (1982:66-86), not exhaustively but more extensively than the three theories briefly discussed above because Vennemann approaches some phonological problems in a different way. Vennemann's presentation is meant to provide an outline (*Skizze*) only of a 'word-phonological theory' (p. 66), and it may be for this reason that some details of his theory are not completely clear to us. Thus, our presentation of the theory may not faithfully reconstruct all details as intended by the author.

The primitive notions which Vennemann makes use of are as follows (our reconstruction and translation):

(i) the set of phonological features,
(ii) the function of coefficient assignment,
(iii) the downstep-operator,
(iv) the upstep-operator,
(v) the set of phonetic states,
(vi) the set of normal utterances of possible words,
(vii) the relation of phonological satisfaction,
(viii) the relation of homophony,
(ix) the function of phonologization,
(x) the set of natural numbers,
(xi) the set of real numbers.

A *phonological feature* could be interpreted as a phonetic dimension or parameter in our sense, i.e. as a set of homogeneous phonetic features (see above, Sec. 4, Def. 1). Examples of phonological features given by Vennemann are Nasality and Vowel height. The *function of coefficient assignment* associates each feature with a natural number. If a feature F happens to be binary, then it is associated with 2, i.e. with the set $\{0,1\}$. The *downstep-* and *upstep-operators* apply to tone levels; their use is restricted to tonology. *Phonetic states* are simply states of articulatory organs, of sound waves, or of auditory processes. Thus, for instance, degree of oral aperture, tongue configurations, fundamental frequencies, etc. are phonetic states located within the respective continua. Phonetic states as conceived by Vennemann are reminiscent of his phonological features. It can be decided by the native user of language system L whether a phonetic event is a (phonetic) *normal utterance of a possible word* in L. The *relation of phonological satisfaction* holds, roughly speaking, between a phonetic event and a phonological word form. If a phonetic event e satisfies a phonological word form ϕ, then the phonetic properties expressed by ϕ apply to e. More precisely, the relation of phonological satisfaction connects a sequence of phonetic events $\langle e_i \rangle_{i \leq n}$ and a phone sequence contained in ϕ only if the phone sequence has length n and there is a phonetic event e such that $\langle e_i \rangle_{i \leq n}$ is a segmentation of e. The *relation of homophony* is understood as the set of pairs of normal utterances of expressions of (language system) L. These utterances form a subset of phonetic events. The *function of phonologization* associates equivalence classes of the relation of homophony with appropriate phonological word forms. Primitive notions (x) and (xi) are no longer phonological.

Vennemann defines a fairly large number of phonological notions, in particular:

(i) the feature catalogue
(ii) the relation of feature specification
(iii) a feature matrix
(iv) a syllable indicator
(v) a syllabification indicator
(vi) a syllabification inducer
(vii) a syllable
(viii) the set of accentuations
(ix) the set of tone levels
(x) the set of tones
(xi) the set of phonological word forms
(xii) the set of phonetic events
(xiii) the function of segmentation

Some of these notions appear to be motivated by linguistic intuitions that are somewhat doubtful. Thus, the definition of *feature matrix* may not yet be adequate. Such matrices are formed by feature specifications, i.e. pairs consisting of a feature and its coefficient; the specifications are interpreted as properties of segments. A feature matrix is ultimately identified with a *phone*. But how do we obtain the information necessary to identify the feature specification of a particular matrix so that the segments corresponding to the phone are sufficiently characterized? It is largely left to the linguist to imagine which feature specifications should be combined into feature matrices, and which matrices into phone sequences that are components of phonological word forms. This problem could be solved by granting the phone the status of a primitive notion or by introducing an operation that transforms a specific subset of feature specifications into a unit, i.e. a phone.

Next consider the notion of syllable. It is defined by using the concepts of *syllable indicator*, *syllabification indicator*, and *syllabification inducer*. A syllable indicator is a pair $\langle \mu, \nu \rangle$, where

(a) μ is a pair $\langle m, m'\rangle$ of natural numbers,
(b) ν is a pair $\langle n, n'\rangle$ of natural numbers, and
(c) $m \leq n \leq n' \leq m'$.

For example, if $\langle\langle m_i, m'_i\rangle, \langle n_i, n'_i\rangle\rangle$ is a syllable indicator, then m_i and m'_i indicate, respectively, the beginning and the end of a syllable, and n_i and n'_i the beginning and the end of the syllable's nucleus. If $\sigma = \langle\mu, \nu\rangle$ is a syllable indicator, then μ is the basis and ν the nucleus indicator. A *syllabification indicator* is a sequence of syllable indicators such that there are no gaps between the bases of any two neighbouring syllable indicators. If a syllabification indicator $s = \langle\sigma_i\rangle_{i \leq j'}$ with $\mu_{j'} = \langle m_{j'}, m'_{j'}\rangle$ as basis indicator of $\sigma_{j'}$ is associated with a feature matrix sequence $p = \langle M_i\rangle_{i \leq j'}$ such that $m'_j = j$, then s is called a *syllabification inducer* for p.

This definition of syllabification inducer presents a serious problem: how to associate effectively a given syllabification indicator with an appropriate sequence of feature matrices. How can we perfom this operation successfully if the method of syllable identification within a sequence of feature matrices, i.e. a sequence of phones, is not available beforehand? In other words, how should we, in such a sequence, recognize the bases of syllables and their nuclei? Since the notion of syllable is not available prior to the notion of syllable indicator, the members of an indicator cannot in this framework be correctly associated with the right parts of a syllable. Even worse, since the concept of syllable indicator is introduced independently of the concept of syllable, there is, in principle, an infinite number of syllable indicators which may be considered for a single syllable. We thus need an operation that associates a given syllable with its appropriate syllable indicator, an operation missing from Vennemann's primitive notions. To be adequate, the definition of a syllable indicator would require additional information on the structure of a syllable. It turns out, then, that syllable indicator, syllabification indicator, and syllabification inducer all presuppose the notion of syllable, rather than conversely. The notion of syllable should therefore be taken as primitive, and Vennemann's system modified accordingly.

A similar suggestion may be made with respect to the notion of a phonetic event. As intended by Vennemann a phonetic event should be a continuous, non-repeatable physical entity that lasts during a certain time interval and passes through various phonetic states. Thus, it has a certain extension in time. Vennemann formally defines a phonetic event as any function whose domain is in the set of real numbers, which represent points of time, and whose range is in the set of phonetic states. A phonetic event thus appears to be essentially construed as a temporal sequence of phonetic states. However, it may be objected that several phonetic states may cooccur at a single point in time. Construing phonetic events as arrangements of phonetic states, we must allow such arrangements to be both sequential and simultaneous (asequential). Thus, they cannot be functions in Vennemann's sense but must be functions whose values are *sets* of phonetic states. Generally, it may be safer to treat phonetic states as primitive entities in Vennemann's system.

We also feel uncomfortable with Vennemann's concept of segmentation; an adequate definition of such a concept should require a prior notion of segment. Vennemann does specify formal conditions that a segmentation should fulfil but does not touch upon the problem of the size of segments, i.e. the relation of elementary to unit-length segments.

It follows from these objections that the ontological status of some phonological entities in Vennemann's theory does not always agree with our own intuitions, and we do feel that specifying the properties of these entities is not simply a matter of taste.

Our remarks on Vennemann's phonological theory have been mainly critical but it would be quite wrong to conclude that we take a negative attitude towards the theory. On the contrary, Vennemann's formal approach, which renders possible pertinent discussion and clearly reveals not only shortcomings but also important achievements of his theory, meets our highest approval. We also believe that Vennemann's theory could be easily given a format similar to the one chosen by Batóg for his own theory.

Many phonological theories are informal, and all informal phonological theories are not yet mature enough for axiomatic reconstruction. In order to become accessible to formalization, such a theory may have to be reinterpreted, or changed in even more essential ways because it is not yet satisfactory on various accounts: it may abound in vague and ambiguous terms, have definitions that are imprecise or inadequate, and theorems that lack a clear sense. Such a situation, which is due to the unstable foundations of the discipline, cannot be tolerated indefinitely in theoretical phonology. Foundational research in this field is therefore more than welcome.

In this context we would like to emphasize the importance of Lieb's work (e.g. 1988) for theoretical phonology as well as for the methodology of this discipline. We briefly consider his 1988 study, which outlines part of a general phonological theory and is meant to provide a theoretical foundation for a phonological method (BEVA-TON — Berlin procedure for auditive pitch analysis; cf. Lieb (ed.) 1988 for details). Opposing methodological naïvety, Lieb attempts to develop an exact method for studying language entities that involve the intentionality of the human mind, which is also true of phonological objects.

Speaking is an action, and each action, according to Lieb, has an intention as one of its necessary components (an intention-in-action, to use Searle's term whom Lieb follows). The relevant properties (articulatory, acoustic, auditive) of speech sound events are directly or indirectly determined by the intention of speaking. Adhering to an exact methodology Lieb inquires into such fundamental phonological notions as phones, tones, syllables, the interrelationships between tone and syllable, sound segments and tone segments, as well as tone segments and syllable segments. The solutions which Lieb offers are certainly a challenge to established phonological science. Let us here adduce at least his conception of a *phone* (sound) as a set of auditive functions, i.e. functions which associate with each person an auditive property of sound events that is relativized to this person. While such a conception has undeniable virtues, it may still seem a bit antiintuitive, and one might wish to look for some other way to incorporate the problem of intentionality into theoretical phonology.

However, regardless of our agreeing or disagreeing with the contents of Lieb's theory, we cannot help but appreciate its precise and explicit formulation which, eliminating ambiguities, does not leave much room for guess-work. This may well be one of the roads on which new structuralism in phonology should proceed.

6 Is generative phonology reducible to structuralist phonology?

Generative phonology appears to be a consequence of structuralist phonology: this is the claim that will now be argued in greater detail. Generative phonology, which was developed in oppositon to American structuralism, adopted several ideas from the Prague School, in particular, Trubetzkoy's concept of the phoneme as a set of distinctive features; his concept of archiphoneme; and the concept of feature itself. All these proved fertile notions for generative phonology, which attempted to formulate synchronic generalizations in terms of phonological rules. It is the feature approach to phoneme and archiphoneme that allowed the formulation of rules determining variants, i.e. allowed general statements on the transformation of phonological representations into phonetic ones. This transformation, and corresponding rules, are at the core of generative phonology.

Remember that the generative phonological approach associates each morpheme (with certain exceptions) with exactly one phonological representation, and specific allomorphs of the morpheme with one or more phonetic representations. The allomorphs of a single morpheme form a morphonological paradigm, for which the phonological representation of the morpheme is the morphonological deep structure or underlying form.

A *phonological representation* is a linear structure, a sequence of phonemes, a *phonetic representation* a sequence of sounds. A *sound* is a set of phonetic features, and a *phoneme* should contain only those features which are distinctive and distributionally unpredictable. Phonological rules, which associate phonemes with the corresponding sounds, thus operate on distributionally unpredictable features and supply the predictable ones.

Phonemization rules are to associate the phonetic representations of a morphonological paradigm with the phonological representation of this paradigm. As a matter of fact, such rules were not or could not be given, due to the theoretical principles that were adopted. Thus, it is not rare that the construction of phonological representations appears to be left to the fancy of the linguist, or else one cannot help suspecting that phonological representations take the form they do for a single reason: guarantee the derivation of phonetic representations by applying the phonological rules.

Given the lack of phonemization rules, the phonological representations often give the impression of imaginary structures. For example, *divine* [di'vayn] ~ *divinity* [di'viniti], and *vary* ['vɛəri] ~ variety [və'rayəti] each belong to a single morphonological paradigm and are thus each derived from a single underlying form. In the first case, the morphonological alternation *ay/i* is thus reduced to an imaginary phoneme, the tense long /ī/, which does not appear in the phonetic representations. From underlying /ī/, [ay] is derived by diphthongization, and [i] by laxing. In the second case, the morphonological alternation *i/ay* is reduced to an underlying /i/ that, under stress before a vowel, becomes long and tense and is then diphthongized.

Phonological description tended to be regularized at any prize, which often led to postulation of imaginary phonological representations that are quite absurd from the point of view of synchronic language consciousness. No doubt that language consciousness does establish morphonological relationships between, say, [ay] in *divine* and [i] in *divinity* but this does not mean it derives the alternating sounds from an imaginary entity /ī/.

Still, the automata-theoretical approach of generative phonology to the description of phonological reality is of interest. It demonstrates, for one thing, what absurd phonological representations must often be resorted to if phonological reality is to be described in terms of the proposed rules. While this may even be useful for some purposes, we are convinced that generative phonology could be given a form that avoids its recent absurdities.

In order to prove that generative phonology is a consequence of structuralist phonology we must:

(i) define in terms of phonemization the operation of variant specification (allophonization), i.e. the operation that converts the phonological representation of a word into its phonetic representation;

(ii) prove that the phonetic representation of any word is derivable from its phonological representation; for this we must first prove that any phoneme has at least one variant;

(iii) formulate generative rules in terms of variant specification.

For reasons of space our argument cannot be completely explicit in a formal way. For this we would also have to enrich Trubetzkoyan phonology by a few distributional concepts. In a general way, though, we are going to show how a generative phonological approach can be accomodated within the structuralist framework of Trubetzkoy's phonology, without going beyond it (cf. Bańczerowski 1990).

Remember that both Zgółka's and Lieb's reformulations of Trubetzkoy's theory operate with phonetic and phonological representations. The phonetic representation of a word can be transformed into its phonological representation by phonemization. This operation associates a given sound with an appropriate phoneme and can be defined within Zgółka's and Lieb's theories. In order to perform the inverse transformation, we need an operation of variant specification to associate a given phoneme in a given environment with exactly one variant (or with all free variants) in this environment. Such an operation can be defined in terms of phonemization, provided that the concepts of sound and phoneme environment are available. This is no problem since distribution is compatible with Trubetzkoyan phonology and is implicit in the phonetic and phonological representations.

Given variant specification, we may now retransform the phonological representation of a word into a corresponding phonetic one. And since each phoneme has at least one variant, the phonetic representation of any word is derivable from its phonological representation.

Obviously, the generative phonology that emerges in this way is a consequence of structuralist phonology. Generative phonology was implicit in structuralist phonology, waiting to be developed and finally making its appearance as a natural complement to the latter. In summary, the relation of variant specification is basic to generative phonology. It can be defined in terms of structuralist concepts. Generative rules can be formulated in terms of variant specification. Therefore, the generative phonological framework does not transcend the structuralist.

Generative phonology, as here considered, could be modified and developed in various directions. The content of rules for variant specification depends on what entities are used in the construction of phonological representations. Such representations may be composed of real and 'imaginary' phonemes and archiphonemes, 'imaginary' in a technical sense. Once the transformation of phonetic representations of words into phonological ones is defined, the inverse transformation is also given, and conversely. Phonemization and variant specification are not independent from each other. In conclusion, then, generative phonology appears to be just one form of structuralism in phonology.

The tragedy of generative phonology is partly due to the inadequate metaphonological (metatheoretic) knowledge of its adherents, which prevented them from correctly evaluating their own linguistic practice: they were not completely aware of what they were really doing (something that is not rare at all in the field of science).

What generativists really achieved in trying to discredit structuralist phonology is, at best, extending its domain in a natural way by developing rules of variant specification, which, as pointed out above, were inherently present in structuralist phonology. Since such rules are inconceivable without distributional information on phonemes, they in fact testify to the perserverance of the distributional tradition. Thus, generative phonologists failed to jump over their structuralist shadow, despite their amazing efforts.

The desire to conquer the phonological market proved irresistible. The theory was given a deceptive mentalist coating so as to justify a phonological practice that was claimed to be new and revolutionary. This was to create the impression that structuralism and mentalism are imcompatible. On closer inspection it is, however, obvious that generative phonological practice is easily reconciled with structuralist practice. Recognizing this fact does not diminish the value of the generative phonological approach but puts it in a proper linguistic perspective. Thus, we do not have the slightest intention to start a crusade against generative phonology but strongly recommend approaching it without prejudice, be it positive or negative. Phonological metatheory must be unprejudiced; it investigates all phonological theories evenly, uncovering both virtues and deficiencies.

7   Concluding remarks

It has been one of our objectives to emphasize the usefulness of the axiomatic method for the new structuralist approach to phonology. In view of the current explosive growth of phonological information and a mushrooming of new phonological theories, the axiomatic method is more important than ever.

The axiomatization of competing theories will result in the elimination of apparent rather than true differences, and will reveal whatever original and essential contributions they may contain; it will contribute to the survival of those theories which are of genuine linguistic value.

Axiomatization may also serve as a kind of Occam's razor for phonological information, eliminating what is superfluous by retrieving shared content from different formulations: "informatio non est multiplicanda praeter necessitatem"; information should be reduced to what is necessary.

The axiomatic method is of course no panacea, no magic wand that may be waived to dissolve all fundamental problems of structuralist phonology: like any other method it has its built-in limitations, of which we are aware. The set of axioms of a theory is not sufficient for proving all its true propositions (cf. Gödel 1931; Tarski and Lindenbaum 1934-35). In addition, the set of axioms needed for a complete characterization of a given domain allows for an indefinite number of interpretations including non-intended ones (cf. Skolem 1941): reality is too rich for full axiomatization. Despite its limitations the axiomatic method has great advantages over other methods of formulating theories, which should be exploited. No better method has yet been discovered both for systematizing knowledge and for alleviating the effects of informational inflation.

In characterizing linguistic structuralism we used a system of basic philosophical and methodological dimensions that also allowed to take into account relationships between structuralist theories of language and theories of neighbouring disciplines. We believe that structuralism itself may serve in linguistics as a system of reference for determining the philosophical and methodological status of any linguistic theory developed either before or after the 'structuralist period' in the narrow historical sense.

We have argued for the persistence of structuralism, giving as reasons, among others, the development of the theory of phonological oppositions; logical reconstructions of classical structuralist theories; and the emergence of generative phonology, which, in fact, is reducible to structuralism.

Changes within the area of structuralism derive mainly from different interpretations of the content of structuralism. For reconstructing fundamental notions, theorems, and definitions, a multi-dimensional philosophical and methodological approach is required.

The heritage of linguistic structuralism has been so versatile and rich that it is bound to remain, for a long time to come, an inexhaustible source of linguistic inspiration.

8 Appendix: Lieb's Nine Principles of New Structuralism

In what follows we would like briefly to discuss some aspects of Lieb's conception of new structuralism as reflected in his Nine Principles, which are of special importance for evaluating the chances of the contemporary reorientation of structuralism. No doubt Lieb's conception deserves to be regarded as a break-through in the history of linguistics in the sense that from now on each structuralist theory of language will have to determine its status with respect to the Nine Principles by either accepting or rejecting them (acceptance and rejection may of course be partial). Consequently we, too, feel an obligation to define our position towards Lieb's approach.

Generally, Lieb's Principles are acceptable to us, provided we do understand them as intended by their author. This proviso seems appropriate because it is a common experience that people may say the same thing and still not mean it. The following comments may serve to clarify our position and also give a more precise interpretation to some of the Principles.

Both Principle 3 and Principle 5 is seen as a consequence of Principles 1 and 2. It would be difficult to show in a formal way that 3 and 5 follow from 1 and 2. Rather, Principle 1 should be interpreted so as to exclude contradiction between 1 and Principles 3 and 5; similarly, for Principle 2.

All Principles have a metascientific character, as is also obvious from Lieb (this vol., Section I). They raise a number of problems. One problem concerns the descriptive adequacy of the Principles with respect to structuralism in a historical sense: to what extent do historically attested linguistic theories, traditionally considered as structuralist, satisfy the requirements of the Nine Principles?

Lieb's Principles formulate conditions for the development of structural linguistics; thus, they map a direction for its development. Hence, the properties of future structuralist theories are no minor issue. Following Lieb, New Structuralism allows for an indefinite number of theories of language; this raises the problem of how they are interrelated. In the present paper an attempt was made to show correspondences between Prague School phonology and generative phonology.

There appears to be a certain dilemma inherent in the Nine Principles. By Principle 1 the objects of linguistics must be the objects actually studied by practising linguists. Considering both the past and the future, should we indeed allow all objects actually studied in structuralist theories into the domain of structuralism? We continue to suspect that a cumulative approach to the domain of structuralism may cause difficulties. Any linguistic object has existence only relative to the theory within which it is either postulated or defined. Even fundamental objects such as the phoneme may have different status in different theories (cf. the concept of phoneme in mentalist or cognitivist theories on the one hand and distributionalist ones on the other).

Linguistic structuralism as it exists is heterogeneous from various points of view. It includes distributionalist theories with a physicalist tinge and a preference for segmentation and classification procedures, as well as glossematics, emphasizing the non-reducibility of the subject matter of linguistics to the level of 'substance'. This highlights the following problem: may we indeed assume a single basis for the subject matter of linguistics which may then be made obligatory for all structuralist theories? A metascientific point of view does not have to favour a cumulative solution by which any category attested in the history of linguistics must be included.

As a matter of fact, Lieb's Nine Principles do restrict, quite radically, the kind of objects allowed as the subject matter of linguistics: they should be abstract, extra-mental, have derived spatiotemporal properties, and should be required by the content of intentional mental states. This restriction raises a basic question: is it adequate with respect to structuralism as it exists, and adequate for its future development? For an answer, past linguistic theories will have to be studied more thoroughly. All structuralist theories of the past may not satisfy the requirements imposed by the Principles on the objects of linguistics; for example, the requirement of derived spatiotemporal properties could be hard to meet in glossematics.

Most of Lieb's Principles determine properties of objects in the domain of theories that conform to new structuralism. The class of these theories is relatively vast; it excludes theories whose domain contains mentalistic objects, but should include certain algebraic theories.

Principles 3 and 4 advocate the autonomy of linguistics, i.e. its non-reducibility to other disciplines such as psychology and biology (and, by extension, to sociology) while establishing a definite relation to such disciplines, Lieb's non-reducibility stance is, of course, very attractive to linguistics, and is, on the whole, compatible with traditional structuralism (Jakobson 1941 could be interpreted as adopting reductionist postulates, which are not entirely absent from structuralist work).

Principle 7 — linguistic diversity, both within and between languages, is fundamental — may be the most controversial, at least for some structuralists. Sociolinguists have frequently attacked structural linguistics based on the *langue-parole* distinction, both for accepting 'Saussure's paradox', arising the postulated homogeneity of *la langue*, and for restricting the subject matter of linguistics to *la langue* in the first place. On this view, postSaussurean structuralist linguistics does not take into account the internal diversity of languages but instead describes the system of languages as being a reconstruction of an ideal object, a homogeneous *langue*. This is the major objection raised by sociolinguists: in focusing on *la langue*, structuralists overlook the internal diversity of languages. Principle 7 thus appears to agree with the stand taken by sociolinguists, rather than with existing structuralist theories. Incorporating Principle 7 into New Structuralism might therefore seriously weaken its links with traditional structuralism.

Lieb's Nine Principles define a scientific perspective that may apply to many different theories. On the whole the Principles do mirror principles present in various approaches within traditional structuralism. The major novel feature of his conception of new structuralism is, however, its metascientific character. Lieb's Principles have not only a historical-descriptive value, they are, first and foremost, projective. The conditions imposed upon linguistic objects may be satisfied by some traditional structuralist theories but not satisfied by others (cf. glossematics).

The metascientific framework proposed by Lieb is essentially a theory of structuralist linguistic theories; it is not directly a theory of language. It remains to be seen which linguistic theories will eventually form the class defined by the Nine Principles.

Bibliography

Adamus, Marian. 1967. *Phonemtheorie und das deutsche Phoneminventar*. Wrocław; Prace Wrocławskiego Towarzystwa Naukowego.
Antal, László. 1978. "Psychologismus und Objektivismus in der Sprachwissenschaft". In: Mohammad Ali Jazayery, Edgar Polomé and Werner Winter (eds). *Linguistic and Literary Studies*. In Honour of Archibald A. Hill. The Hague: Mouton. 51-61.
Anttila, Raimo. 1973. "Onko strukturalismin aika kielitieteessä jo ohi?" *Vitittäjä* 2.109-122.
—. 1978. "Who is structuralist". In: Mohammad Ali Jazayery, Edgar Polomé and Werner Winter (eds). *Linguistic and Literary Studies*. In Honour of Archibald A. Hill. The Hague: Mouton. 63-73.
Apresjan, Yurij. 1966. *Idei i metody sovremennoj strukturnoj lingvistiki*. Moscow: Prosveščenije.
Baltaxe, Christiane A. M. 1978. *Foundations of distinctive feature theory*. Baltimore: University Park Press.
Bańczerowski, Jerzy. 1980. "A contribution to the system-theoretic approach to language". *Lingua Posnaniensis* 23.33-41.
—. 1982. "Über einen formalen Ansatz zur theoretischen Phonologie". In: Theo Vennemann (ed.). *Silben, Segmente, Akzente*. Tübingen: Niemeyer. 9-35.
—. 1983. "On some morphonological relations". *Biuletyn Polskiego Towarzystwa Językoznawczego* 40.25-33.
—. 1985. "Phonetic relations in the perspective of phonetic dimensions". In: Ursula Pieper and Gerhard Stickel (eds). *Studia Linguis-*

tica Diachronica et Synchronica. Berlin/New York/Amsterdam: Mouton de Gruyter. 25-40.
—. 1989. "Undular aspect of phonological space-time". *Studia Phonetica Posnaniensia* 2.
—. 1990. "Is generative phonology consequent upon the structural one?". In: Jacek Fisiak and Stanisław Puppel (eds). *Phonological Explorations*. Amsterdam: John Benjamins. [To appear].
—, Pogonowski, Jerzy, and Tadeusz Zgółka. 1982. *Wstęp do językoznawstwa*. Poznań: Adam Mickiewicz University.
Bartsch, Renate, and Theo Vennemann. 1982. *Grundzüge der Sprachtheorie*. Eine linguistische Einführung. Tübingen: Niemeyer.
Batóg, Tadeusz. 1967. *The Axiomatic Method in Phonology*. London: Routledge and Kegan Paul.
—. 1969. "A reduction in the number of primitive concepts of phonology". *Studia Logica* 25.55-60.
—. 1971a. "On the definition of phonemic basis". *Studia Logica* 27. 117-122.
—. 1971b. "A formal approach to the semantic theory of phoneme". *Studia Logica* 29.27-42.
—. 1978. "On the classical concept of phonemic basis". *Lingua Posnaniensis* 21.53-64.
Bierwisch. Manfred. 1966. "Strukturalismus. Geschichte, Probleme und Methoden". *Kursbuch* 5.77-152.
—. 1971. *Modern Linguistics*. The Hague: Mouton.
Bloch, Bernard. 1948. "A set of postulates for phonemic analysis". *Language* 24.3-46.
Bloomfield, Leonard. 1926. "A set of postulates for the science of language". *Language* 2.153-164.
—. 1933. *Language*. New York: Holt, Rinehart and Winston.
Brainerd, Barron. 1971. *Introduction to the Mathematics of Language Study*. New York: American Elsevier. (Mathematical Linguistics and Automatic Language Processing 8).
—. 1974. "Etic systems and phonological theory". *Cahiers de Linguistique Théoretique et Appliquée* 11.25-34.
Bühler, Karl. 1933. "Die Axiomatik der Sprachwissenschaften". *Kantstudien* 38.24-90.

Bzdęga, Andrzej Z. 1974. "Zum Linearitäts- und Invarianzprinzip der klassischen Phonologie". *Kwartalnik Neofilologiczny* XXI.333-342.

Carr, Philip. 1990. *Linguistic Realities. An Autonomist Metatheory for the Generative Enterprise.* Cambridge etc.: Cambridge University Press. (Cambridge Studies in Linguistics 53).

Chomsky, Noam. 1965. "Some controversial questions in phonological theory". *Journal of Linguistics* 1.97-138.

—, and Morris Halle. 1968. *The Sound Pattern of English.* New York: Harper and Row.

Crothers, John. 1973. *On the Abstractness Controversy.* Bloomington: Indiana University Linguistics Club.

Dingwall, William O. (ed.). 1971. *A Survey of Linguistic Science.* College Park: University of Maryland.

Ehrmann, Jacques (ed.). 1970. *Structuralism.* Garden City, N. Y.: Doubleday. (Anchor Books A 719).

Fischer-Jørgensen, Eli. 1966. "Form and substance in glossematics". *Acta Linguistica Hafniensia* 10.1-33.

—. 1975. *Trends in Phonological Theory.* Copenhagen: Akademisk Forlag.

Fisiak, Jacek. 1976. "Generative phonological contrastive studies". *Kwartalnik Neofilologiczny* 23.119-124.

Fraisse, R. 1982. "Les axiomatiques ne sont elles qu'un jeu?" Penser les mathématiques. *Séminaire de philosophie et mathematiques de l'Ecole normale superieure du Seuil* 44.

Gardies, Jean L. 1985. *Rational Grammar.* Munich/Vienna: Philosophie Verlag.

Giedymin, Jerzy. 1964. *Problemy. Założenia. Rozstrzygnięcia.* Poznań: PTE.

Gleason, Henry. 1961. *An Introduction to Descriptive Linguistics.* New York: Holt, Rinehart and Winston.

Gödel, Kurt. 1931. "Über formal unentscheidbare Sätze der Principia Mathematica und verwandter Systeme". *Monatshefte für Mathematik und Physik* 38.173-198.

Graumann, Carl, and Theo Hermann (eds). 1984. *Karl Bühlers Axiomatik — Fünfzig Jahre Axiomatik der Sprachwissenschaften.* Frankfurt a.M.: Klostermann.

Greenberg, Joseph H. 1959. "An axiomatization of the phonologic aspect of language". In: L. Gross (ed.). *Symposium on Sociological Theory.* Evanston, Ill: Row, Peterson and Co. 437-480.
Guchman, M. M., and V. N. Jarceva (eds). 1964. *Osnovnye napravlenija strukturalizma.* Moscow: Nauka.
Gussmann, Edmund. 1980. *Introduction to Phonological Analysis.* Warsaw: Państwowe Wydawnictwo Naukowe.
Harris, Zellig S. 1941. Review of Trubetzkoy 1939. *Language* 17.345-349.
—. 1951. *Methods in Structural Linguistics.* Chicago: University of Chicago Press.
Hymes, Dell H. 1972. "On communicative competence". In: J. B. Pride and J. Holmes (eds). *Sociolinguistics.* Harmondsworth: Penguin. (Penguin Modern Linguistic Readings).
Itkonen, Esa. 1978. *Grammatical Theory and Metascience.* Amsterdam: Benjamins.
Jakobson, Roman. 1941. *Kindersprache, Aphasie und allgemeine Lautgesetze.* Uppsala. (Språkvetenskapliga Sällskapets i Uppsala Förhandlingar, 1940-42).
—. 1961. *Selected Writings I: Phonological Studies.* The Hague: Mouton.
—. 1971. "The Kazań school of Polish linguistics and its place in the international development of phonology". In: *Selected Writings II: Word and Language.* The Hague: Mouton. 394-428.
—, and Morris Halle. 1956. *Fundamentals of Language.* The Hague: Mouton.
Jankowsky, Kurt. 1972. *The Neogrammarians.* A Reevaluation of Their Place in the Development of Linguistic Science. The Hague/ Paris: Mouton.
Jassem, Wiktor. 1978. "On the distributional analysis of pitch phenomena". *Language and Speech* 21:4.362-372.
Jones, Daniel. 1950. *The Phoneme: Its Nature and Use.* Cambridge: Heffer.
Kamp, R. 1977. *Axiomatische Sprachtheorie.* Wissenschaftstheoretische Untersuchungen zum Konstitutionsproblem der Einzelwissenschaften am Beispiel der Sprachwissenschaftstheorie Karl Bühlers. Berlin: Duncker & Humblot.

Kanger, S. 1964 . "The notion of a phoneme". *Statistical Methods in Linguistics* 3.43-48.
Katz, Jerold J. 1981. *Language and Other Abstract Objects*. London: Blackwell.
Kiefer, Ferenc. 1968. *Mathematical Linguistics in Eastern Europe*. New York: Elsevier.
Kiparsky, Paul. 1972. "Explanation in phonology". In: S. Peters (ed.). *Goals in Linguistic Theory*. New Jersey: Prentice Hall. 189-227.
—. 1974. "From paleogrammarians to neogrammarians". In: Dell Hymes (ed.). *Studies in the History of Linguistics*. Traditions and Paradigms. Bloomington: Indiana University. 331-334.
Kmita, Jerzy. 1974. "Marxism and the controversy between realism and instrumentalism". *Studia Metodologiczne* 11.5-33.
Koerner, E. F. K. 1972. "Hermann Paul and synchronic linguistics". *Lingua* 29.274-307.
—. 1975. "European structuralism: Early beginnings". *Current Trends in Linguistics* 13.707-827.
Kortlandt, Frederik H. H. 1972. *Modelling the Phoneme: New Trends in East European Phonemic Theory*. The Hague: Mouton.
Lakatos, Imre. 1970. "Falsification and the methodology of scientific research programmes". In: Imre Lakatos and A. Musgrave (eds). *Criticism and the Growth of Knowledge*. Cambridge: Cambridge University Press. 135-164.
—. 1971. "History of science and its rational reconstructions". In: R. Buck and R. Cohen (eds). *Boston Studies in the Philosophy of Science* 8. Dordrecht: Reidel. 55-98.
Lane, Michael. 1970. *Introduction to Structuralism*. New York: Basic Books.
Lass, Roger. 1981. *On Explaining Language Change*. Cambridge: Cambridge University Press.
Lepschy, Giulio G. 1970. *A Survey of Structural Linguistics*. London: Faber and Faber.
Lieb, Hans-Heinrich. 1974. 1976. "Grammars as theories: the case for axiomatic grammar". *Theoretical Linguistics* 1.39-115; 3.1-98.
—. 1979. "Some basic concepts of Trubetzkoy's phonology". *Forum Linguisticum* 4:1.1-25.

—. 1986. "Language is external — a reply to Helmut Schnelle". *Theoretical Linguistics* 13:3.239-255.
—. 1988. "Auditives Segmentieren: Eine sprachtheoretische Grundlegung". In: H.-H. Lieb (ed.). 1988. 147-192.
—. (ed.). 1988. *BEVATON — Berliner Verfahren zur auditiven Tonhöhenanalyse*. Tübingen: Niemeyer. (Linguistische Abeiten 205).
Lomtev, Timofej Petrovič. 1972. *Fonologia sovremennogo ruskogo jazyka*. Moscow: Vysšaja Škola.
Lyons, John. 1962. "Phonemic and non-phonemic phonology: some typological reflections". In: V. Makkai (ed.). *Phonological Theory*. New York: Holt, Rinehart and Winston. 275-281.
Maher, J. Peter. 1977. *Papers on Language Theory and History*. Part I: *Creation and Tradition in Language*. Amsterdam/Philadelphia: John Benjamins. (Current Issues in Linguistic Theory 3).
Marcus, S. 1963. "Un model matematic al fonemului". *Studii și Cercetări Matematice* 14.405-421.
—. 1966. "Le modelage mathématique en phonologie. Méthodes, résultats, signification". *Cahiers de Linguistique Théorique et Appliquée* 3.109-116.
—. 1967. *Introduction mathématique à la linguistique structurale*. The Hague: Mouton.
—, and E. Vasiliu. 1960. "Mathématique et phonologie. La théorie des graphes et le consonantism de la langue roumaine". *Revue roumaine de mathématiques pures et appliquées* 5.319-340, 681-703.
Morciniec, Norbert. 1968. *Distinktive Spracheinheiten im Niederländischen und Deutschen*. Wrocław: Ossolineum.
Mulder, J. W. F. 1968. *Sets and Relations in Phonology*. An Axiomatic Approach to the Description of Speech. Oxford: Clarendon Press.
—. 1989. *Foundations of Axiomatic Functionalism*. Berlin: Mouton de Gruyter.
Nebeský, L. 1966a. "K odnoj matematičeskoj modeli fonemy". *Revue roumaine de mathématiques pures et appliquées* 11.453-456.
—. 1966b. "On the notion of relevant features". *The Prague Bulletin of Mathematical Linguistics* 6.35-43.
Newmeyer, Frederick J. 1980. *Linguistic Theory in America*. New York: Academic Press.

Pak, T. Y. 1971. "Convertibility between distinctive features and phonemes". *Linguistics* 66.97-114.
Pateman, T. 1987. *Language in Mind and Language in Society.* Oxford: Clarendon Press.
Paul, Hermann. 1880. *Prinzipien der Sprachgeschichte.* Halle (Saale): Niemeyer.
Peterson, Gordon E., and F. Harary. 1961. "Foundations of phonemic theory". In: *On the Structure of Language and Its Mathematical Aspects. Proceedings of the 12th Symposium on Applied Mathematics.* Providence, R. I.: American Mathematical Society.
Piaget, Jean. 1968. *Le structuralisme.* Paris: Presses Universitaires de France. (Que sais-je? 1311).
Pilch, Herbert. ^{3}1974. *Phonemtheorie.* 1. Teil. Basel, etc.: S. Karger.
—. 1986. "The function-substance antinomy in phonetics". *Zeitschrift für Phonetik, Sprachwissenschaft und Kommunikationsforschung* 39:3.339-356.
Pogonowski, Jerzy. 1985. "A contribution to the theory of linguistic oppositions". *Lingua Posnaniensis* 28.117-135.
—. 1987. "Similarity relations as a tool for the description of sound systems". *Studia Phonetica Posnaniensia* 1.69-79.
Popper, Karl R. 1959. *The Logic of Scientific Discovery.* London: Hutchinson.
—. 1972. *Objective Knowledge.* Oxford: Clarendon Press.
Postal, Paul. 1968. *Aspects of Phonological Theory.* New York: Harper and Row.
Qvarnström, Bengt-Olov. 1979. *Formalisations of Trubetzkoy's Phonology.* Åbo: Åbo Akademi. (Publications of the Research Institute of the Åbo Akademi Foundation 42).
Revzin, I. I. 1977. *Sovremennaja strukturnaja lingvistika.* Problemy i metody. Moscow: Nauka.
Rubach, Jerzy. 1976. "The concept of an underlying representation". *Biuletyn Polskiego Towarzystwa Językoznawczego* 34.101-109.
Ruszkiewicz, Piotr (ed.). 1978. *Phonology.* Part I: *An Anthology of European Structuralism.* Katowice: Uniwersytet Śląski.
—. (ed.). 1981. *Phonology.* Part II: *An Anthology of Generative Phonology.* Katowice: Uniwersytet Śląski.

Sabol, Ján. 1983. "The interrelation between a phone, a phoneme and a morpheme". *Prague Studies in Mathematical Linguistics* 8.173-177.
Sadock, J. M. 1974. *Towards a Linguistic Theory of Speech Acts*. New York: Holt.
Saussure, Ferdinand de. 1916. *Cours de linguistique générale*. Lausanne/Paris: Payot.
Schaff, Adam. 1964. *Sprache und Erkenntnis*. Vienna, etc.: Europa Verlag.
—. 1972. *Gramatyka generatywna a koncepcja idei wrodzonych*. Warsaw: Książka i Wiedza.
—. 1975. *Szkice o strukturalizmie*. Warsaw: Książka i Wiedza.
Schane, Sanford A. 1971. "The phoneme revisited". *Language* 47.503-521.
Schiwy, Günther. 1969. *Der französische Strukturalismus*. Mode, Methode, Ideologie, mit einem Textanhang. Hamburg: Rowohlt. (Rowohlts Deutsche Enzyklopädie 310-311).
Skolem, T. 1941. "Sur la portée du théorème de Skolem-Löwenheim". *Les Entretiens de Zürich sur les Fondements des Sciences Mathématiques*. 25-47.
Šaumjan, S. K. 1968. *Problems of Theoretical Phonology*. The Hague: Mouton.
Šreider, Yu. A. 1972. "Topologičeskije modeli jazyka". In: *Problemy strukturnoj linguistiki 1971*. Moscow: Nauka. 47-67.
Tarski, Alfred, and Adolf Lindenbaum. 1934-35. "Über die Beschränktheit der Ausdrucksmittel deduktiver Theorien". In: *Ergebnisse eines mathematischen Kolloquiums*. Vol. 5. 15-22. [Translation in: Tarski, Alfred. 1966. *Logic, Semantics, Metamathematics*. Oxford: Clarendon Press. 384-392].
Trubetzkoy, N. S. 1939. *Grundzüge der Phonologie*. (Travaux du Cercle Linguistique de Prague 7). [Reprinted Göttingen: Vandenhoeck & Ruprecht, 1958 etc.].
—. 1958. *Anleitung zu phonologischen Beschreibungen*. Göttingen: Vandenhoeck & Ruprecht.
—. 1969. *Principles of Phonology*. Berkeley: Univ. of California Press.
Ungeheuer, G. 1959. "Das logistische Fundament binärer Phonemklassifikationen". *Studia Linguistica* 13.69-97.

Uspenskij, V. A. 1964. "Odna model dlja ponjatija fonemy". *Voprosy Jazykoznanija* 13:6.39-53.
Vennemann, Theo. 1972. "On the theory of syllabic phonology". *Linguistische Berichte* 18.1-18.
—. 1980. "Universalphonologie als partielle Sprachtheorie". In: H.-H. Lieb (ed.). *Oberflächensyntax und Semantik*. Tübingen: Niemeyer. 125-133.
—. 1986. *Neuere Entwicklungen in der Phonologie*. Berlin, etc.: Mouton de Gruyter.
—. 1988. *Preference Laws for Syllable Structure and the Explanation of Sound Change*. Berlin, etc. Mouton de Gruyter.
Verburg, P. 1974. "Vicissitudes of paradigms". In: Dell Hymes (ed.). *Studies in the History of Linguistics: Traditions and Paradigms*. Bloomington: Indiana University. 191-230.
Wójcicki, Ryszard. 1982. *Wykłady z metodologii nauk*. Warsaw: Państwowe Wydawnictwo Naukowe.
Zgółka, Tadeusz. 1976. *O strukturalnym wyjaśnianiu faktów językowych*. Warsaw/Poznań: Państwowe Wydawnictwo Naukowe.
—. 1980. *Język, kompetencja, gramatyka*. Studium z metodologii lingwistyki. Warsaw: Państwowe Wydawnictwo Naukowe.

The Structuralist Heritage in Natural Morphology

Wolfgang U. Wurzel
Forschungsschwerpunkt Allgemeine Sprachwissenschaft, Berlin

1 Natural morphology

The approach to grammar known today as 'natural morphology' began to emerge in the mid-seventies in a series of studies by Dressler, Mayerthaler and Wurzel.[1] It took as a model the concept of naturalness in phonology as developed in different ways by Stampe and Donegan-Miller on the one hand, and Bailey on the other.[2] While the first studies in natural morphology remained rather heavily indebted to their point of departure, the approach increasingly developed its own theoretical profile, shared by natural phonology in Europe which has been pursued in close connection with natural morphology so that, strictly speaking, there is a joint approach of natural morphology and phonology based on a uniform concept of naturalness. It has recently been shown, in particular by Stein, that such a concept can also be extended to syntax.[3] I will, however, restrict myself to the problems of natural morphology, which seem particularly relevant to the problems discussed at the Round Table.

I begin by a brief characterization of natural morphology, omitting many points, not all of them inessential:

(1) The theoretical core and point of departure of natural morphology is the assumption that morphological phenomena can be evaluated by their naturalness or markedness. Such evalua-

tion does not treat naturalness and markedness as either-or phenomena. Rather, they give rise to a graded scale of maximally natural/unmarked to maximally unnatural/marked.

(2) In both its structure and change, the morphology of a language is subject to universal principles of morphological naturalness (markedness principles, preference principles) that relate to different parameters of morphological structuring. Principles of system-independent naturalness may be distinguished from principles of system-dependent naturalness. The first class includes, among others, the principles of constructional iconicity, the principle of morphosemantic transparency, the principle of uniformity and distinctiveness, and the principle of serialization iconicity; the second class includes the principle of inflectional-class motivation and the principle of system congruity. Accordingly, there is no undifferentiated naturalness/markedness of morphological phenomena but relativization to individual principles of morphological naturalness.

(3) It is assumed that, due to specific properties of morphology (its smallest units, the morphemes, are genuine language signs), the morphological naturalness principles are motivated semiotically. Thus semiotics as a general theory of signs assumes the role of a metatheory for morphology.

(4) Although uniformly motivated semiotically, the various principles of morphological naturalness relate to parameters of structuring that are largely independent of each other and may therefore point in different directions: a phenomenon that is natural with respect to one naturalness principle can be marked with respect to another, and vice versa. This is how intramorphological contradictions or conflicts of naturalness develop. Typically, there will be a conflict between principles of system-independent and of system-dependent naturalness, e.g. the naturalness principles of constructional iconicity and those of system-congruity. There appears to exist a fixed hierarchy of priorities of naturalness principles by which intramorphological naturalness conflicts may be resolved in a

uniform way and which, in particular, gives priority to principles of system-dependent naturalness over those of system-independent naturalness.

(5) Natural morphology forms an integral part of a conception of grammar whose starting-point is the fact that each component of the language system is shaped by specific naturalness principles, which results in a relative autonomy of individual components; compare morphology, with its semiotically motivated naturalness principles, and phonology, with principles that are motivated articulatorily or perceptually. Because of this difference, morphological and phonological naturalness principles necessarily point in different directions, and contradictions or conflicts of naturalness will arise between the components. The naturalness principles of morphology and of phonology are not integrated into a (uniform) hierarchy of priorities. Since morphological and phonological principles are related to different groups of facts, a naturalness principle of one type may prevail irrespectively of the principles of the other type, which results in a continous struggle between phonological and morphological principles, with changing 'directions of attack'.

(6) Naturalness principles (of any component) have the character of universals that are tendencies, or more strictly speaking, they are *Gesetzmäßigkeiten* having the character of tendencies, i.e. statistical laws in the epistemological sense of "law".[4] It is really these universals that are of interest to the theory of grammar because, differently from postulated 'strict' universals, their functioning can be observed and described.

(7) Natural morphology construes the language system and its components as a continuously changing entity that develops through time as a structure in progress. Accordingly, it rejects as inadequate any strict dichotomy of synchrony and diachrony. The essential properties of natural languages are not covered unless the description of languages also includes language change, one of their necessary characteristics. It is

in language change that the effects of naturalness principles are most clearly revealed. That is why facts of language change, far from being 'external' evidence, play a crucial role in the theory and practice of natural morphology.

(8) Language change as a rule proceeds not in an abrupt but in a gradual manner, not as a sudden transition of language units from one class to another but as a change of individual properties. This means that in natural languages we do not normally have an opposition between disjoint classes with clearly marked boundaries but gradual transitions between classes. Therefore, beside prototypical representatives of classes, there are also transition phenomena with properties characteristic of entities of different classes (compare e.g. the distinction between inflection and derivation, between monomorphemic and bimorphemic words, between nouns and adjectives, etc.).

(9) Natural morphology, as characterized in (1) to (8), has considerable explanatory potential covering both synchronous and diachronous relationships. This potential derives from considering two types of data: first, frequency of occurrence of various morphological phenomena in the languages of the world and implicative relationships between them and second, the occurrence, course, and results of morphological changes.

2 Natural morphology and generative grammar

The characteristics of natural morphology obviously imply a number of essential differences between natural morphology and generative grammar in any of its varieties, differences whose careful specification would require a separate study. The following three, which are of special importance, may here be mentioned:

(1) While natural morphology assumes that the nature of language is expressed first and foremost in the naturalness principles as universal tendencies, it is well known that generative grammar defines the nature of language by strict universals. Unfortunately, there are very few truly strict universals in

morphology, and most of these have little explanatory value. Furthermore, universal tendencies have the advantage of explaining language change, which is impossible by definition for strict universals. Hypothetical universal tendencies are easily verified through language change, whereas strict universals may be justified only indirectly by lack of falsification. Naturalness principles, being tendencies, may contradict each other, which is, of course, ruled out for strict universals.

(2) For natural morphology language change follows from the continuous interaction of the naturalness principles: thus, it results directly from the very nature of the language system. Any spoken language is subject to such change. Therefore, explaining the grammatical aspect of language change requires no additional principles. For natural morphology, the distinction between synchrony and diachrony has no basis in language itself; it is only of a methodological nature. An adequate theory of grammar must therefore be 'panchronic' (using a somewhat outdated term). In contradistinction, it is well known that generative grammar postulates a strictly synchronic theory of grammar where language change does not result from the very nature of the language system but somehow affects it 'from outside'. What appears as normal on this view is not change but persistence.

(3) There are also differences in the classification of language units. Natural morphology, as stated above, starts from the fact of gradual transitions between classes of language units, allowing a given unit to be in one class with respect to one property and in another class with respect to another. Generative grammar, on the other hand, assumes strictly disjoint classes where the class membership of units is uniquely determined.

3 The structuralist heritage

Although natural morphology differs in its basic assumptions not only from generative grammar but also from other contemporary schools of grammar, it is of course not an entirely 'new' development but follows certain linguistic traditions. It continues ideas and conceptions that have been discussed in linguistics again and again from various points of view. Interestingly, such ideas and conceptions were discussed as early as in Plato's "Kratylos", one of the earliest documented attempts at a scientific treatment of language. In more recent times, Schleicher, Paul, Sapir, and Skalička should be mentioned as some of the linguists who have had a lasting influence on natural morphology.[5]

Last but not least among the traditions that have influenced the basic assumptions of natural morphology, is European structuralism, especially through its basic assumption that not all morphological phenomena occurring in languages are 'equally good' but that some may be more preferred, i.e. more natural, than others. It is above all the trend-setting ideas of two linguists that must here be mentioned, the ideas of Jakobson and Coseriu, which natural morphology could follow directly, as will now be explained in greater detail but still omitting a number of interesting prints.

3.1 Jakobson: semiotics — motivation — iconicity

After treating questions of semiotics, iconicity and motivation in natural language over a period of decades,[6] Jakobson summarized his views on these problems in a work with the title, certainly not arbitrary, "Quest for the essence of language" (1965, republished in *Selected writings II* 1971). The influence of Jakobson's ideas has been most pronounced in the theory of language change and in historical linguistics (Andersen, Anttila), and in the research on universals and typology (Greenberg and coworkers).[7]

In his "Quest", Jakobson uses Peirce's theory of signs to throw light, once again, on the old Platonic question concerning the relationship between the meaning and the form of language units: is it "natural" (φύσει) or "conventional" (θέσει)? and in this context he also discusses Saussure's concept of arbitrariness. He arrives at the result (suggested by the title) that the various motivation phenomena concern "the essence of language". Even if natural language is mainly symbolic, the iconic and indexical components of language signs should not be underestimated, let alone, disregarded if the essence of language is to be accounted for. Following Jakobson, morphology along with syntax is in that area of the language system where motivation is definitely prototypical: "Yet on a plain, lexical level the interplay of sound and meaning has a latent and virtual character, whereas in syntax and morphology (both inflection and derivation) the intrinsic, diagrammatic correspondence between the signans and signatum is patent and obligatory" (1971:355). Saussure's dogma of the fundamental importance of arbitrariness, claimed to dominate, along with linearity, the entire mechanism of language, thus proves untenable to Jakobson.

True enough, while emphasizing arbitrariness, Saussure also stresses the importance of the relative motivation of complex language signs, and for him, too, the domain of relative motivation is morphology (excluding syntax). Thus languages with an elaborate morphology (such as Sanskrit) exhibit a high degree of relative motivation. Again, for Saussure there is no language without relative motivation. On the whole, though, Jakobson is right in his criticism of Saussure for whom the best sign is, admittedly, a completely arbitrary one, that is, a symbolic sign, claimed to be best suited for an optimal semiotic process.[8] Natural morpholoy has since proved that the opposite is true.

Jakobson discusses mainly phenomena of diagrammatic iconicity, mostly in morphology, partly also in syntax. Diagrammatic iconicity functions according to the general principle of the diagram: "The relations in the signans correspond to the relations in the signatum" (1971: 350). Following Peirce, diagrams are "veridically iconic, *naturally analogous* to the thing represented" (l.c., emphasis mine, W. U. W.). Jakobson gives examples for nearly all types of diagrammatic iconicity now studied in the framework of natural morphology; naturally, he does not yet determine their specific properties nor does he provide a classification or systematization. The phenomena of diagrammatic iconicity are considered already by him as "universalistic propensities" (1971:350), that is, as universal tendencies. There is a more detailed discussion by Jakobson of the following types of diagrammatic iconicity (here denoted by terms from natural morphology).

(a) Uniformity and transparency
Uniformity and transparency are emphasized not only as essential characteristics of any morphological structuring — there would be practically no morphology without them — but are also construed as essentially gradual, in opposition to

Saussure, who allows only language units that are either completely arbitrary or else are motivated, i.e. partly motivated. Thus, Jakobson points out that Saussure's well-known French example *berger* is not completely arbitrary since it clearly contains the suffix *-er* that also occurs in *vacher* etc.; it is, therefore, partly transparent. There may also be partial uniformity (identity) of language signs; for instance, all Polish instrumental morphemes have the phonological feature of nasality in their last segments, be they consonants or vowels.

(b) Constructional iconicity

"Morphology is rich in examples of alternate signs which exhibit an equivalent relation between their signantia and signata. Thus in various Indo-European languages, the positive, comparative, and superlative degrees of adjectives show a gradual increase in the number of phonemes, e.g. *high — higher — highest, altus — altior — altissimus*. In this way the signantia reflect the gradation gamut of the signata" (1971:352). Jakobson cites as another example conjugation in French and Polish, where the plural form of each person is longer than a corresponding singular form. More generally, and with reference to markedness, Jakobson had stated already at Greenberg's 1961 universals conference (published in 1963): "In general, the 'iconic symbols' of language display a particularly clear-cut universalistic propensity. Thus, within a grammatical correlation the zero affix cannot be steadily assigned to the marked category and a 'non-zero' (real) affix to the unmarked category"; and: "Briefly, language tends to avoid any chiasmus between pairs of unmarked/marked categories on the one hand, and pairs of zero/non-zero affixes (or of simple/compound grammatical forms) on the other hand" (1963:213). As Greenberg himself had shown at this conference by way of his two famous universals of number and case symbolization (universals 35 and 38), Jakobson's important theses on the role of constructional iconicity stand the test of a comprehensive corpus of languages (see Greenberg 1963:74f).

(c) Serialization iconicity
Serialization iconicity is first established for syntax: "The temporal order of speech events tends to mirror the order of narrated events in time or in rank" (1971:350). Starting from this fact, Jakobson demonstrates that there is serialization iconicity also within the word, that is, in the area of morphology. For instance, the substantial semantic contrast between word roots as lexical morphemes and affixes as grammatical ones is expressed in their different position in the word (1971:352). Once again, reference to Greenberg is appropriate, who showed by his universals that there are more far-reaching and more specific relationships of serialization iconicity in natural languages: see his universals 28 and 39: "If both the derivation and inflection follow the root, or they both precede the root, the derivation is always between the root and the inflection"; and: "Where morphemes of both number and case are present and both follow or both precede the noun base, the expression of number almost always comes between the noun base and the expression of case" (Greenberg 1963:73ff). Note that Greenberg offers no explicit iconic evaluation of these phenomena.

(d) Morpheme class iconicity
The phenomenon of morpheme class iconicity is treated by Jakobson in connection with serialization iconicity and is described as follows: "... affixes, particularly inflectional suffixes, in languages where they exist, habitually differ from the other morphemes by a restricted and selected use of phonemes and their combinations" (1971:352). For example, just four of 24 Russian obstruents occur in inflectional suffixes.

(e) Diagrammatic alternations in stems
"There are ... specimens of analogous grammatical 'diagrams' with a manifestly iconic value in the alternants themselves" (1971:355). Manifestations adduced by Jakobson are reduplications of stems in plural, iterative, durative and augmentative forms, and occurrence of diffuse (high) vowels in the formation of diminutives and of compact (low) vowels in augmentatives.

For the sake of completeness, it should also be mentioned that in addition to diagrammatic iconicity, sound iconicity/sound symbolism is also counted among the motivation phenomena by Jakobson though not considered of equal relevance to natural languages because of its comparatively "latent and virtual" nature (1971:355; see also above).

Jakobson did not himself apply, in a systematic way, his ideas on the topics of semiotics, motivation, and iconicity to language change. This was done by several of his disciples, highly creditably so by Andersen and Anttila whose conceptions of language change are crucially based on Jakobson's (and Peirce's) semiotic concepts, as evidenced by a typical statement from Anttila: "... most change is due to the iconic features of a language" (1972:19).

All of Jakobson's ideas outlined above, each embodying a deep insight into the essence and functioning of morphology, have in one form or other found their way into the theory of natural morphology, partly by direct and conscious reference to Jakobson, and partly by resuming his ideas as further developed and systematized by linguists like Andersen, Anttila, and Greenberg. In addition, some insights of Jakobson's were literally 'rediscovered' by representatives of the emerging approach of natural morphology. It was subsequently noticed with satisfaction rather than disappointment that natural morphologists had been following in the tracks of a great linguist all along.

Reconsidering the crucial role of iconic phenomena for morphological structuring, emphasized by Jakobson over and over again, was one of the points of departure of natural morphology. As an important example, take Mayerthaler's book *Morphologische Natürlichkeit* (published only in 1981 but written in large part as early as in 1975/77). Mayerthaler assigns absolute priority to constructional iconicity, defined as the mapping of a semantic markedness asymmetry of two morphological categories onto a constructional symbolization asymmetry of the same categories (1981:23). Especially noteworthy is Mayerthaler's attempt to provide a theoretical justification for the semantic markedness of categories, mainly based on plausibility considerations in the case of Jakobson. Mayerthaler also showed that constructional iconicity is a gradual phenomenon. For him, morphological naturalness is essentially constituted by constructional iconicity, uniformity, and transparency; in addition, reduplication and phonetic iconicity are treated as natural morphological means. Within natural morphology it has been Dressler above all who examined in detail uniformity and transparency, showing, in particular, the gradual character of these phenomena and working out the structure of the relevant scales; see his *Morphonology* (1985). Serialization iconicity and morpheme class iconicity, discussed only briefly (among other naturalness principles) in Wurzel's paper "Zur Determiniertheit morphologischer Erscheinungen" (1985), remain to be studied in detail. For a natural morphology treatment of diagrammatic alternations in stems, Wurzel's Paper "Was bezeichnet der Umlaut im Deutschen?" (1984b) may be mentioned where it is shown that German 'grammatical umlaut' symbolizes the semantic markedness of categories. The motivation phenomena to which Jakobson drew attention are effective over the morphological systems of arbitrary languages; they are thus fundamental to what would be called, from a current point of view, "system-independent naturalness".

3.2 Coseriu: system dependence — system congruity

The neo-grammarians, especially Paul, had a notion of *Systemzwang* for explaining certain 'analogous' changes, particularly in morphology, relating them to more general properties of the language system in question: general properties of the language system that take precedence over individual phenomena shape individual morphological phenomena. By this notion the neo-grammarians tried to grasp a major factor of morphological structuring without yet realizing its true importance; there is no precise determination of *Systemzwang*, let alone a definition; the term is partly used just to refer to detailed analogies.

There was a new approach to such phenomena offered by Hjelmslev, be it with different aims, through his distinction of system and norm (as part of the system/norm/use triad), meant to resolve the antinomy of synchrony and diachrony. This approach was resumed, worked out in detail, and systematized by Coseriu, especially in his two basic studies *Sincronía, diacronía e historia* (1958), translated into German as *Synchronie, Diachronie und Geschichte* (1974), and "Sincronía, diacronía y tipología" (1965), German version "Synchronie, Diachronie und Typologie" (1975).

It is the distinction of system and norm in grammar that is of crucial importance. Coseriu's notion of norm covers anything realized by tradition (1975:141) at a given point of time and is recognized by the language community, whereas his notion of system covers the basic structural properties of the language, its general grammatical structure. The system does contain phenomena actually occurring at a given point of time but is still a system of possibilities. It embodies the grammatical potential of the language, put differently, the rules that underlie the realization of language phenomena, more specifically, the productive rules in their general form, i.e. without the restrictions and exceptions that are due to the norm. In his 1965 study Coseriu supplemented his norm and system by the notion of language type. This comprises "die funktionalen Prinzipien, d. h. die Verfahrenstypen und die Kategorien von Oppositionen des Systems, und stellt somit die zwischen den einzelnen Teilen des Systems feststellbare funktionelle Kohärenz dar" (1975:141). Also, the language type contains not only phenomena occurring in the system but "auch Verfahren, die im System noch nicht existieren, wohl aber möglich wären, in Übereinstimmung mit schon als solchen vorhandenen Kategorien der Sprachtechnik" (1975:142). In this way, the language type embodies the typological potential of language. It comprises the general typological structure of language, the general principles underlying the (productive) rules. For Coseriu, all three "Stufen der Grammatikalität" (1975:141) are objectively existing levels of language structure. Typically, the relationship between system and norm is highly asymmetrical in many languages. On the one hand, the system is wider than the norm because it contains not only what is actually realized, i.e. the norm, but also what is possible due to structural properties (productive rules). From this angle, not all grammatical phenomena covered by the system are realized by the norm. On the other hand, the system is narrower than the norm because it contains not only grammatical phenomena that conform to the system but also archaic elements that no longer conform to the system but reflect its earlier states. Language type and language system are related in a similar way. The asymmetry of system and norm is characteristic of inflecting (fusing) languages, which as a rule have a non-uniform and complex structure. In comparison, (truly) agglutinative languages have a uniform and less complex structure; in such a language anything that is possible, i.e. inheres in the system, is also realizable, i.e. is in agreement with the norm. The asymmetries between levels are an important reservoir for language change: the norm tends to utilize the possibilities of the system, the system tends to utilize the possibilities of the language type. Thus, anything gravitating towards the norm is also contained in the system, and anything gravitating towards the system is also contained in the language type. More generally: "Was vom Standpunkt einer bestimmten strukturellen Ebene her diachronisch ('Wandel') ist, erscheint auf einer anderen, höheren Ebene als synchronisch ('Funktionieren')" (1975:143), a statement from which it also appears why language change, at least from a certain point of view, is predictable.

It was for developing the concept of system-dependent naturalness that Coseriu's theory of the three levels of grammaticalness became fruitful in natural morphology: languages turned out to abound quite regularly in morphological changes that cannot be explained by system-independent naturalness as based on iconicity (and used in its 'classical' form in Mayerthaler 1981), worse, that even run counter to it. Natural morphology seemed to fail in its explanatory claim. Closer study revealed that changes of this type are due to the nature of an individual language. They can be explained if the specific properties of a given morphological system are taken into account: morphological constructions or construction types that are sufficiently predominant in the system are extended to new instances. There are two main types of changes that must be distinguished. The first type is an extension of grammatical rules to new instances, the second type an extension of more general structural properties. We are obviously dealing here with phenomena that made Coseriu establish his norm/system/language type triad. Using Coseriu's terminology we may say that in the first type of change potential forms that are inherent in the system (due to the existence of appropriate rules) are moved to the norm; in the second type of change, structural principles inherent in the language type give rise to new rules, and the forms generated by these rules are then moved to the norm. In natural morphology these phenomena are called class stability (or class motivation) vs. system congruity. As an effect of the principle of class stability, forms from unstable construction classes (e.g., inflectional classes) tend to be replaced by forms from stable ones; and as an effect of the principle of system congruity, morphological phenomena that do not conform to higher-order structural properties defining the system, tend to be replaced by morphological phenomena that do conform. Class stability and system-defining structural properties can be determined independently, due to quantitative relationships in the morphological system. Corresponding changes are thus predetermined in part by the morphological system. Class stability and system-congruity are principles of system-dependent naturalness. Being principles of naturalness, they are universal, just as the principles of system-independent naturalness are. They differ from the latter in a dependence on specific properties of individual languages; it is such properties that determine the direction in which the principles take effect. Just as the various types of iconicity, class stability and system-congruity are motivation phenomena; they are cases of 'systemic motivation'. Coseriu has contributed much to our understanding of what is now called 'system-dependent naturalness'. Partly proceeding from his inspirational ideas, Wurzel introduced into natural morphology 'systemic motivation' in a number of studies (see esp. his *Flexionsmorphologie und Natürlichkeit*, 1984a) where it was also shown that system-dependent naturalness prevails over system-independent naturalness in cases of conflict. Principles of system-dependent naturalness are therefore crucial to morphological structuring.

4 Conclusion

By a discussion of Jakobson's ideas of iconicity and Coseriu's concept of the norm/system/language type triad, it was shown that European structuralism has done much to develop 'natural' positions in grammar and particularly, in morphology. It should not be surprising that these positions should have been rediscovered and adopted, first, by linguists such as Andersen and Anttila, and then by the adherents of natural morphology as it began to emerge since the mid-seventies. 'Postgenerative rethinking' could not but focus on characteristics of natural language that had been ignored or underestimated by generative grammar, and it was precisely such characteristics that had been studied by European structuralists. In this way 'natural morphologists' came to pay attention to the structuralist heritage, or as Andersen put it (1980a:

201): "Natural theory is moving towards traditional structuralist positions". I submit that this is a move ahead.

Notes

1. Of course not all works of natural morphology can be listed here but compare, in particular, Mayerthaler (1981), Wurzel (1984a) and Dressler (1985). A fair overview is given in Dressler, Mayerthaler, Panagl and Wurzel (1987). For further relevant studies, see the bibliographies of these books.
2. Compare especially Donegan and Stampe (1979) and Bailey (1973).
3. Compare especially Stein (1985).
4. Compare Hörz and Wessel (1983:107ff).
5. Cf. Wurzel (1987), for Plato's "Kratylos", and Wurzel (1988), for Paul.
6. Remember that Jakobson is also one of the 'fathers' of the markedness concept. See the relevant studies listed in Jakobson (1962).
7. Compare, on the one hand, Anttila (1972) and Andersen (1975) and (1980a) and, on the other, Greenberg (1963) and (1978).
8. For Saussure's concept of arbitrariness and motivation in language, see Saussure (1931:79ff and 156ff).

References

Andersen, H. 1975. "Towards a typology of change: Bifurcating changes and binary relations". In: J. M. Anderson and Ch. Jones (eds). *Historical Linguistics*. Amsterdam: North Holland. 2.18-62.
—. 1980a. "Morphological change: towards a typology". In: J. Fisiak (ed.). *Historical Morphology*. The Hague/Paris/New York: Mouton. 1-50.
—. 1980b. "Typology and genetics of language: Summing up". In: T. Thrane, V. Winge, L. Mackenzie, U. Canger and N. Ege (eds). *Typology and Genetics of Language*. Copenhagen: The Linguistic Circle. 197-210.

Anttila, R. 1972. *Introduction to Historical and Comparative Linguistics*. New York/London: Macmillan.
Bailey, Ch.-J. N. 1973. *Variation and Linguistic Theory*. Arlington: Center for Applied Linguistics.
Coseriu, E. 1974. *Synchronie, Diachronie und Geschichte*. Das Problem des Sprachwandels. München: Hueber. [German translation of: *Sincronía, diacronía e historia*. Montevideo: Universidad de la República 1958].
—. 1975. "Synchronie, Diachronie und Typologie". In: D. Cherubim (ed.). *Sprachwandel*. Reader zur diachronischen Sprachwissenschaft Berlin/New York: de Gruyter. 134-149. [German translation of: "Sincronía, diacronía y typología". In: Actas del XI Congreso Internacional de Lingüística y Filología Románicas, Madrid 1965, I. Madrid: C. S. J. C. 1968. 269-283].
Donegan, P., and D. Stampe. 1979. "The study of natural phonology". In: D. Dinnsen (ed.). *Current Approaches to Phonological Theory*. Bloomington: University Press. 126-173.
Dressler, W. U. 1985. *Morphonology*. Ann Arbor: Caroma.
—, Mayerthaler, W., Panagl, O., and W. U. Wurzel. 1987. *Leitmotifs in Natural Morphology*. Amsterdam/Philadelphia. Benjamins.
Greenberg, J. 1963. "Some universals of grammar with particular reference to the order of meaningful elements". In: Greenberg (ed.). 1963. 58-90.
—. (ed.). 1963. *Universals of Language*. Cambridge, Mass.: M. I. T. Press.
—. (ed.). 1978. *Universals of Human Language*. Vol. 3: *Word Structure*. Stanford: Stanford University Press.
Hörz, H., and K. F. Wessel. 1983. *Philosophische Entwicklungstheorie*. Berlin.
Jakobson, R. 1962. *Selected Writings*. Vol. 1. The Hague/Paris: Mouton.
—. 1963. "Implications of language universals for linguistics". In: Greenberg (ed.). 1963. 208-219.
—. 1971. "Quest for the essence of language". In: R. Jakobson. *Selected Writings*. Vol. 2: *Word and Language*. The Hague/Paris: Mouton. 345-359.

Mayerthaler, W. 1981. *Natürliche Morphologie*. Wiesbaden: Athenaion.
Saussure, F. de. 1931. *Grundlagen der allgemeinen Sprachwissenschaft*. 2. Aufl. Berlin: de Gruyter.
Stein, D. 1985. *Natürlicher syntaktischer Sprachwandel*. München: tuduv.
Wurzel, W. U. 1984a. *Flexionsmorphologie und Natürlichkeit*. Berlin: Akademie-Verlag. (Studia Grammatica XXI). [English: *Inflectional Morphology and Naturalness*. Dordrecht/Boston/London: Kluver 1989].
—. 1984b. "Was bezeichnet der Umlaut im Deutschen?". In: *ZPSK* 37/6.647-663.
—. 1985. "Zur Determiniertheit morphologischer Erscheinungen. Ein Zwischenbericht". In: *Acta Linguistica Academiae Scientiarum Hungaricae* t. 34 (1/2).151-168.
—. 1987. "Platos 'Kratylos'-Dialog oder: Von der Motiviertheit der morphologischen Formen". In: W. Neumann and B. Techtmeier (eds). *Bedeutungen und Ideen in Sprachen und Texten*. Werner Bahner gewidmet. Berlin: Akademie-Verlag. 120-134.
—. 1988. "Analogie: Hermann Paul und die natürliche Morphologie". In: *Zeitschrift für Germanistik* 9.537-544.

What are Language Histories Histories of?*

Roger Lass
University of Cape Town

1 Problemstellung

My title question could have a simplistic or definitional answer: they're obviously histories of languages. More sharply, they could be histories of 'aspects' or 'parts' of languages: sounds (*Lautgeschichte*), etc., combined to form a *Sprachgeschichte*. These are familiar and traditional terms, though they need exegesis, especially in the light of this volume's basic concerns.

A *Lautgeschichte* is clearly not a history of 'sounds' as such, which are evanescent; there must be some type/token thinking behind such a notion. The things we tell stories about are categories whose spatio-temporal manifestations are sounds, and so on. That is, on the most superficial analysis, histories of (parts of) languages are histories of (parts of) systems of categories, or elements (sounds, phonemes, morphs, words, constructions, meanings).

But what is the ontological status of these items whose stories we tell? Or, since the notion 'language history' is problematical, what other familiar, perhaps ontologically more perspicuous kinds of histories are language histories like? Like political histories (sequences of (collective) events)? Art or music histories (sequences of styles, devices, conventions)? Biological histories (sequences of genotypes, phenotypes, genotype/phenotype and other ecological interactions)? Geological histories (sequences of physical states interfaced by state-changing operations)?

None of these is self-evidently compelling; there is a basic difficulty, which is the proper exegesis of the term 'linguistic structure'. What level are we operating on when we talk about this, and what are the implications of a choice when it comes to doing linguistic history? And, we might add, is any one of the choices mentioned above necessarily appropriate for all kinds of linguistic change?

The major concern of this volume is with exploring the consequences of a 'new structuralist' view: the idea that 'cognitivism' (Lieb, this vol., Section I) is a failure or even an obfuscation as a basic orientation for linguistics, and that perhaps we ought to return to 'structuralism' proper: if in a more sophisticated version. Put another way, what is involved is a shift from the now dominant concern with what Chomsky (1986) calls 'I-languages' to the traditional concern with 'E-languages'.

During the 1987 Round Table on 'Prospects for a New Structuralism' (Lieb 1990), a set of 'Principles of New Structuralism' were enunciated, of which the following are relevant here (numbering as in original):

(1) The objects of linguistics are the objects actually studied by the practicing linguist [...] They cannot be prescribed independently of linguistic practice.

(3) Neurophysiological or mental mechanisms do not belong to the objects of linguistics.

(5) The objects of linguistics, in particular, languages, their systems, and linguistic structures, are abstract and extra-mental.

(6) Despite their abstract nature the objects of linguistics may have derived spatial and temporal properties, based on spatial or temporal properties of objects or events in spacetime.

(8) Traditional structuralism was right in — mostly — construing the objects of linguistics as extra-mental and emphasizing their structural (system-based) properties. Traditional structuralism was wrong where it failed clearly to recognize their abstract nature [...]

This much I agree with, and it will be supported in what follows. But two points raised in the 'Principles' may be inappropriate (in part) for the historian:

(2) Something is an object of linguistics only if it is needed for describing the content of intentional (directed) mental states or events that are connected with (a) speaking, (b) understanding speech, or (c) judging speech from a communicative point of view.

And a last portion of (8): traditional structuralism was wrong where it failed to recognize the 'basis in human intentionality' of the objects of linguistics.

I will suggest that even this much 'mentalism' — however valid it may be for synchronic linguistics — is out of place or irrelevant for certain major historical concerns. At least this will be the case for one major type of change — phonological — which will be my main concern here. (I will, however, largely as a matter of trying to achieve a refined preliminary taxonomy, also discuss briefly some types of change which seem to come closer to involving 'mental states' of some kind.)

2 Language and mind(s), mind(s) and metalanguage

Some linguists in every generation have been concerned with trying to specify an underpinning ontology for their subject. In what Rudolph Botha has aptly called the 'metaphysics market' (1989, 1990), language is perpetually being sold 'as' something: as physical, as behaviour, as a platonic entity, as a system of interpersonal norms ('social fact'), as an epiphenomenon of discourse, as a 'mental organ' ... the list goes on and on. It has even been sold as (virtually) nothing but a product of linguists' transactions with certain kinds of behavioural data, as in the instrumentalist extreme espoused by Zellig Harris (1960).

Most of these classic monist positions are of course vulgar-reductionist: in saying that language 'is' X one most often ends up saying it's 'nothing-but' X. Such reductionist accounts usually treat some preselected properties elegantly, but relegate others (which on different interpretations may be central) to the marginal or epiphenomenal. So for Chomsky discourse is presumably a performance use of pre-existing structure; for Givón (1979) structure itself arises from the exigencies of discourse.

A non-reductive but supportable ontology has been a long time coming; we don't have a fully developed one yet. Much pioneering work has been done by H.-H. Lieb over the past two decades or so (see particularly Lieb 1970, 1983: Part A). What I am going to suggest here is in many ways at least compatible with Lieb's work, though couched in somewhat different terms; it is a matter for future research to what extent our approaches may in the end be close to the same. At any rate, one possibly fruitful approach, as I first suggested a decade ago (Lass 1980a: Ch. 4) is by way of a kind of (neo)Popperian 'interactionism'. That is, a view in which language is an object-type *sui generis*, which interacts with and is interacted with by human psyches, social aggregations, etc., without compromising its autonomy, or theirs. I later argued (1987a) that some such account is necessary to handle even the surface phenomenology of linguistic change, at least for such macro-phenomena as long-term convergences, 'conspiracies', and drifts. Most recently, Philip Carr (1990) has developed a much clearer interactionist or 'autonomist' framework, against the background of a trenchant criticism of other (mostly reductionist) positions. This paper in a way is a diachronic pendant to Carr's largely synchronic argument.

In anticipation, I want to push the view, with reference to language change and what the historical linguist is supposed to make of it, that the best approach is a pluralist interactionism. By discriminating between different kinds of historical (and hence by reflection synchronic) phenomena, we can set up a framework in which language 'itself' remains autonomous, but speakers' involvement with it varies. In other words the lump category 'change' is not as simple as it looks, and there seem to be at least three major types: (a) those that crucially involve (properties of) speakers as individuals; (b) those that crucially involve (properties of) groups of speakers; and (c) others — perhaps the bulk of what historians usually busy themselves with — that primarily involve 'structures' or 'systems', and where the role of human agents, individually or collectively, is at best marginal. It is this last type that will be my main concern here, as its justification is perhaps less obvious, and its contrast to the other types not entirely clear. (It may not be at the end, either, but this is a preliminary attempt to make sense of a fuzzy and complex domain.)

Now if language is, as mentalists would have it, a strictly mental object, and therefore in its outward form a 'mirror of mind', then language change, which by reductive definition is simply the behaviour of that mind over time, may also be a source of information about it.[1] Transformations of linguistic structure in this view may therefore be clues to 'optimal' states, or in other ways allow access to the regularities, structural principles, etc., of 'mind', just as the principles of Chomskyan UG, the permissable/preferred ranges of parameter-settings, etc., are supposed to do. Some such assumption has certainly been an element of the generativist approach to historical linguistics, from the primitive 'rules-added-to-competence' discourse of the 60s (Kiparsky 1968, King 1969) to recent more sophisticated versions of what is essentially the same thing (e.g. Lightfoot 1979 on 'opacity' and the like).

But as I have argued elsewhere (Lass 1987a), it is curious that despite some attempts at showing definite connections, and a lot of mentalist meta-commentary, ranging from dutiful throwaway lines about 'competence' or 'knowledge' to more serious concerns with 'learnability', mentalist language and thinking have traditionally been alien to the discourse of 'core' historical linguistics. In our trade we typically talk about linguistic objects, change in linguistic systems or parts of them — not about changes in 'mental representations' or things that speakers 'know' or 'do'. We talk about vowel-raising, lenition, attrition of morphology, restructuring, not about what may (presumably) be going on in the heads of individuals whose behavioural output (or 'data') in one way or another suggests that these things have occurred.

It may be of course that non-mentalist language is easier, and that's all there is to it. So in describing the spirantization subpart of Grimm's law, for instance 'IE */p/ > Gmc /f/' is merely an 'informal abbreviation' for something mental, just as '[p], [f]' are informal abbreviations for feature-bundles — which in turn represent a 'mental content' with certain 'real-world' correlates.

But we could ask whether the choice of figurative terminology ('vowel-raising', 'language change') in a given domain as the normal *façon de parler*, as sanctioned practice, good heuristic, etc. doesn't in fact say something interesting about what the domain is really like. Do domains perhaps choose their optimal descriptors? If so, this kind of (relatively) forced choice may reflect something deeper, it may point to a corporate (if inexplicit) ontological intuition — even one that goes counter to the prevailing explicit commitment. At worst it can suggest the range of appropriate possibilities for ontological ascription, in cases where (regardless of what the participants in a foundational polemic may claim) the nature of the ontological ground is far from obvious.

Now a synchronic 'structural' linguist (generative or other) may of course avoid commitment to any particular position on the ontology of his objects of inquiry.[2] The same may be true of the 'abstract' linguistic historian, who refuses to grant phonetic or even phonological reality to his starred representations (e.g. Zawadowski 1962). But the less fanatically agnostic historian, whether reconstructor, chronicler, or both, may not have this option. If his job is to tell stories about successive 'events', or even 'states', then surely the objects in his narrative are — if obscurely — spatiotemporally localized. And I assume that an '"unreal" spatiotemporally located object' is a nonsense.

This is a way of saying that the synchronist appears on one (permissive) reading to have special privileges: he can avoid ontological commitment, at least in the sense that while his data is in some 'real' world as a matter of fact, his constructs, representations, operations do not have to reflect anything outside the model that generates them. In fact any 'projection' to other planes ('psychological reality', etc.) is beside the point.[3] For the unreflecting at least, a clean, parsimonious, insightful analysis tends to look more or less the same regardless of what its producer thinks the projection is, or even if he thinks there's none, or doesn't care. Bloomfield's Menomini analysis (1939) might be about the 'competence' of Menomini speakers, the history of Algonquian, or how to do neat process (morpho)phonology; and it stands or falls on the last set of criteria (which is why of course it's a classic), not on any of the others. Bloomfield explicitly takes the internal-reconstruction-like look of his product as coincidental or irrelevant (1939:106, and cf. Lass 1977a:8f for discussion).

The question that might arise now is whether the historian can be allowed the same freedom, whether he can do his work as an agnostic, or espouse a non-psychologistic, non-social ontology. Is Grimm's Law for instance just an 'algebraic' coding of a relation holding over correspondence sets like L *piscis*, Gothic *fisks*, or L *plēnus*, Gothic *fulls*? Or is it a claim that (a) there were in the past (as there still are) localized real phonetic forms with property clusters like [labial, stop] and [labial, fricative] in initial position, plus a certain semantic common core? And (b), that the 'law' (say *[p] > [f], or [-continuant] > [+continuant]) is a real event, relating at least 'surface forms' or imagined speaker outputs at one time to the same class of phenomena at another. If both (a, b) are even trivially true, then historians are perforce realists at the level of speaker output, whatever they think about what they do, and however idealized their representations are. History is about 'what speakers said' (or might have said) in some sense, hence it is realist, and even more so is 'about' individual humans and their activities, and probably the mental realia underwriting these activities.

It is however possible to maintain that these obvious facts do not determine an entire ontological stance; that it is possible, and indeed desirable, not to have individual speakers (or even collectives), with all their psychosocial clutter, centrally involved in the main business of language change. There is as we will see an argument to the effect that in *this* kind of change anyhow, as well as others, our concern is really not with output proper (cf. Sec. 1), but with categories (non-mentally) 'underlying' that output — even if we presuppose ('privately', as it were) the output, and historically assume that it would have been there as a stimulus for our positing of the categories. (A synchronic linguist dumped from a time-machine into the Proto-Germanic community would take this point of view.) Is it possible, perhaps, that we can view speakers, in other words, as not centrally involved in our business, rather perhaps as 'carriers' of change (cf. Lass 1987a)? In line with Richard Dawkins' famous dictum that a hen is an egg's way of making another egg, perhaps a speaker is a language's way of making the next language-state.

To be a bit more precise: assuming at least the minimum function of speakers as carriers (since there is no genetic code for language, but only intergeneration or cultural transmission), is there any deeper individual involvement, such that changes must perforce be seen as alterations in individual 'internalized grammars'? Even if there is, is this central? And in our current state of knowledge, is it a profitable or meaningful way of talking about change? I suggest that the history of a language is more than, and perhaps in essence something different from, a mere summation over the 'acts' (in whatever sense) of speakers.

3 Speaker 'involvement': a sketch for a model

The hypostasis of 'language' as something over and above and independent of its users is not just a linguist's way of talking; it is a normal convention, especially in the historical realm. Just sticking to English, we find as early as the 14th century a mode of speech quite congenial to most historical linguists — here in a poet's comment on change (Chaucer, *Troilus and Criseyde*, II, 22ff):

> Ye knowe ek that in forme of speche is chaunge
> Withinne a thousand yeer, and wordes tho
> That hadden pris, now wonder nyce and straunge
> Us thinketh hem, and yet thei spake hem so [...]

And in a normative and dramatic but no less relevant vein, Dr Johnson in the preface to his *Dictionary* (1755) remarks on the fact that language is 'apt to decay'; it does things in spite of what we want it to do:

> If the changes that we fear be thus irresistible, what remains but to acquiesce with silence, as in the other insurmountable distresses of humanity. It remains that we retard what we cannot repel [...] tongues, like governments, have a natural tendency to degeneration [...]

The lack of 'blame' cast on speakers is the point: the reification here is as natural to linguists as it is to the layman. What is interesting is why it is so congenial to both sets of users, especially the professionals.

It's not enough just to ascribe this to tradition and let it go at that; there are questions to ask about traditions. Just because a usage has been normal and apparently useful for ages, should we keep it up? (Should I vote Tory only because my father did?) Even the question of 'truth' can come up here: do traditional acceptance and apparent fruitfulness correlate with truth? (There are probably more people in the world who cure — and induce — disease by witchcraft than by western medicine.) So granted that linguists have for ages talked about 'languages changing' rather than speakers doing things with or to them, that it's 'the history of English' rather than 'changing mental representations in the English-speaking community' that we study, it might be worth asking why. Leaving aside the obvious pretheoretical existence of individual speakers, communities, etc., can we do historical linguistics in such a way that these can — at least for some major types of change — be relegated to some place out of the limelight?

I propose here to look at some test cases which might help to establish a cline of 'speaker-involvement' in processes of change — at least on the levels of phonology and morphology. This will suggest that the major part of the historiographical endeavour can (and perhaps should) be done as it always has, without recourse to the user. Consider for instance the standard 'neogrammarian' reconstruction (say comparative method), and the history that flows from it. We can begin with a factual (or more safely pretheoretical) universe that everyone would probably agree represents something like the total set of variables that might possibly be involved in language change — a set of potential interactants, an ecosystem if you will. We might represent it as in (1) below.

(1)

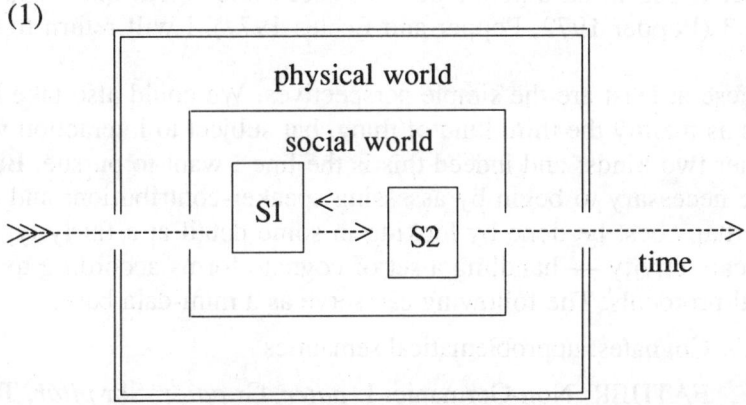

That is, a physical universe with spatiotemporal coordinates 'in which' everything we're interested in can — or ought to be able to — be located. Within this, a 'social world' (whatever its precise nature), in which members of a speech community interact: and a dyad, consisting of two speakers S-1 and S-2 (or better speaker/hearers) who interact. And these of course have their own individual minds.

Beyond this our problems begin. Most important, where are our primary objects of study, linguistic systems, located? Does each individual own one? On this reading, S-1 and S-2 are Leibnizian monads with universal and particular grammars packed inside, subject to the contingent possibility of encountering each others' outputs, i.e. the 'use' of their 'internalized grammars'. (I assume this is *au fond* the Chomskyan position.) This is of course a reasonable and respectable kind of speculative metaphor, but its popularity nowadays doesn't mean we have to take it seriously. Indeed, it's probably the worst starting point for historical (not to mention sociohistorical) linguistics one could imagine.

Alternatively, we could allow language systems their 'full' existence only interpersonally.[4] This would make language some kind of 'social fact', not an intrapsychic one. The Labovian 'community grammar' would probably fit here.

Finally, we could put systems ('languages' in the linguist's usual sense) somewhere else: they could be Katzian platonic objects; or better, objects of a third kind, 'objective' but not social, physical or intrapsychic, living in an autonomous but accessible world like Popper's World 3 (Popper 1972, Popper and Eccles 1977). I will return to this below.

These at least are the simple perspectives. We could also take languages as mainly the third kind of thing, but subject to interaction with the other two kinds; and indeed this is the line I want to pursue. But it will be necessary to begin by assessing speaker-contribution; and this can perhaps best be done by looking in some detail at a fairly typical historical activity — handling a set of cognate forms according to traditional protocols. The following can serve as a mini-data base:

A. Cognates: unproblematical semantics

1. FATHER. Non-Germanic: L *pater*, Gr *patḗr*, Skr *pitár*, Toch *pačar*. Germanic: OE *fæder*, ON *faðir*, Sw *far*, Du *vader*. Celtic: OIr *athir*.

2. PORK. Non-Gmc: L *porcus*, Gr *porkós*, Lith *par̃šas* 'castrated pig', OCS *prasę*. Gmc: OE *fearh* 'pig', OHG *farah*, G *Ferkel* 'piglet', E *farrow*, Du *vark*. Celtic: OIr *orc* 'pig'.

3. FOOT. Non-Gmc: L *ped-*, Gr (gen sg) *podós*, Skr *pād-*, Lith *pãdas*. Gmc: Go *fōtus*, OE *fōt*, OHG *fuoʒ*, E *foot*, Du *voet*.

4. FULL. Non-Gmc: L *plēnus*, Gr *plérē*, Lith *pìlnas*, OCS *plŭnŭ*, Skr *pūrṇa-*. Gmc: OE *full*, Go *fulls*, ON *fullr*, G *voll*.

B. More tenuous semantics (Cultural Archaeology)
1. E *feather*: L *(acci)piter* 'hawk', Gr *ptéruks* 'wing', Skr *pátati* 'he flies', L *pro(p)teruus* 'vehement', petō 'I attack, rush at', later 'demand'.
2. OE *fǣmne* 'woman': Avestan *paeman* 'milk', Gr *pīón* 'fat, juice', Skr *páyate* 'teems, abounds with'. See D below.
3. E *farrow*: *fearh*, *Ferkel*, etc. as above. Add now OE *furh* 'furrow' > ModE *furrow*; L *porca* 'field-drain, earth between furrows', Lith *pra-paršas* 'ditch, trench', Armenian *herk* 'fallow land' (Arm /h/ = L /p/ = Gmc /f/).

C. A, B as loan-diagnostics
1. FATHER. E *father* vs. *paternal, patrimony, patriot, allopatric*.
2. FOOT. E *foot* vs. *pedal, sesquipedalian, impede, pedestrian, podiatrist, arthropod, centipede*.
3. FULL. E *full* vs. *plenum, plenary, plenty, plethora, plenitude, implement*.
4. PORK. E *farrow, furrow, furlong* < OE *furh-lang* vs. *pork, porcine, porcupine* (OF *porc-espin*), *porpoise* (OF *porc-peis*, i.e. L *porcus* + *piscis*: cf. G *Meer-schwein*); hence *fish* vs. *piscatorial, piscina, piscary* 'fishing-rights in common'.

D. A, B as filter for 'false' relations

OE *fǣmne* 'woman', OFris *famne/femne*, Old Saxon *fēmea*, ON *feima*. NOT related to L *fēmina* 'woman', *fēmininus*, E *feminine*, etc. REGULARITY: L *fēlare* 'suckle', Gr *thḗlus* 'female', *thēlḗ* 'breast', Skr *dhātrī* 'nurse'; cf. L *foris* 'outside', Gr *thúrā* 'portal'; L *faciō* 'do', Gr *(tí)thēmi* 'place'.

This is all familiar enough in type, and is based on a set of protocols deriving from a highly restrictive theory of change. If its interpretive claims (e.g. in the first instance that some pair X, Y of forms are cognate, and in the second that therefore some other pair A, B are likely to be, and some other pair C, D cannot be) are true, then they are true by virtue of system-internal criteria. That is, they fit within the bounds of an attractive and well-defined praxis. They involve — as such — no necessary subsidiary claims (or even notions) about 'where' this is all happening. At this point the game is coherent even without an arena.

Section A is clearly a picture of 'filiation', with the familiar conceptual geometry of a genealogical stemma:

(2)

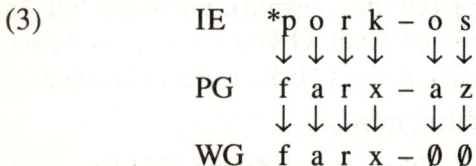

In this framework, a sound change is nothing more than a function from one 'time-indexed' set to another; an etymology is a set-theoretic construct, the sum of the mappings between the constituent corresponding segments of a lexical item. So for one member of the PORK set, E *farrow*, the beginning of the etymology would be one-to-one segmental mappings between IE and PGmc, and between PGmc and WGmc (the latter including, as can be seen below, a mapping of two segments — the nom sg affix — onto the null element):

(3)   IE   *p o r k – o s
             ↓ ↓ ↓ ↓   ↓ ↓
        PG   f a r x – a z
             ↓ ↓ ↓ ↓   ↓ ↓
        WG   f a r x – ∅ ∅

And so on, with each new sound change a new mapping. Sound change then is 'regular' in the classic sense, and maps input to output determinately. We can now go ahead with our database as follows:

(i) If X > Y regularly, we can project from the clear-cut semantics in A to more tenuous instances in B, underwritten by the correspondences. The relatedness of 'pig' and 'castrated pig' is clear enough; unlike, at first, that between 'pig' and 'furrow'. But in the latter case we can use the regularity assumption, plus what — using the same techniques — we've reconstructed of IE word-formation and morphophonology, to get us into a crude 'archaeosemantics'. If OE *fearh*, L *por-*

cus, OE *furh* are regular developments, the first two imply an *o*-grade and the third a zero-grade of the same root, */pork- ~ pr̥k-/. The regularity hypothesis, plus a simplicity criterion of sorts (don't invoke homonymy when polysemy or even minor variations of the same basic sense are available) makes good history of the data. Given the well-known IE proclivity for naming animals after prototypical attributes or activities (cf. *bull*: *phallus*), the pig is 'The Furrower'.[5]

Similar argumentation will give the proper results in the rest of B — even if we have trouble deciding what the 'primitive' sense of a lexical root might be, i.e. which of the ones suggested by its history.

(ii) With this established, C is now a diagnostic for loans vs. native formations. The regularity idea has heuristic value as a creator of historical depth and a detector of diachronic stratification in the lexicon; and this with no need for any knowledge of the details (or even the existence) of the actual contact situation in the real world that would make the borrowings likely or even possible. If we knew nothing of Germanic/Latin contacts, or in the extreme case, if Latin itself were unattested but most of the rest of IE were intact, we could still claim (rightly) that if *father, foot, full* are native, *paternal, pedal, plenum* (cognate *ex hypothesi*) must come from elsewhere.

(iii) It's now possible, as in D, to filter out adventitious resemblances, even in the presence of what looks like semantic congruence. An English or other Germanic native /f/ simply can't correspond to a Latin /f/; but since in this set we have L /f/ = Greek /th/ (as opposed to sets where L /f/ = Gmc /b/, like *break*: *frēg-ī*, which would entail Gr /ph/); and since in the case of L /f/ = Gr /th/ the cognates in Germanic would have to have /d/ (Gr *thúrā*, L *foris*, E *door*), we can exclude OE *fæmne* as having anything to do with L *fēmina* and its derivatives.

Now observe that all this historical depth and heuristic richness requires no (individual, human) ontological projection. The theory behind it (never mind whether it's true or not) could be unprojected, or could be projected to an autonomous, self-existent 'language', divorced from speakers or social groupings. Consider three possible 'pure' models of the locus for change:

(4)

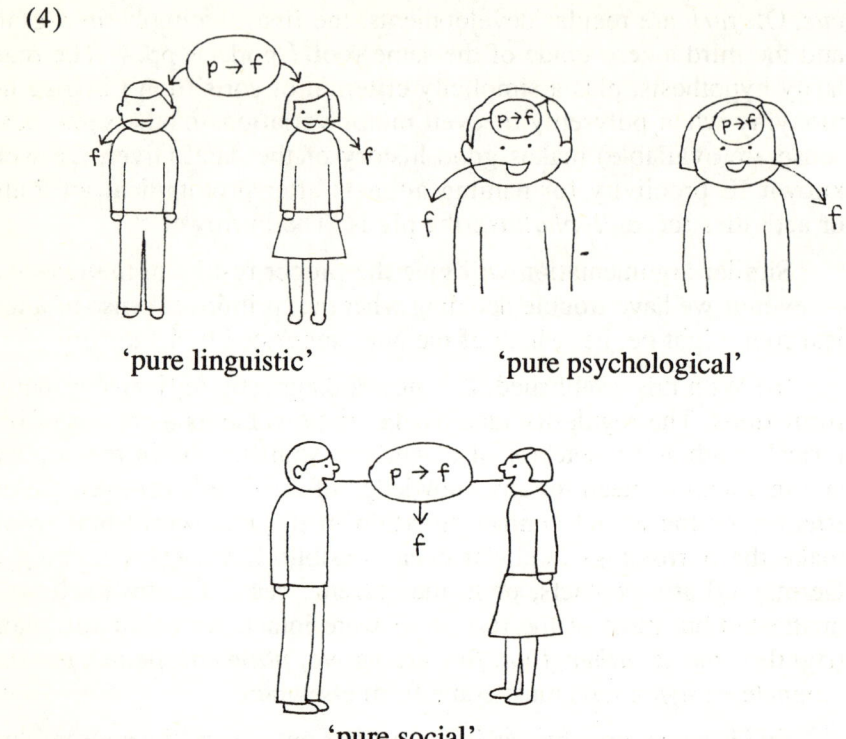

'pure linguistic'　　　　'pure psychological'

'pure social'

This is a cartoon version of how classical exceptionless change might come about: an event in real time, with three possible loci, hence three possible dimensions of control. But at this stage the choice of localisation has no consequences for the fruitfulness of the theory for its particular purposes, i.e. as a descriptive or predictive device that orders a complex class of phenomena. An autonomous linguistic locus, an intrapsychic (individual) or a social (collective) one — or even none at all — will have the same results. Like any good tool, comparative method doesn't care why it's being used, only that it's being used correctly. (When it comes to 'understanding' changes, or making our understanding fit with certain kinds of empirical evidence, as we'll see, the result may be somewhat different.)

In other words, ontological specificity at this stage is beside the point; the machine makes good history, regardless of how we think it might work. Speculations about 'minds', or attempts to involve 'agents', simply fudge the issue. The first point where we are tempted to projection is where 'irregularities' or perturbations in the pattern occur. For there are all kinds of exceptions to regular ('mechanical') change, as even the Neogrammarians knew perfectly well. But the way in which temptations to extralinguistic interpretation arise is instructive, and will help to suggest a model of what some kinds of change might really be like.

Neogrammarian-style attempts to cope with irregularities are not deviations from the regularity principle; rather a set of forced hedges which allow projection to nonlinguistic domains to creep in at the edges. 'Normal' or non-marginal data is neutral with respect to ontology, but marginal phenomena of some kinds introduce, if equivocally, a desire for interpretation. Or better, some classes of data look funny without extralinguistic localisation, and we want then to invoke (some aspects of) speakers.

One type of irregularity, which does not require any special explanation, is the 'inherently sporadic' process, like dissimilation or metathesis, which is not generally expected to result in *Lautgesetze*. So L *peregrinus* > F *pèlerin*, L *arbor* > Sp *árbol*, L *miraculum* > Sp *milagro*, OE *bridd* > ModE *bird* do not follow any 'sound laws' in the usual sense: Romance /r ... r/ tends to /r ... l/ or /l ... r/, OE /CrVC/ tends to /CVrC/, etc. But no non-instance is a counterexample to anything, since these are outside the pattern, marginal anomalies that can safely be carried along because of their low frequency and lack of structural import. They do not affect the hard core of the theory, but are simply garbage that is tidied away as part of procedural good housekeeping. (Of course an exception to a 'regular' dissimilation like Grassmann's Law counts like any other, and would be a problem.)

The other kinds are something different, and provoke attempts to tie them in with speakers or communities. Some of the most important seem to be:

(i) *Analogy*. Despite general regularity, we get non-phonetically motivated exceptional developments: L *honor*/*honoris*, earlier *honos*, etc. The 'normal' reflex of IE */-s/ in Latin is of course /s/ (*custo-s*, *die-s*). Here the classical account is in terms of 'impulse' or 'motivation' for the aberrant behaviour; regularising of irregular paradigms, minimising allomorphy in this case. And there is a natural psychological interpretation for such behaviour, connected with memory preferences, 'desire for symmetry', optimality of form/meaning biuniqueness, and so on. This applies not only to levelling but to extension as well: OE *wulf/wulfas, sunu/suna, hnutu/hnyte,* ModE *wolf/wolves, son/sons, nut/nuts.* These and other analogical phenomena (e.g. L *novem* instead of **noven* 'because of' *decem,* etc.) can be seen as teleological, even 'rational' (perhaps in the sense of Itkonen's 1983 'unconscious rationality') rather than 'mechanical', a response to a need, or whatever.

But not necessarily. They can be viewed just as well as instances of system-homeostasis, patching-up operations within a (not too efficiently) self-maintaining system.[6] 'Failures' of analogy then are the linguistic counterpart of periodic benign hypoglycemia: the boundary conditions for the system are ill-defined and allow for some flux, and a range of tolerances such that 'metabolic imbalances' fit (mostly) within these boundaries, and do not lead to pathology. Or if they might, the system as it were burns some glycogen, turns off the insulin factories, and so on. This could all be handled in terms of a non-projected autonomous system or set of structural relations, with no necessary reference to 'users' of the system.

Where users come in is not in the inception of the change itself, but in its spread throughout the linguistic 'on-line' systems of individual speakers, e.g. through mechanisms like lexical diffusion or variable implementation. Such mechanism are in principle different from inception; let's suggest for the moment that a change 'occurs' within the autonomous system, and the user's job is to follow whatever procedures are necessary to get it established in his own system. Or this might hold for the collective of users, in which case we get various 'social' mechanisms of spread, sociolinguistic evaluation and weighting, and other properties of users-in-aggregates.

(ii) *Dialect borrowing.* There are cases where regular developments appear to be short-circuited or deflected by importations from neighbouring dialects. E.g. given the *Lautgesetze,* the reflex of OE /ɑː/ in Scots ought to be [e(ː)] (with length depending on context: Lass 1987c: Sec. 5.7.1). So [hem] 'home', [seːr] 'sore', [meːr] 'more' < OE *hām, sār, māra.* This should hold as well for *goat, bone* < OE *gāt, bān*;

but even in the broadest urban Central Belt dialects the latter two are typically [gɔt], [bɔn]. The usual southern English reflex of OE /ɑː/ is of course [əʊ] or [œʊ] now, but used to be [ou], and up to the early 19th century was [oː]. The Scots [o]-forms are clearly borrowings from prestigious or 'conquering' English, phonetically accomodated to the nearest Scots vowel type.

Such borrowings typically occur along prestige gradients, in multidialectal or even diglossic situations, and must presuppose the interaction at least of speech communities, each with its own norms (if not, necessarily, of individuals). They have, that is, no genuine (strictly) intrasystemic interpretation. For this reason they can be relegated to the 'historical sociology' of the linguistic area in question, and purged from (intrasystemic) diachronic linguistics proper. Each system evolves according to its own internal pattern, and the fact that two systems have undergone contact, and bits of one have leaked into the other, is neither here nor there. The results, in terms of pattern-disruption, from the historian's long-term or 'God's-eye' view, are not part of the language 'itself', and stand outside the macroevolutionary line. The 'history itself' can still be seen as the action of a self-regulating autonomous system. This is why borrowing (unlike analogy, perhaps) is a benign escape-hatch: the bulk of linguistic evolution, what 'serious' or 'core' historical linguistics is about, is internal or endogenous, *structural* evolution in the strict sense.

The internal/external dichotomy, which is both expository convenience and reflection of an intuitively felt divide (for many linguists) allows us to refrain from bringing the human agent or his society centre-stage. This is entirely proper, I think, and certainly conduces both to parsimony and heuristic elegance (see Lass and Wright 1986). The distinction between internal history, which is genuinely structural, and external history, which from a linguistic point of view is contingent or largely so, is a real one: neglect of it leads to incoherent story-telling. (Not of course when we deal with pidgins and creoles, or any genuine *Mischsprache* cases; these I maintain are not 'normal', but exceptional, and not proper models in any case for how to do language history.)

But now consider the case of what looks like morphosyntactic interference with regular sound change. There are two subtypes: one involves communicationally neutral 'morphological conditioning', the other issues like 'avoidance of homophony', 'loss of distinctiveness', etc.

(iii) Consider Yiddish /ə/-deletion (see Lass 1980b for details). At some point in the post-medieval evolution of Yiddish, final unstressed -*e* was generally deleted (Yi *harts, gas, erd, ix gej* vs. G *Herze, Gasse, Erde, ich gehe*). This deletion failed (a) in attributive adjectives with a predeterminer (*di grojse štot* 'the big city' vs. *dos štot iz grojs* 'the city is big'); (b) in diminutives (*gas/gesele* 'little street', *kats* 'cat'/*ketsele*); (c) in words of non-MHG origin whose plurals are in -*s* (*kaše/kaše-s* 'question', *šikse/-s* 'gentile girl' < Hebrew, *bobke/-s* 'bean, goat-turd', *luže/-s* 'puddle' < Slavic, *historje/-s* 'history', *roze/-s* 'rose' < Romance), and in a small class of borrowed verbs in the present 1 sg (*burčen* 'grumble', pres 1 sg *ix burč-e*, vs. the native type *kratsen* 'scratch', *ix krats*).

There is clearly a 'global' or cross-component involvement of the grammar here; we could visualize it as the operation of some kind of comparison or checking procedure, say like this:

(5) CHECKING ROUTINE EXIT: -ə#
 1. Diminutive? Y (exit); N (2)
 2. Inflected Adj? Y (exit); N (3)
 3. Plural in -*s*? Y (exit); N (4)
 4. Verb of -*e* class? Y (exit); N (5)
 5. Default; -∅#

On the most simple-minded interpretation this presupposes an 'agent' to do the checking; but it could, on reflection, just as easily be an autonomous non-conscious device, unspecified except in terms of its behaviour: an (agnostic) black box, or a dedicated autonomous intrasystemic computer. It might seem *a priori* that the best candidate for such a computational device would be a psyche, not an abstract 'system'; but this is just a weak preference-statement for non-autonomy, not an argument.

(iv) PIE */s/ deletes intervocalically in Ancient Greek, e.g. *génos* 'kind', gen sg *gén-e-os* < */gén-es-os/ (cf. L *genus/gen-er-is*). This 'natural' change fails in a certain class of verbal futures (*inter alia*): pres 1 sg *lú-ō* 'loose', future *lǘ-s-ō* vs. pres *stéll-ō* 'place', future *stel-é-ō* < */stel-és-ō/. That is, /s/ deletes just in case there is *another* marker which will keep the future distinct from the present (for discussion, Lass 1980a:67ff).

This kind of exception — apparently an 'avoidance' of an otherwise regular process for (on one interpretation) communicational reasons, seems to presuppose a social arena, or at least a dyad. The task that would not be performed if present and future were to merge is the minimally dyadic one of signalling a difference, i.e. the field of operation appears to be semiotic, and an object isn't a sign unless it's a sign *for* someone, as the doctrine goes. The same appears to be true of so-called 'taboo-avoidance': if OE *scyttan* 'shut' had developed in the normal way, with OE /y/ > /ɪ/ (cf. *mycg* > *midge*, *brycg* > *bridge*), it would merge with *shit*. Hence this word was recycled via a minor development to short /u/, thus avoiding the homophony.[7]

These instances are subject to my earlier stricture against functional and avoidance arguments (Lass 1980a and 1987b); I still hold to the position taken there, that neither type of explanation is coherent, at least not if one is looking at any kind of primary mechanisms.

What we might be dealing with here, of course, is material outside the macro-trajectory of changes, which would allow invocation of speakers and communicational exigencies: the material is given by the system, but speakers can tinker at the edges if they want/need to. To revert to an earlier example, pigs as furrowers: the connection is in a sense 'resident' in the system, and it's up to speakers to recognize it or not. The option was easily available to IE speakers, and perhaps to early Germanic ones as well; it certainly isn't to English speakers, because *farrow* is now pretty much a technical term, or restricted only to young pigs, and hence is out of the system, which is built on the quite different root in *pig*. Semiosis is non-primary and non-systemic; it belongs to the domain of use, not that of structure. (This far at least I suppose I'm more of a 'Chomskyan' than an adherent of other sorts of ideologies.)

4 Time and change: diffusion and population-thinking

Whatever ontological position we take, however rich or poor we assume the speaker's innate equipment is, one thing is clear: the language (as 'primary linguistic data') is available in the first instance only as a 'presentation': as something handed down, given. Whatever its historicity, in the synchronic dimension it is indefeasible, a *fait accompli*.

I have argued elsewhere (Lass 1987a) that one of the strongest motivations for not seeing the speaker as the primary locus of change is the obverse of this condition: the existence (from the historian's perspective only) of long-term, transgenerational evolutionary patterns (drifts, conspiracies, discontinuous repetitions of change types with long gaps between implementations). The 'life-span' of such patterns is typically longer than that of any conceivable human carrier, and the information concerning it can therefore not be stored in a brain; it requires a longer-lasting memory. An autonomous World-3 system is — at least *faute de mieux* — just such a facility.

Much of course depends on how you visualize things; since a World-3 object is in no way 'demonstrable' (by definition it has no spatiotemporal location), the acceptance criteria are non-experimental, i.e. argumentative and/or aesthetic. But some of the consequences of accepting such a characterization even provisionally are interesting.

Let us consider another type of 'exception' to neogrammarian 'regular' change: the very common case where an etymological category appears to have several disjoint developments, not attributable to borrowing or to any particular determinate conditioning. My example is the development in southern British and related Englishes of ME /oː/ (as in *food*, *blood*, *good*). The majority development is to ModE /uː/ via the Great Vowel Shift; but there are, as the examples given suggest, two sets of short-vowel reflexes, which fall in with the (also complex) reflex set for ME short /u/ (*blood* with *but*, *good* with *wool*). A representative (but not exhaustive) list:

(6) a. Unshortened: ModE /uː/
  (i) PRE-LABIAL: broom, bloom, doom, groom, loom, proof, roof, hoop, loop
  (iii) PRE-CORONAL: food, mood, fool, tool, boot, brood, booth, boon, moon, moor, noose, pool, poor, stool, tooth
 b. Early shortening: ModE /ʌ/
  (i) PRE-LABIAL: glove (*perhaps also* love)
  (ii) PRE-CORONAL: blood, flood, stud

c. Late shortening: ModE /ʊ/
   (i) PRE-LABIAL: hoof (*some varieties* broom, roof)
   (ii) PRE-CORONAL; good, stood, soot, foot, hood (*some varieties* root)
   (iii) PRE-VELAR: book, brook, cook, crook, hook, look, rook, took

The only determinate phonological conditioner is a following /k/; except in the North, all ME /oː/ words shorten here in a quite *regelrecht* manner. It also seems that a following coronal predisposes to shortening, and a following labial does much less strongly. We can model this development in at least *two different ways*:

(i) Consider a change, no matter how long it takes, or precisely how it proceeds, as a kind of ideal trajectory: this is one interpretation of the (generally true) statement that 'ME /oː/ > ModE /uː/':

(7)
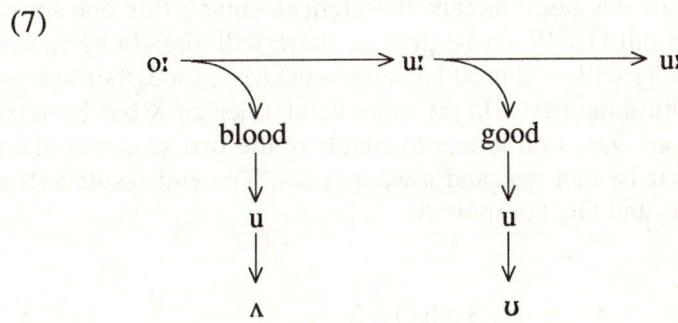

A segment or etymological category travels through time on a vector, and subvectors ('deviations') arise as particular subclasses of items 'drop off' the main vector. On this view the change (overall) of ME /oː/ to /uː/ is what's 'real'; the other developments are 'perturbations' but do not affect the general historical picture in a major way.

(ii) Now take the opposite view, where the trajectory is epiphenomenal (an artefact), and the changes themselves are all that is 'real'. Imagine the lexicon to be a bag of items, and a change to be (say) a snake with particular dietary preferences and a particular metabolism. The snake enters the bag, eats items of a certain shape, and emits 'transformed' items. It wanders (randomly?) through the bag, looking for appropriate items.

But (a) the snake is allowed only a certain time to finish eating — it has a life-span; (b) not all snakes have the same eating-speed or robustness of health; and (c) a snake may die before he finishes eating. So, take a snake who eats Xs and emits Ss:

(8)

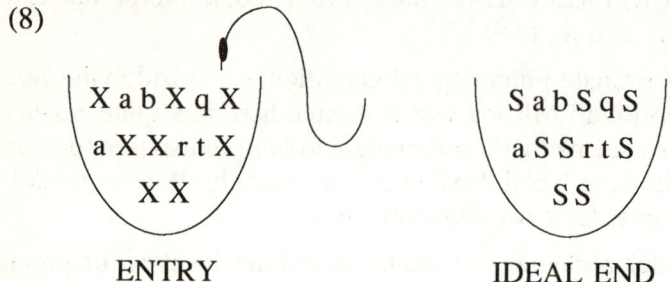

ENTRY   IDEAL END

Now assume that while the first snake is in the bag, another (feebler) one with the same dietary preferences enters; this one however emits not Ss but Os. When he gets in, there will already be fewer Xs for him, and he will — due to lateness, weakness, food-shortage — always lag behind the first. On the other hand, once an X has been transformed into an O, it's no longer available to the first snake; so the second eats what he can get, and always loses. The end result will be a mixture of Ss and Os, but more Ss:

(9)

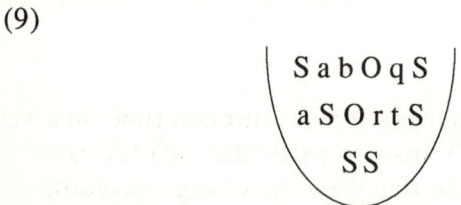

END OF TWO-SNAKE COMPETITION

(UNEQUAL MATCH)

Extend it to three snakes, and we have the scenario for ME /oː/.

There is another spinoff: suppose two equally voracious snakes get in together and compete for the same resources. If the two emit different waste products, we get another, apparently gross, violation of neogrammarian regularity — an apparently unprincipled and virtually equal distribution of Ss and Os. Such cases do occur: a good example is the development beginning in late Middle English, where final /x/ either went to /f/ (*rough, tough, cough*) or deleted, leaving a lengthened vowel (*through, bough, plough*).

The two models (trajectories vs. snakes) have quite different ontological implications. If we reify the trajectory (as in fact we normally do, whether we mean to or not), we get a model that can really only be interpreted autonomously. If we reify the lexicon and take changes as 'agents' with limited life-spans, we open the way to psychological interpretation. We can ask 'where' the lexicon is, and consider the (final) changes as the summation of sets of 'actions' or 'choices' on the part of the possessors of the lexicon (or of lexica: this may not be the same thing). Thus trajectories are vectors in an uninterpreted space, lexica as primes suggest (just) the possibility of psychological projection. Whether this is individualist or collectivist is of course open, but I will not discuss that any further here. Psychologism however is still only one option, and not a forced choice. Indeed, it's difficult to see how, in the present state of our knowledge, adopting a psychological perspective actually buys us anything at all — except a change in attitude and a different choice of (quasi-, pseudo-)explanatory terminology. There may be no genuine claims being made at all, only the expression of a stylistic or aesthetic preference.

'Neogrammarian' exceptionless change is not a mechanism, but a byproduct or effect. Given enough time, changes tend to *become* exceptionless (see Chen 1972 for the classic formulation, and Lass 1981 for some examples). The implementation of change typically involves not 'catastrophic' replacement of old by new material, but cumulative, directionally weighted variation, whose output — in time — is replacement. And because changes normally have variable rates as well, their temporal trajectories are characteristically sinusoidal: an initial 'lag phase' where the change is gaining impetus, a 'log phase' of rapid spread, and a falling-off either to completion, or towards an asymptote (cf. Lass 1984:322-329). The Neogrammarian Effect (= *Ausnahmslosigkeit*) then is the result of intersecting the curve at two points: before the start of the lag phase, and after completion or close to the asymptote.

Given this picture, there are two historiographical perspectives. In one we look at the beginning and end points of the curve and calculate a function from one to the other; this gives the 'X > Y' format of a sound law or other change of this type. In the other, we relegate the beginning and end to background, and look at the mode of implementation. These perspectives are complementary and non-reducible; there is no good argument to the effect that only the implementation-process is 'real', while the 'X > Y' change is epiphenomenal, an artefact of procedure (cf. Lass 1976a, 1987c:20ff).

That is, macrohistory and microhistory are two sides of the same coin, differing in level of abstraction and idealisation, and in ontological locus — but not in 'reality'. The same kind of macro-/microcomplementarity is patent in other historical disciplines, e.g. in palaeobiology. So from the macro-perspective one group of reptiles 'became mammals', and a new taxon arose. From the micro-perspective, this taxonomic saltation was achieved gradually, over a long transitional period in which the small bones of the lower jaw migrated to form the auditory ossicles, scales were replaced by hair, etc. Both the transitional mechanism and the systematic outcome are equally worthy of study, and indeed neither fully makes sense without the other.

Now in historical biology we do not have to invoke any abstract or World-3 objects. Concepts like 'species', *Bauplan* and the like are expository/heuristic conveniences, and in the end (nearly) fully reducible. So 'species' ultimately reduces to concepts on the molecular and sub-cellular levels (a particular DNA constitution, deployment of genes at particular loci, a chromosome number) as well as at population level (possessors of the specified configurations that interbreed, form a functional gene pool). Similarly, *Baupläne* are given in the genotype, and their specific expressions can be more or less calculated on the basis of 'ecological' information *sensu lato* (timing of gene-expression, interaction with the environment, etc.).

But with language this is not possible; in fact the situation may be argued to be precisely the reverse. There is no doubt that there exist long-term patterns of change like drifts and conspiracies, repetitions of specifiable change-types with long gaps between, recrudescences of certain 'favoured' segment- or structure-types ('centres of gravity': Lass 1977b). All of these, as I have argued elsewhere (Lass 1987a), conduce to a view that linguistic history is a transindividual study, in which the perspective of the participating individual is of little interest (as Sapir saw seventy years ago: 1921:155, and cf. the discussion in Lass 1987a:163ff).

The mentalist (hence individualist) perspective is incapable of handling this kind of time-extension, since the objects of history transcend the temporal boundaries of individual minds. *Mechanisms* (microhistory) may be individual; ultimately of course (see below) they must be, since change emerges in the last analysis from the individual's output. Changes themselves however must be trans- and/or meta-individual; since minds do not (as far as we know, except in religious world-views which are irrelevant here) outlast their physical possessors, long-term developments cannot be 'mentally' coded.

In fact the most appropriate framework for looking at change is the one familiar from 'variationist' sociolinguistics. Just as the individual in (evolutionary) biological historiography has been superseded by the population as primary locus of interest, so in linguistic history a kind of 'population-thinking' gives us the clearest view of the implementation process. A language for a historian is a population of variants, certain of which are 'selected' (though not by functional or 'fitness' criteria) over time, and survive, while others vanish.

5 Postlude and prelude

This paper has been programmatic and, perhaps, polemical; it has not been an attempt to lay out a theory of change. I've been interested mainly in chipping away at the edges of 'mentalist' views of change, and trying to show how the kind of interactionist programme suggested inchoately in my earlier work (Lass 1980a, 1987a) and given philosophical and argumentative underpinnings by Carr (1990) might be incorporated into the background thinking of historical linguists. In a sense, of course, I've done nothing more than try to put some flesh on the linguistic bones of ordinary usage concerning change, both lay and professional, on the assumption that there is a solid if poorly defined and largely unconscious basis for that usage. In this final section I will not be a whole lot more precise, but I will try to say something about how I imagine that the 'interaction' lying at the heart of both Carr's and my views might work, and what it says about the relation of speakers to change.

In principle, an interactionist/World-3 view of change suggests that there are two givens: the language-system itself (historically presented, culturally mediated), and the population of agents who 'acquire' and use it. The system serves as the repository of linguistic properties (those that change as well as those that don't), as well as in some yet-to-be-specified way a coding for 'drifts' and other long-term phenomena. That is, in some way at least certain developmental trends or tendencies, as well as the foundations of large-scale changes like vowel-shifts or major typological transformations, are implicit in the historically given object. How speakers might find this out is a mystery: but no worse than assuming that such things occur without any sort of information being present. It looks very much as if, in a wider perspective, language evolutions are partly 'canalised', there are predefined paths or 'chreods' (Waddington 1977) along which changes optimally proceed. These are of course in no way universal; they are language-specific and even periodic-specific; but for any historian sensitive to the overall shape of a linguistic history there can be little doubt that such things are an important part of what he works with, and need to be described, even if one is at a loss about just what they really are, or how they get into the behaviour of the speakers.[8]

We can however at least loosely imagine the speaker's relation to processes of change in the language as follows: he has to cope, by and large, with what's given, constrained by his own cognitive limitations, and the boundary conditions on successful use of a language. E.g. if the system orders him to turn all Xs to Ys, this can't be done as 'ordered', because neither his memory nor the accepted norms of the community, which are essential to the communicational function of the language, will allow it. I suspect this may be one of the main reasons why change proceeds by variation; it has to sneak in both to the memories of individuals and the norm-systems of communities, without being perceived as damaging.

It is the individual's having to cope, as it were, with signals 'from above' that ultimately gives to much linguistic history the appearance of being controlled by an 'invisible hand' (Keller 1990). The 'efforts' of individual speakers, in their different ways, to deal with structural/

evolutionary imperatives leads to a canalisation of performance which shapes (though without any kind of 'foreknowledge', 'planning', or 'intention' with respect to the outcome) the historical object that is handed down to the next generation.

Assuming a self-existent, historically given but mutable language system avoids the platonist trap of 'inaccessibility' that Katz (1981) falls into (cf. Carr 1990:114ff); it also allows both for the 'abstract object' or World-3 status of language, and for the undoubted fact that knowledge of language is 'crucially objective knowledge, intersubjectively constituted', as Carr (124) puts it.

The central question is whether we really need to understand the producer in order to understand the artefact. This is similar to the question that arises in art criticism of various kinds about whether the biography of a writer or composer is crucial to the understanding of the work. If we know about the state of Beethoven's hearing in 1806, we may understand something different about the 'fate' motif in the 5th symphony; but this is fundamentally external to understanding the symphony itself; the first movement is a sonata form of a particular kind regardless of the special sense Beethoven (might have) wanted us to read into it, it has a particular structure, even a particular emotional effect on us, completely aside from any 'literary' importations we might want to bring to it.

Something similar might be suggested for certain kinds of large-scale structural change in language. In a basic sense, the material is there, in the data or our theoretical formulations of the data; invoking persons and their minds and societies may help us to understand certain features of the implementation of a change, or even supply a motivation for certain low-level developments (mainly in pragmatics); but with respect to the larger evolutionary currents this extra information is largely decorative and inessential, not really the basic stuff history is made of.

Notes

* I am grateful to H.-H. Lieb for comments on an earlier draft, and for nearly saintly patience in waiting for this to get on paper. And to my wife Jaime for livening things up with the drawing in (4). More indirectly, I owe a debt to Phil

Carr for much correspondence, and for work of his that has clarified my own thinking (I hope) on a number of issues.

[1] Nonhistorically, that is. I leave aside the question of whether there can be anything like 'diachronic psychology': I doubt it.

[2] Though he may not coherently be able to espouse a pure instrumentalism. See Carr (1990: Ch. 3) for arguments against the tenability of instrumentalism.

[3] The term 'projection' is borrowed from Hjelmslev. See the discussion in Lass (1980a:115ff).

[4] This might be one way of avoiding the notorious 'private language' problem. See Carr (1990: Ch. 5) on Itkonen with respect to this issue.

[5] There is of course some borderline psychology in such a metaphorization; but this is as far as we need to go. Nothing crucial hangs on it, and we can if we wish see senses developing 'automatically' for all the good any invocation of cognitive properties would do here.

[6] This would perhaps involve assuming the possibility of some kind of 'ontology of (pure) systems', perhaps in the manner of the General Systems Theory tradition (Bertalanffy 1968).

[7] For discussion of this very complex case see Lass (1980a:75ff), and the controversy between M. L. Samuels and myself (Samuels 1987, Lass 1987b).

[8] For some earlier arguments to this effect, with supporting data, see the discussion of 'metarules' and the shape of Germanic vowel shifts in Lass (1976b: Ch. 2).

References

Bertalanffy, L. von. 1968. *General Systems Theory*. Harmondsworth: Penguin Books.
Bloomfield, L. 1939. "Menomini Morphophonemics". In: *Études phonologiques dédiées à la mémoire de M. le Prince N. S. Trubetzkoy*. Prague: Jednota Českých Matematiků A Fysiků. (TCLP 8).
Botha, R. P. 1989. "The metaphysics market. 1, Merchandizing language as matter". *Stellenbosch Papers in Liguistics* 20.
—. 1990. "The metaphysics market. 2, Billing language as behavioural". *Stellenbosch Papers in Linguistics* 21.

Carr, P. 1990. *Linguistic Realities*. An Autonomist Metatheory for the Generative Enterprise. Cambridge: Cambridge University Press.
Chen, M. 1972. "The time dimension: contribution toward a theory of sound change". *Foundations of Language* 8.457-498.
Chomsky, N. 1986. *Knowledge of Language: Its Nature, Origin, and Use*. New York: Praeger.
Givón, T. 1979. *On Understanding Grammar*. New York: Academic Press.
Harris, Z. S. 1960. *Methods in Structural Linguistics*. Chicago: University of Chicago Press.
Johnson, S. 1755. *A Dictionary of the English Language*. 2 vols. London: J. F. & C. Rivington et al.
Itkonen, E. 1983. *Causality in Linguistic Theory*. London: Croom Helm.
Katz, J. J. 1981. *Language and Other Abstract Objects*. Oxford: Basil Blackwell.
Keller, R. 1990. *Sprachwandel*. Von der unsichtbaren Hand in der Sprache. Tübingen: Francke Verlag.
King, R. D. 1969. *Historical Linguistics and Generative Grammar*. Englewood Cliffs: Prentice-Hall.
Kiparsky, P. 1968. "Linguistic universals and linguistic change". In: Bach, E., and R. T. Harms (eds). *Universals in linguistic theory*. New York: Holt, Rinehart & Winston. 171-202.
Koopman, W., v. d. Leek, F., Fischer, D., and R. Eaton (eds). 1987. *Explanation and linguistic change*. Amsterdam: Benjamins.
Lass, R. 1976a. "Variation studies and historical linguistics". *Language in Society* 5.219-229.
—. 1976b. *English Phonology and Phonological Theory*. Synchronic and Diachronic Studies. Cambridge: Cambridge University Press.
—. 1977a. "Internal reconstruction and generative phonology". *Transactions of the Philological Society (1975)*. 1-26.
—. 1977b. "'Centers of gravity' in language evolution". *Die Sprache* 23.11-19.
—. 1980a. *On Explaining Language Change*. Cambridge: Cambridge University Press.
—. 1980b. "Paradigm coherence and the conditioning of change: Yiddish 'schwa-deletion' again". In: Fisiak, J. (ed.). *Historical Morpho-*

logy. The Hague: Mouton. 251-272.
—. 1981. "Undigested history and synchronic 'structure'". In: Goyvaerts, D. (ed.). *Phonology in the 1980s*. Ghent: E. Story-Scientia. 524-544.
—. 1984. *Phonology. An Introduction to Basic Concepts*. Cambridge: Cambridge University Press.
—. 1987a. "Language, speakers, history and drift". In: Koopman et al. (eds). 1987. 151-176.
—. 1987b. "On sh*tting the door in Early Modern English". In: Koopman et al. (eds). 1987. 251-256.
—. 1987c. *The Shape of English. Structure and History*. London: J. M. Dent.
—, and S. Wright. 1986. "Endogeny vs. contact: 'Afrikaans influence' on South African English". *English World-Wide* 7: 201-224.
Lieb, H.-H. 1970. *Sprachstadium und Sprachsystem*. Umrisse einer Sprachtheorie. Stuttgart: Kohlhammer.
—. 1983. *Integrational Linguistics*. Vol. I: *General Outline*. Amsterdam: Benjamins. (CILT 17).
—. 1990. "Rundtisch/Round Table 12. Prospects for a New Structuralism". In: W. Bahner, J. Schildt, and D. Viehweger (eds). *Proceedings of the Fourteenth International Congress of Linguists, Berlin/GDR, August 10 – August 15, 1987*. Vol. I. Berlin: Akademie-Verlag. 325-328.
Lightfoot, D. 1979. *Principles of Diachronic Syntax*. Cambridge: Cambridge University Press.
Popper, K. R. 1972. *Objective Knowledge: An Evolutionary Approach*. Oxford: Clarendon Press.
—, and J. Eccles. 1977. *The Self and Its Brain*. Berlin: Springer International.
Samuels, M. L. 1987. "The status of the functional approach". In: Koopman et al. (eds). 1987. 239-250.
Sapir, E. 1921. *Language*. New York: Harcourt, Brace and Company.
Waddington, C. H. 1977. *Tools for Thought*. London: Jonathan Cape.
Zawadowski, L. 1962. "Theoretical foundations of comparative grammar". *Orbis* 11.5-20.

Index of Names

Numbers in brackets refer to page numbers of author's contribution in this volume.

A
Adamus 216
Albrecht 179
Andersen 230, 234, 238f
Antal 216
Anttila 216, 230, 234, 238–240
Apresjan 216

B
Bailey 225, 239f
Ballard 40, 70
Baltaxe 216
Bańczerowski v, 10f, 185, 200, 210, 216
Bartsch 202, 217
Batóg 193, 200–202, 206, 217
Běličová 78, 86
Bertalanffy 270
Bickle 66, 70
Bilgrami 8, 13
Bierwisch 79, 86, 217
Bloch 200, 217
Bloomfield 75, 95, 199f, 217, 248, 270
Botha 245, 270
Brainerd 200, 217
Brettschneider 80, 89, 122–125
Broschart 111–113, 123
Budde 130, 179
Bühler 94, 96, 217–219
Butt 141, 180
Buyssens 131, 179
Bzdęga 218

C
Carnap 47, 70, 81
Carr vf, 8f, 11, 13, [17–32], 36, 67, 70, 134, 179, 218, 246, 267, 269–271

Carrier 66f, 70
Chaucer 250
Chen 265, 271
Choi 130, 179
Chomsky 9, 12f, 17, 20, 27, 31, 35f, 38–40, 44, 52, 66f, 69-71, 76f, 134, 179, 181, 188, 218, 261, 271
Coseriu 11, 25, 31, 79, 86, 97, 134, 179, 230, 235–238, 240
Craig 123
Crothers 218

D
Daneš 80, 83, 86
Dingwall 218
Dirven 31, 86, 89
Dokulil 78, 80, 86
Donegan 225, 239f
Dressler 86, 180, 225, 235, 239f
Droste 12f

E
Eaton 271
Eccles 67, 71, 252, 272
Ehrmann 218
Eisenberg 129f, 141, 179f

F
Falkenberg 130, 180
Farmer 41, 70
Feldman 40, 70
Ferguson 77, 123
Fillmore 82
Fine 47, 70
Firbas 85f
Fischer, B. 130, 174, 180,
Fischer, D. 271
Fischer-Jørgensen 218
Fisiak vi, 217f, 239, 271
Fodor 40, 70

INDEX OF NAMES

Foley 104, 123
Fraisse 218
Fried 86, 89

G
Gabelentz 83
Gardies 188, 218
Giedymin 187, 218
Givón 115, 123, 245, 271
Gleason 218
Gödel 212, 218
Graumann 218
Greenberg 120, 123, 125, 219, 230, 232f, 239f
Groot 78, 87
Guchman 219
Gussmann 219

H
Hajičová 80, 87–89
Halle 10, 13, 218f
Harary 222
Harris, R. 128, 180,
Harris, Z. 188, 200, 219, 245, 271
Hasenclever 117, 122f
Havránek 76f, 87
Heger v, 9, [91–98], 100, 123, 132, 180
Hjelmslev 75, 79, 235, 270
Hoepfner 130, 180
Hörz 239f
Hudson 134, 180
Hurford 27, 31
Hymes 190, 219f, 224

I
Itkonen 20, 22–24, 31, 219, 258, 270f

J
Jakobson 11, 78, 83, 87, 215, 219, 230–235, 238–240
Jankowsky 189, 219
Jarceva 219
Jassem 219
Jespersen 83
Johnson 250, 271
Jones 219
Joos 69f
Joseph 12f

K
Kac 12f
Kamp 219
Kanger 220
Katz vf, 8, 12f, 20, 23f, 27, 31, 35f, 38, 66f, 70, 220, 252, 269, 271
Keller 268, 271
Kendzia 130, 180
Kiefer 220
King 247, 271
Kiparsky 220, 247, 271
Kmita 186, 220
Koerner 31f, 220
Koj 81, 87
Koktova 85, 87
Koopman 271f
Kortlandt 220
Koschmieder 91f, 94, 97
Kuroda 85, 87
Kuryłowicz 78, 87

L
Labov 252
Lakatos 220
Lakoff 122f
Lane 220
Langendoen 24, 31, 36, 70
Lass v, 20, 24, 27f, 31, 220, [243–271]
Leek 271
Lehmann 25, 31, 120, 123, 125
Leibniz 251
Lepschy 220
Leška 83, 87
Lieb v, vi, [1–13], 20, 24f, 27, 29, 32, [33–72], 82–85, 87, 91, 95, 97–99, 103, 121, 123, [127–182], 199–202, 207, 210, 213–216, 220f, 224, 244, 246, 269, 272
Lightfoot 247, 272
Lindenbaum 212, 223
Lomtev 221
Luelsdorff 78, 86, 88
Lutzeier 130, 182
Lyons 221

M
Maher 221
Marcus 200, 221
Margolis 76, 88

INDEX OF NAMES

Materna 83, 88
Mathesius 76, 80, 83, 88
Mayerthaler 225, 234, 237, 239–241
McCawley 85, 88
McClelland 40, 71f
Mittelstraß 66f, 70
Montague 12, 78f, 82
Moravcsik 123
Morciniec 221
Mudersbach 94, 97
Mulder 200, 221

N
Nebeský 200, 221
Newmeyer 221
Nichols 115, 124

P
Pak 222
Panevová 80, 87, 89
Pateman 27, 32, 222
Paul 189, 220, 222, 230, 235, 239, 241
Pauliny 78, 88
Peirce 118f, 230f, 234,
Penrose 40, 71
Peters 130, 134, 182
Peterson 222
Petkevič 82, 88
Piaget 222
Pilch 222
Plato 8, 20, 24, 27, 35, 230, 239, 241, 245, 252, 269
Pogonowski [185–224]
Popper 8, 11, 13, 18–22, 24f, 32, 67, 71, 222, 246, 252, 272
Posner 79, 88, 181
Postal vi, 8, 12f, 24, 31, 35f, 38, 70, 85, 88, 222
Premper 102, 108, 125
Pylyshyn 38, 40, 70, 72

Q
Quine 95
Qvarnström 200, 222

R
Raible 97, 123, 125
Revzin 200, 222
Richter 130, 166, 173, 182

Rittner 124f
Ross 111f, 124
Rubach 222
Rumelhart 40, 71f
Ruszkiewicz 222

S
Sabol 223
Sadock 190, 223
Sampson 23, 32
Samuels 270, 272
Sapir 230, 267, 272
Şasse 122, 124
Saumjan 223
Saussure 7, 26, 76, 79, 92, 94f, 131, 187, 215, 223, 230–232, 239, 241
Schaff 223
Schane 223
Schiwy 223
Schleicher 230
Schlerath 124f
Schnelle 32, 41, 71f, 82, 88f, 221
Schooneveld 78, 89
Searle 8, 13, 39–42, 49f, 52, 67, 72, 83, 89, 207
Seiler v, 9, 80, 89, [99–126]
Sgall v, 9f, [75–90]
Skalička 78, 89, 230
Skolem 212, 223
Şoames 36, 72
Sreider 200, 223
Stachowiak 120, 125
Stampe 225, 239f
Steele 110, 125
Stein 239, 241
Stimm 97, 123, 125
Swiggers 26, 32

T
Tarski 212, 223
Tesnière 80, 82, 89, 95, 98
Toffoli 70
Togeby 95
Trnka 79, 89
Trubetzkoy 10, 78, 181, 192–195, 197–201, 208, 210, 219f, 222f, 270

U
Ungeheuer 223

INDEX OF NAMES

Uspenskij 224

V
Vachek 84, 89f
Van Valin 104, 123
Vennemann 200, 202–206, 216f, 224
Verburg 224

W
Waddington 268, 272

Walter 111, 126
Wessel 239f
Wójcicki 186, 224
Wolfram 70
Wright 259, 272
Wurzel v, 7, 11, [225–242]

Z
Zawadowski 248, 272
Zgółka [185–224]

In the CURRENT ISSUES IN LINGUISTIC THEORY (CILT) series (Series Editor: E.F. Konrad Koerner) the following volumes have been published thus far, and will be published:

1. KOERNER, E.F. Konrad (ed.): *The Transformational-Generative Paradigm and Modern Linguistic Theory*. Amsterdam, 1975.
2. WEIDERT, Alfons: *Componential Analysis of Lushai Phonology*. Amsterdam, 1975.
3. MAHER, J. Peter: *Papers on Language Theory and History I: Creation and Tradition in Language*. Foreword by Raimo Anttila. Amsterdam, 1977.
4. HOPPER, Paul J. (ed.): *Studies in Descriptive and Historical Linguistics: Festschrift for Winfred P. Lehmann*. Amsterdam, 1977. Out of print.
5. ITKONEN, Esa: *Grammatical Theory and Metascience: A critical investigation into the methodological and philosophical foundations of 'autonomous' linguistics*. Amsterdam, 1978.
6. ANTTILA, Raimo: *Historical and Comparative Linguistics*. Amsterdam/Philadelphia, 1989.
7. MEISEL, Jürgen M. & Martin D. PAM (eds): *Linear Order and Generative Theory*. Amsterdam, 1979.
8. WILBUR, Terence H.: *Prolegomena to a Grammar of Basque*. Amsterdam, 1979.
9. HOLLIEN, Harry & Patricia (eds): *Current Issues in the Phonetic Sciences, Proceedings of the IPS-77 Congress, Miami Beach, Fla., 17-19 December 1977*. Amsterdam, 1979. 2 vols.
10. PRIDEAUX, Gary (ed.): *Perspectives in Experimental Linguistics. Papers from the University of Alberta Conference on Experimental Linguistics, Edmonton, 13-14 Oct. 1978*. Amsterdam, 1979.
11. BROGYANYI, Bela (ed.): *Studies in Diachronic, Synchronic, and Typological Linguistics: Festschrift for Oswald Szemerényi on the Occasion of his 65th Birthday*. Amsterdam, 1980.
12. FISIAK, Jacek (ed.): *Theoretical Issues in Contrastive Linguistics*. Amsterdam, 1980.
13. MAHER, J. Peter with coll. of Allan R. Bomhard & E.F. Konrad Koerner (ed.): *Papers from the Third International Conference on Historical Linguistics, Hamburg, August 22-26, 1977*. Amsterdam, 1982.
14. TRAUGOTT, Elizabeth C., Rebecca LaBRUM, Susan SHEPHERD (eds): *Papers from the Fourth International Conference on Historical Linguistics, Stanford, March 26-30, 1980*. Amsterdam, 1980.
15. ANDERSON, John (ed.): *Language Form and Linguistic Variation. Papers dedicated to Angus McIntosh*. Amsterdam, 1982.
16. ARBEITMAN, Yoël & Allan R. BOMHARD (eds): *Bono Homini Donum: Essays in Historical Linguistics, in Memory of J. Alexander Kerns*. Amsterdam,.1981.
17. LIEB, Hans-Heinrich: *Integrational Linguistics*. 6 volumes. Amsterdam, 1984-1986. Vol. I available; Vol. 2-6 n.y.p.
18. IZZO, Herbert J. (ed.): *Italic and Romance. Linguistic Studies in Honor of Ernst Pulgram*. Amsterdam, 1980.
19. RAMAT, Paolo et al. (eds): *Linguistic Reconstruction and Indo-European Syntax. Proceedings of the Coll. of the 'Indogermanische Gesellschaft' Univ. of Pavia, 6-7 Sept. 1979*. Amsterdam, 1980.
20. NORRICK, Neal R.: *Semiotic Principles in Semantic Theory*. Amsterdam, 1981.
21. AHLQVIST, Anders (ed.): *Papers from the Fifth International Conference on Historical Linguistics, Galway, April 6-10, 1981*. Amsterdam, 1982.

22. UNTERMANN, Jürgen & Bela BROGYANYI (eds): *Das Germanische und die Rekonstruktion der Indogermanische Grundsprache.* Akten, Proceedings from the Colloquium of the Indogermanische Gesellschaft, Freiburg, 26-27 February 1981. Amsterdam, 1984.
23. DANIELSEN, Niels: *Papers in Theoretical Linguistics.* Edited by Per Baerentzen. Amsterdam/Philadelphia, 1992.
24. LEHMANN, Winfred P. & Yakov MALKIEL (eds): *Perspectives on Historical Linguistics. Papers from a conference held at the meeting of the Language Theory Division, Modern Language Ass., San Francisco, 27-30 December 1979.* Amsterdam, 1982.
25. ANDERSEN, Paul Kent: *Word Order Typology and Comparative Constructions.* Amsterdam, 1983.
26. BALDI, Philip (ed.) *Papers from the XIIth Linguistic Symposium on Romance Languages, University Park, April 1-3, 1982.* Amsterdam, 1984.
27. BOMHARD, Alan: *Toward Proto-Nostratic.* Amsterdam, 1984.
28. BYNON, James: *Current Progress in Afroasiatic Linguistics: Papers of the Third International Hamito-Semitic Congress, London, 1978.* Amsterdam, 1984.
29. PAPROTTÉ, Wolf & René DIRVEN (eds): *The Ubiquity of Metaphor: Metaphor in Language and Thought.* Amsterdam, 1985.
30. HALL, Robert A., Jr.: *Proto-Romance Morphology.* Amsterdam, 1984.
31. GUILLAUME, Gustave: *Foundations for a Science of Language.* Translated and with an introd. by Walter Hirtle and John Hewson. Amsterdam, 1984.
32. COPELAND, James E. (ed.): *New Directions in Linguistics and Semiotics.* Houston/Amsterdam, 1984. No rights for US/Can. *Customers from USA and Canada: please order from Rice University.*
33. VERSTEEGH, Kees: *Pidginization and Creolization: The Case of Arabic.* Amsterdam, 1984.
34. FISIAK, Jacek (ed.): *Papers from the VIth International Conference on Historical Linguistics, Poznan, 22-26 August 1983.* Amsterdam, 1985.
35. COLLINGE, N.E.: *The Laws of Indo-European.* Amsterdam, 1985.
36. KING, Larry D. & Catherine A. MALEY (eds): *Selected Papers from the XIIIth Linguistics Symposium on Romance Languages.* Amsterdam, 1985.
37. GRIFFEN, T.D.: *Aspects of Dynamic Phonology.* Amsterdam, 1985.
38. BROGYANYI, Bela & Thomas KRÖMMELBEIN (eds): *Germanic Dialects: Linguistic and Philological Investigations.* Amsterdam, 1986.
39. BENSON, James D., Michael J. CUMMINGS & William S. GREAVES (eds): *Linguistics in a Systemic Perspective.* Amsterdam, 1988.
40. FRIES, Peter Howard and Nancy (eds): *Toward an Understanding of Language: Charles C. Fries in Perspective.* Amsterdam, 1985.
41. EATON, Roger, et al. (eds): *Papers from the 4th International Conference on English Historical Linguistics.* Amsterdam, 1985.
42. MAKKAI, Adam & Alan K. MELBY (eds): *Linguistics and Philosophy. Essays in honor of Rulon S. Wells.* Amsterdam, 1985.
43. AKAMATSU, Tsutomu: *The Theory of Neutralization and the Archiphoneme in Functional Phonology.* Amsterdam, 1988.
44. JUNGRAITHMAYR, Herrmann & Walter W. MUELLER (eds): *Proceedings of the 4th International Hamito-Semitic Congress.* Amsterdam, 1987.
45. KOOPMAN, W.F., F.C. VAN DER LEEK, O. FISCHER & R. EATON (eds): *Explanation and Linguistic Change.* Amsterdam, 1987.

46. PRIDEAUX, Gary D., and William J. BAKER: *Strategies and Structures: The Processing of Relative Clauses*. Amsterdam, 1986.
47. LEHMANN, Winfred P.: *Language Typology 1985. Papers from the Linguistic Typology Symposium, Moscow, 9-13 Dec. 1985.* Amsterdam, 1986.
48. RAMAT, Anna Giacalone (ed.): *Proceedings of the VII International Conference on Historical Linguistics, Pavia 9-13 September 1985.* Amsterdam, 1987.
49. WAUGH, Linda R. & Stephen RUDY (eds): *New Vistas in Grammar: Invariance and Variation.* Amsterdam/Philadelphia, 1991.
50. RUDZKA-OSTYN, Brygida (ed.): *Topics in Cognitive Linguistics.* Amsterdam/Philadelphia, 1988.
51. CHATTERJEE, Ranjit: *Aspect and Meaning in Slavic and Indic.* Amsterdam/Philadelphia, 1988.
52. FASOLD, Ralph & Deborah SCHIFFRIN (eds): *Language Change and Variation.* Amsterdam/Philadelphia, 1989.
53. SANKOFF, David (ed.): *Diversity and Diachrony.* Amsterdam, 1986.
54. WEIDERT, Alfons: *Tibeto-Burman Tonology. A Comparative Analysis.* Amsterdam, 1987.
55. HALL, Robert A. Jr.: *Linguistics and Pseudo-Linguistics.* Amsterdam, 1987.
56. HOCKETT, Charles F.: *Refurbishing our Foundations. Elementary Linguistics from an Advanced Point of View.* Amsterdam, 1987.
57. BUBENIK, Vít: *Hellenistic and Roman Greece as a Sociolinguistic Area.* Amsterdam/Philadelphia, 1989.
58. ARBEITMAN, Yoël L.: *FUCUS. A Semitic/Afrasian Gathering in Remembrance of Albert Ehrman.* Amsterdam/Philadelphia, 1988.
59. VOORST, Jan van: *Event Structure.* Amsterdam/Philadelphia, 1988.
60. KIRSCHNER, Carl and Janet DECESARIS (eds): *Studies in Romance Linguistics.* Amsterdam/Philadelphia, 1989.
61. CORRIGAN, Roberta, Fred ECKMAN and Michael NOONAN (eds): *Linguistic Categorization.* Amsterdam/Philadelphia, 1989.
62. FRAJZYNGIER, Zygmunt (ed.): *Current Progress in Chadic Linguistics.* Amsterdam/Philadelphia, 1989.
63. EID, Mushira (ed.): *Perspectives on Arabic Linguistics I. Papers from the First Annual Symposium on Arabic Linguistics.* Amsterdam/Philadelphia, 1990.
64. BROGYANYI, Bela (ed.): *Prehistory, History, and Historiography of Language, Speech, and Linguistic Theory.* Amsterdam/Philadelphia, 1992.
65. ADAMSON, Sylvia, Vivien A. LAW, Nigel VINCENT and Susan WRIGHT (eds): *Papers from the 5th International Conference of English Historical Linguistics.* Amsterdam/Philadelphia, 1990.
66. ANDERSEN, Henning and Konrad KOERNER (eds): *Historical Linguistics 1987. Papers from the 8th International Conference on Historical Linguistics, Lille, August 30-September 4, 1987.* Amsterdam/Philadelphia, 1990.
67. LEHMANN, Winfred (ed.): *Language Typology 1987. Systematic Balance in Language. Papers from the Linguistic Typology Symposium, Berkeley, 1-3 December 1987.* Amsterdam/Philadelphia, 1990.
68. BALL, Martin, James FIFE, Erich POPPE and Jenny ROWLAND (eds): *Celtic Linguistics / Ieithyddiaeth Geltaidd. Readings in the Brythonic Languages. Festschrift for T. Arwyn Watkins.* Amsterdam/Philadelphia, 1990.
69. WANNER, Dieter and Douglas A. KIBBEE (eds): *New Analyses in Romance Linguistics. Papers from the XVIII Linguistic Symposium on Romance Languages, Urbana-Champaign, April 7-9, 1988.* Amsterdam/Philadelphia, 1991.

70. JENSEN, John T.: *Morphology. Word Structure in Generative Grammar.* Amsterdam/Philadelphia, 1990.
71. O'GRADY, WILLIAM: *Categories and Case. The sentence structure of Korean.* Amsterdam/Philadelphia, 1991.
72. EID, Mushira and John McCARTHY (eds): *Perspectives on Arabic Linguistics II Papers from the Second Annual Symposium on Arabic Linguistics.* Amsterdam/Philadelphia, 1990.
73. STAMENOV, Maxim (ed.): *Current Advances in Semantic Theory.* Amsterdam/Philadelphia, 1992.
74. LAEUFER, Christiane and Terrell A. MORGAN (eds): *Theoretical Analyses in Romance Linguistics.* Amsterdam/Philadelphia, 1992.
75. DROSTE, Flip G. and John E. JOSEPH (eds): *Linguistic Theory and Grammatical Description.* Amsterdam/Philadelphia, 1991.
76. WICKENS, Mark A.: *Grammatical Number in English Nouns.* Amsterdam/Philadelphia, 1992.
77. BOLTZ, William G. and Michael C. SHAPIRO (eds): *Studies in the Historical Phonology of Asian Languages.* Amsterdam/Philadelphia, 1991.
78. KAC, Michael B.: *Grammars and Grammaticality.* Amsterdam/Philadelphia, 1992.
79. ANTONSEN, Elmer H. and Hans Henrich HOCK (eds): *STÆFCRÆFT: Studies in Germanic Linguistics.* Amsterdam/Philadelphia, 1991.
80. COMRIE, Bernard and Mushira EID (eds): *Perspectives on Arabic Linguistics III.* Amsterdam/Philadelphia, 1991.
81. LEHMANN, Winfred P. & H.J. HEWITT (eds): *Language Typology 1988. Typological Models in Reconstruction.* Amsterdam/Philadelphia, 1991.
82. VAN VALIN, Robert D. (ed.): *Advances in Role and Reference Grammar.* Amsterdam/Philadelphia, 1993.
83. FIFE, James & Erich POPPE (eds): *Studies in Brythonic Word Order.* Amsterdam/Philadelphia, 1991.
84. DAVIS, Garry W. & Gregory K. IVERSON (eds): *Explanation in Historical Linguistics.* Amsterdam/Philadelphia, 1992.
85. BROSELOW, Ellen, Mushira EID & John McCARTHY (eds): *Perspectives on Arabic Linguistics IV.* Amsterdam/Philadelphia, 1992.
86. KESS, Joseph L.: *Psycholinguistics. Psychology, Linguistics, and the Study of Natural Language.* Amsterdam/Philadelphia, 1992.
87. BROGYANYI, Bela & Reiner LIPP (eds): *Historical Philology: Greek, Latin, and Romance Papers in Honor of Oswald Szemerényi II.* Amsterdam/Philadelphia, 1992.
88. SHIELDS, Kenneth.: *A History of Indo-European Verb Morphology.* Amsterdam/Philadelphia, 1992.
89. BURRIDGE, Kate: *Syntactic Change in Germanic. A study of some aspects of language change in Germanic with particular reference to Middle Dutch.* Amsterdam/Philadelphia, 1992.
90. KING, Larry D.: *The Semantic Structure of Spanish. Meaning and grammatical form.* Amsterdam/Philadelphia, 1992.
91. HIRSCHBÜHLER, Paul and Konrad KOERNER (eds): *Romance Languages and Modern Linguistic Theory. Selected papers from the XX Linguistic Symposium on Romance Languages.* Amsterdam/Philadelphia, 1992.
92. POYATOS, Fernando: *Paralanguage: A linguistic and interdisciplinary approach to interactive speech and sounds.* Amsterdam/Philadelphia, n.y.p.

93. LIPPI-GREEN, Rosina (ed.): *Recent Developments in Germanic Linguistics.* Amsterdam/Philadelphia, 1992.
94. HAGÈGE, Claude: *The Language Builder. An essay on the human signature in linguistic morphogenesis.* Amsterdam/Philadelphia, 1993.
95. MILLER, D. Gary: *Complex Verb Formation.* Amsterdam/Philadelphia, 1993.
96. LIEB, Hans-Heinrich (ed.): *Prospects for a New Structuralism.* Amsterdam/Philadelphia, 1992.
97. BROGYANYI, Bela and Reiner LIPP (eds): *Comparative-Historical Linguistics: Indo-European and Finno-Ugric. Papers in honor of Oswald Szemerényi III.* Amsterdam/Philadelphia, n.y.p.
98. EID, Mushira and Gregory K. IVERSON: *Issues in Language and Grammar. Papers in honor of Gerald Sanders.* Amsterdam/Philadelphia, n.y.p.
99. JENSEN, John T.: *English Phonology.* Amsterdam/Philadelphia, n.y.p.
101 EID, Mushira and Clive HOLES (eds): *Perspectives on Arabic Linguistics V. Papers from the Fifth Annual Symposium on Arabic Linguistics.* Amsterdam/Philadelphia, n.y.p.

OHIO UNIVERSITY LIBRARY
...k as soon as you have
... it must